THE HUTCHINSON
BUMPER
QUIZ BOOK

THE HUTCHINSON
BUMPER QUIZ BOOK

Helicon

Copyright © Helicon Publishing Ltd 1996

All rights reserved
Helicon Publishing Ltd
42 Hythe Bridge Street
Oxford OX1 2EP

Typeset by Techtype, Abingdon, Oxon
Printed and bound in Great Britain by
Cox & Wyman Ltd, Reading, Berkshire

ISBN 1–85986–194–6

British Cataloguing in Publication Data
A catalogue record for this book is available
from the British Library

Introduction

Welcome to the HUTCHINSON BUMPER QUIZ BOOK and hours of stimulating entertainment and fun. Within each thematic section you will find a range of quizzes covering all aspects of the subject. They are arranged in topics at increasing levels of difficulty – so if you want to find the easier quizzes look at the beginning of each topic, and if you are looking for some tougher quizzes look at the end. There's something for everyone.

And starting on page 377 there's a different type of quiz to challenge even the most experienced quiz fanatic – the Hutchinson Quizlink. Not only do you have to answer the questions, but there is also the added excitement of having to find the link between the answers of each round – the quizlink. You are warned: some of these are quite tricky!

CONTENTS

General Knowledge 7
Mixed Bag 37
  True or False? 38
  Choices 48
  1, 2, 3 ... 54
  Colours 57
  Time 64
  Money 65
  Who, What, or Where? 66
  Crime 69
  Catastrophes and
    Disasters 70
  Fashion 71
  Language 72
  Water, Water, Everywhere 73
  Archaeology 75
  Economics 76
  Cats and Dogs 77
  Name the Year 80
  What's in a Name? 82
Entertainment 85
  General 86
  Music 89
  Jazz 98
  Popular Music 99
  Musical Instruments 106
  Cinema and TV 107
  On the Stage 117
  Comedians and Clowns 123
Sport and Leisure 127
  Sport 128
  Food and Drink 137
  Games and Pastimes 143
Art and Literature 145
  Literature 146
  Art and Artists 157
Around the World 167
  General 168
  UK 174
  USA and Canada 177
  Africa 186
  Asia 192
  Australasia 198
  Europe 204
  South America and the
    Caribbean 210
  Built World 216
History and Politics 221
  History 222
  Kings and Queens 233
  Politics 236
People 245
  General 246
  Murders and
    Assassinations 253
  Conquerors and
    Explorers 256
  Partners 258
  Who Said It? 259
Ideas and Beliefs 265
  General 266
  Bible 275
  Mythology 279
Science 289
  General 290
  Physics 303
  Chemistry 306
  Elements 309
  Energy 312
  Instruments and
    Techniques of Science 315
  Animals and Plants 317
  Human Body 326
  Senses 335
  Medicine and Health 337
  Planet Earth 343
  Space 354
  Technology and
    Transport 366
  Discovery and Invention 374
  Computers 375
Quizlink 377

Answers 421
Quizlink Answers 485

GENERAL KNOWLEDGE

General Knowledge

1

1 What sort of woollen headgear was named after a battle of the Crimean War?

2 Which year (in figures) is displayed by the seven Roman numerals listed in descending order?

3 Whose tomb is situated in Arlington Cemetery, Washington, at the Arc de Triomphe, Paris, and in Westminster Abbey, London?

4 What is the surname of the Hungarian inventor whose multicoloured, rotatable cube became a world cult?

5 What is the set of 26 letters whose name is derived from the names of two Greek letters?

6 How long is the appointed term of office of the secretary general of the United Nations?

7 What is the name common to three Scottish kings, eight popes and three tsars of Russia?

8 Who was elected the first black Anglican archbishop of Cape Town in 1988?

9 What is thrown backhand by the people who contest the championships of the World Flying Disc Association held in the USA?

10 What were first issued in 1950 and allowed people to 'pay by plastic'?

Answers on page 422

General Knowledge

2

1 Who said 'That's one small step for a man, one giant leap for mankind' on 20 July 1969?
2 Which town in Umbria was the birthplace of St Francis?
3 What is the term for a person with assets of over 1,000 million dollars?
4 Who was the Roman Catholic convert arrested on 4 November 1605 in the cellars of the Houses of Parliament?
5 Which school near Elgin was attended by the Duke of Edinburgh and Prince Charles?
6 Carlo Collodi wrote a story about a wooden puppet which became human. What is its title?
7 For which group of people is Romany the native language?
8 What is the acronym for the agency set up in 1923 to provide co-operation between police forces worldwide?
9 Which public official can order an inquest into instances of sudden, violent or suspicious death?
10 What is the Latin word for 'elsewhere' which we use to mean that the person under suspicion was somewhere else when the crime was committed?

Answers on page 422

General Knowledge

3

1. Which 18th-century cattle-thief, smuggler, robber and highwayman was hanged at York in 1739?
2. What is the term used to denote the unauthorized and illegal accessing of computer programs, often with criminal intent?
3. What does the 'MI' of MI5 and MI6 stand for?
4. What was the term popularized by Winston Churchill for the imaginary boundary dividing Europe between the capitalist West and the communist East?
5. On which spring day is a hoax victim referred to as a 'gowk' in Scotland and a poisson d'avril in France?
6. Which nomadic people have an Arabic name which means 'desert-dweller'?
7. Where were Anne Boleyn, Catherine Howard and Lady Jane Grey beheaded?
8. What was the surname of Charles, the dog expert, who organized his first dog show in 1886?
9. What goes after 'People's', 'Atlantic' and 'Citizen's' for three documents drawn up in 1837, 1941 and 1991 respectively?
10. What is the unit used for measuring the fineness of yarn, especially in stockings and tights?

Answers on page 422

General Knowledge

4

1. What stands 320 metres tall in the Champ de Mars and was designed for the 1889 Paris Exhibition?
2. What is printed on most articles for sale and is read by a scanning device to identify the manufacturer and the product?
3. What has three main and seven foundation subjects and is followed in all UK primary and secondary schools?
4. Which Italian city was buried, along with Herculaneum, when Vesuvius erupted in AD 79?
5. Which European country is also known as the Hellenic Republic?
6. What was the dukedom bestowed on Philip Mountbatten on 19 November 1947, the day before his wedding?
7. What was abolished in Britain in 1965 for all crimes except treason?
8. Which emergency device was first used in 1945 and has since saved the lives of more than 5,000 pilots?
9. What is the official monetary unit of the European Community?
10. The Little Mermaid, a statue at the entrance to Copenhagen harbour, is a fairy-tale character created by which writer?

Answers on page 422

General Knowledge

5

1. In which city is the headquarters of the United Nations?
2. What was the title of the memoirs of former intelligence officer Peter Wright, which Britain tried to ban in 1987?
3. What are the Long Man of Wilmington and the Cerne Abbas Giant?
4. Which 1993 film finally won Steven Spielberg Oscars for Best Film and Best Director?
5. What was the pedestrian equivalent of a highwayman?
6. Whose unsuccessful challenge for the Conservative Party leadership in 1990 brought down Margaret Thatcher?
7. Which public holiday is celebrated in the USA on 4 July every year?
8. What was Michaelangelo's first name?
9. Which media tycoon acquired the *Sun*, the *News of the World*, and *The Times*?
10. In which galaxy do we live?

Answers on page 422

General Knowledge

6

1. Which instrument does James Galway play?
2. What is the name of the variation of lawn tennis played by children on a smaller court?
3. Which creature has species called white, tiger, hammerhead and basking?
4. 'Cerebral' refers to which part of the body?
5. The failure of which crop caused famine in Ireland in 1845?
6. Who wrote the science-fiction novel *Brave New World*?
7. Which group of people belong to Equity?
8. Who lives at number 11 Downing Street?
9. Who is the patron saint of travellers?
10. On which inland sea do Russia and Turkey have shores?

Answers on page 422

General Knowledge

7

1. Which international sport uses rings and parallel bars?
2. How many players are there in a netball team?
3. Who issues letters called encyclicals?
4. Who wrote the *Brandenburg Concertos*?
5. Who was the first English printer?
6. Who cut off Samson's hair?
7. Which is the smallest breed of dog?
8. What is the name for a triangle with two sides and two angles the same?
9. What nationality is the tenor Placido Domingo?
10. Which small shark is served in fish and chip shops as 'rock-eel' or 'rock salmon'?

Answers on page 423

General Knowledge

8

1. Who invented the electric light bulb?
2. Which card game, derived from whist, was first played in Britain in 1903?
3. In which war was the Battle of Naseby fought?
4. Of what breed of dogs are King Charles, Sussex and Pekingese varieties?
5. Which animal is the source of cashmere?
6. Which company made the TriStar passenger plane?
7. What is the normal colour of the gem sapphire?
8. What is the popular name for the Central Criminal Court in London?
9. What feature of Cyrano de Bergerac's anatomy added to his fame?
10. Whose first holiday camp opened at Skegness in 1935?

Answers on page 423

General Knowledge

9

1. What other name is given to the Stars and Stripes, the flag of the USA?
2. Which Australian outlaw wore home-made armour?
3. What colour hat is the badge of office of a cardinal?
4. Who was chief of the Greek gods?
5. What kind of creature is an ibex?
6. What was the nickname of the World War I German aviator Manfred von Richthofen?
7. Who wrote about Peter Rabbit, Mrs Tiggy Winkle and Jeremy Fisher?
8. Who commanded the first expedition to sail round the world, but was killed in the Philippines?
9. Which planet in the solar system is more than twice as big as all the others put together?
10. In which West Indian dance does the dancer pass under a low pole?

Answers on page 423

General Knowledge

10

1 What was the ancient kind of cross adopted as the emblem of the Nazi party?

2 What is the record of the survey of England carried out by William the Conqueror?

3 Who was Moby-Dick?

4 In Greek legend, who turned everything he touched to gold?

5 How many millilitres are there in one cubic centimetre?

6 In which town did Jesus grow up?

7 Which former electrician became president of Poland in 1990?

8 Who is the famous brother of actress Shirley MacLaine?

9 What unit of area was originally the size that a yoke of oxen could plough in a day?

10 What name is given to an error in a computer program?

Answers on page 423

GENERAL KNOWLEDGE

11

1. What group of assassins in feudal Japan were reputed in legend to make themselves invisible?
2. What is France's largest vehicle manufacturer?
3. Which creature, discussed since the 15th century, boosts Scottish tourism by £25 million a year?
4. What was the adopted name of Rodolfo Alfonso Guglielmi di Valentina?
5. Who were Harpo, Groucho, Chico, Zeppo and Gummo?
6. Which city was once known as Constantinople?
7. What is the common name for sodium chloride?
8. To what did the Saxe-Coburg-Gotha family change its name in 1917?
9. What is the world's largest inland sea?
10. What is the national sport of Japan?

Answers on page 423

General Knowledge

12

1. In which town did Isaac Newton attend the grammar school, and Margaret Thatcher attend the local girls' school?
2. Who lead the expedition on the raft *Kon-Tiki* in 1947?
3. From which of the nine named planets does the mineral tellurium get its name?
4. Which English physicist and mathematician was born in the same year that Galileo died?
5. What caused the death of John Keats, Frédéric Chopin and Emily Brontë?
6. Which Indian city has a style of riding breeches named after it?
7. Why are the names of the 9th, 10th, 11th and 12th months derived from the Latin for 7, 8, 9 and 10?
8. What was devised by Ludwig Zamenhof in 1887 to make worldwide communication easier?
9. Which British city is the home of the National Museum of Photography, Film and Television?
10. What comes between duke and earl in the ranking of British peers?

Answers on page 423

General Knowledge

13

1 What is the emblem of Islam, displayed, for example, on the national flags of Turkey, Pakistan and Tunisia?

2 What is the English name for the Danish port of Helsinger, the setting for Shakespeare's Hamlet?

3 What is the Italian word for 'scratched drawings' which we apply to unsolicited, public displays of art?

4 Which Portuguese colony was leased from China and will be handed back in 1999?

5 What is Paddy Ashdown's real first name?

6 Which cloth was first manufactured in the French town of Nîmes, from which it got its name?

7 Which UK government-funded body has an official symbol of quality called a 'kite' mark?

8 Which country in the Middle East is the Hashemite Kingdom?

9 What did Tsar Alexander III commission from Fabergé in 1884, as the first of a series of presents for the tsarina?

10 Which is the largest country in area in the British Commonwealth?

Answers on page 424

General Knowledge

14

1. In which town were the investitures of Edward VIII and Prince Charles held, when each was created Prince of Wales?
2. What was the first name shared by Lord Kitchener and Lord Nelson?
3. Which is the only French-speaking republic in the Americas?
4. Who is buried at the Hôtel des Invalides in Paris?
5. In which year was the British Commonwealth established?
6. What is the Russian word for 'dissolute' and the nick-name given to Grigory Efimovich, the illiterate son of a peasant, who had influence over the tsarina?
7. In which city was the world's first skyscraper built?
8. In which building was Winston Churchill born in 1874?
9. What is a unit of thermal insulation used in the textile trade and is often associated with duvets?
10. Which body of people is sometimes referred to as 'The Fourth Estate'?

Answers on page 424

GENERAL KNOWLEDGE
15

1. Which structures have four basic designs – beam, cantilever, arch and suspension?
2. What is the popular name for members of the RCMP?
3. Which sign is the decapod of the zodiac?
4. What is the collective word for a group of companies that limits competition by price-fixing, market-sharing and restricting output?
5. In which Soviet Republic was the space-launch site, the Baikonur Cosmodrome, built?
6. Which country has problems with the drug barons of Medellin?
7. Which Wiltshire country house, famous for its safari park lions, is the seat of Lord Bath?
8. What are the substances in the saliva of vampire bats, leeches and mosquitoes which stop blood from clotting?
9. Which type of edible nut is produced by a variety of hickory tree?
10. What was the name of the pope who introduced the reformed calendar used by the Western world?

Answers on page 424

General Knowledge

16

1. In 1989 the remains of which 17th-century theatre were discovered and excavated near Southwark Bridge?

2. What is the Italian word for 'swank' and the name of an organization that is also known as La Cosa Nostra?

3. Who used the Latin phrase 'cogito ergo sum' ('I think therefore I am') as the foundation for his philosophical theory?

4. Which language is related to both Cornish and Welsh, and is now a recognized language of France?

5. What is the name for all citizens born and brought up in the Western Isles?

6. Which river is poetically called 'Isis' when it flows through Oxford?

7. In which European city are the headquarters of the Red Cross?

8. Which two sets of exams were replaced by the GCSE in 1988?

9. Who was commissioned to redesign 51 London churches burned down in the Great Fire of 1666?

10. What is an important meeting between world political leaders usually called?

Answers on page 424

General Knowledge

17

1. In which country is Transylvania, home of the vampire legends?
2. What is the eye defect strabismus?
3. Which king was dethroned by the Glorious Revolution?
4. Which country was founded by Muhammad Ali Jinnah?
5. Which is the busiest airport in France?
6. Which planet has two moons, Phobos and Deimos?
7. What name is given to a mistake such as saying 'a scoop of Boy Trouts' instead of 'a troop of Boy Scouts'?
8. What surname links a Wimbledon champion, a blues guitarist, an author of horror stories, and a Canadian prime minister?
9. Which modern country did the Romans call Lusitania?
10. What colour are pistachio nuts?

Answers on page 424

General Knowledge

18

1. What nationality was Kurt Waldheim, secretary general of the United Nations from 1972 to 1981?
2. In which modern country are the ruins of Ephesus?
3. In which Italian city is the Rialto bridge?
4. Who was Nazi Germany's minister of propaganda?
5. What kind of sporting event is the Hawaii Ironman?
6. Which river flows through Washington DC?
7. Whose troops were known as *Ironsides*?
8. What colour is the fur of a mink?
9. Which is the first day of Lent?
10. Which cricketer set world records by scoring 61,237 runs and 197 centuries?

Answers on page 424

GENERAL KNOWLEDGE

19

1. For what is the Booker Prize awarded?
2. Where does bossa nova dance music originate?
3. On which day of the week is Ascension Day?
4. To which fish family do pilchards and sardines belong?
5. Against which disease did Edward Jenner develop a vaccine around 1800?
6. Who was the last king of Lydia, famed for his wealth?
7. The Colossus of Rhodes was a statue of which Greek god?
8. Followers of which religion are expected to undertake a pilgramage known as *hajj*?
9. Which two countries are divided by the Kattegat sea passage?
10. What is the art of clipping trees and shrubs into ornamental shapes?

Answers on page 425

General Knowledge

20

1 Which Italian company founded by six brothers withdrew from motor racing in 1957?
2 What is the wind force of a hurricane?
3 What is a hurdy-gurdy?
4 How many squares are there on a draughts (checkers) board?
5 What is the anatomical name for the large flat bone at the front of the chest?
6 What is the Richter scale used to measure?
7 Who led an unsuccessful rebellion against Queen Elizabeth I in 1601?
8 Which semi-divine Trojan prince abandoned Queen Dido of Carthage?
9 Where were the 1932 and 1984 Olympic Games held?
10 To which bird family does the jay belong?

Answers on page 425

General Knowledge

21

1 Which scientist was the first to receive the Nobel prize twice?
2 Who was the model for Citizen Kane?
3 What was the back-kicking dance that originated in the 1920s in South Carolina?
4 What was the nickname of General Norman Schwarzkopf?
5 In which US city did house music originate?
6 What nationality was the composer Chopin?
7 Is a cassowary a large flightless bird, a Maori warclub or an Indian cooking pot?
8 What type of camera was invented by Edwin Land?
9 Who was the Greek god of the sea?
10 What is another name for hydrophobia?

Answers on page 425

General Knowledge

22

1. Who wrote 'The Murders in the Rue Morgue', the first detective story?
2. Who was the British cartoonist whose name is given to clumsily designed machines?
3. How many tusks does a wart hog have?
4. Who in 1969 retired to the village of Colombey-les-Deux-Eglises?
5. What kind of stone is marble?
6. In which country did the poets Keats and Shelley both die?
7. What abrasive rock is produced by gases frothing in lava?
8. In which city on the Mississippi is the Gateway Arch?
9. What is a mixture of 75% potassium nitrate, 15% charcoal and 10% sulphur?
10. How is the island of St Christopher in the Caribbean more familiarly known?

Answers on page 425

General Knowledge

23

1. Who founded The Royal Hospital in Chelsea, London?
2. What popular drink was known in China as early as 2737 BC?
3. Which is the largest city in Switzerland?
4. Did Mahatma Gandhi train as a doctor, a lawyer, or an architect?
5. What kind of creature is a gecko?
6. What is the name given to the chief religious leader of a synagogue?
7. Of which country is Lima the capital?
8. What is the name of the high protein food derived from soya milk?
9. What is another name for the star Polaris?
10. Where would you find an avenue of sphinxes?

Answers on page 425

GENERAL KNOWLEDGE

24

1 What is the general term for the use of computers, telecommunications and microelectronics in the processing and transmission of data?

2 What is the name of the South African movement led by Chief Buthelezi?

3 Which was the first day of the year in the Roman calendar?

4 To which royal house does the royal family of Monaco belong?

5 Which London church is officially the Collegiate Church of St Peter?

6 Who is excluded from succession to the throne in Salic Law?

7 Which boy's name, signalled in Morse code, would be represented by six dashes?

8 What is the study of the relationship between people and their working environment, with the aim of improving performance?

9 Which diamond has a Persian name meaning 'mountain of light'?

10 What do the Sikhs propose to call their separate state, if it ever achieves independence from India?

Answers on page 425

General Knowledge

25

1 What is the ancient Greek name for Troy, from which the title of an epic Homeric poem is derived?

2 What is the Spanish title equivalent to that of a British princess?

3 In which river valley was gold discovered in the Yukon in 1896, causing 30,000 prospectors to rush to the area?

4 What is the name for a Japanese gangster in organized crime, a word meaning 'good for nothing'?

5 Which sign of the zodiac was once part of the adjacent sign, Scorpio?

6 What is identified by its ISBN?

7 On which everyday object would you find the inscriptions 'Decus et tutamen'; 'Nemo me impune lacessit'; or 'Pleidiol wyf i'm gwlad'?

8 What is the collective term for the Spanish, Romanian, Portuguese, Italian and French languages?

9 How do you notate 'multiply by one thousand' in Roman numerals?

10 Who was the author of the *Mary Poppins* stories?

Answers on page 426

General Knowledge

26

1. Of which country is the wattle the national emblem?
2. What was traditionally followed by a beating of the skin with birch twigs, and a roll in the snow?
3. What is the name of the Oxford college founded in 1899 to provide education for working people?
4. What is the name of the world tree that spans heaven and hell in Norse mythology?
5. Which two people, a British fashion designer and a rock music entrepreneur, started the punk movement of the 1970s?
6. What was Jacqueline Kennedy's maiden name?
7. What is the acronym for an independent organization, such as the Equal Opportunities Commission, set up by the government and relying on it for funds?
8. What is the Russian word for 'peace' and the name of the Soviet space station launched in 1986?
9. Where was Nelson Mandela held in prison for 27 years?
10. Which British crown dependency has a government called the Court of Tynwald?

Answers on page 426

General Knowledge

27

1. Who was William IV's queen, after whom an Australian city was named?
2. What is the collective name for the three Low Countries of Europe?
3. What was the code of gallantry and honour that medieval knights were pledged to observe?
4. Which German educationist first opened 'kindergartens' where children learned through play?
5. Which European country has been ruled by Harald V since 1991?
6. Which were the two factions of the Russian Social Democratic Party whose names were taken from the words for 'majority' and 'minority'?
7. Which countries provide the five permanent members of the United Nations Security Council?
8. Who is the patron saint of music?
9. Which principality will become part of France if the reigning Prince dies without producing a male heir?
10. Which day of the week is named after the wife of the Norse god Odin?

Answers on page 426

General Knowledge

28

1. Who did Peeping Tom see naked, according to legend?
2. What is the USA's largest oil concern?
3. For what were Dalmatian dogs once used?
4. What is the world's highest funded art gallery?
5. Of which country is Christmas Island a part?
6. What is a narwhal?
7. Why did Lord Sandwich invent the sandwich?
8. Who was the producer of the *Tom and Jerry* cartoons until 1956?
9. From which boat did Jacques Cousteau conduct his underwater research from 1951?
10. Why were Samuel Pepys's diaries not published until after 1825?

Answers on page 426

General Knowledge

29

1. Which sheikdom is the capital of the United Arab Emirates?
2. What was the codename of the American development of the atom bomb?
3. Which American humorist invented the town of Lake Wobegon?
4. What does the sculptor Christo do to things?
5. Which Christian festival comes 12 days after Christmas?
6. Which American president was famous for his emancipation of slaves?
7. What is 'quasar' an acronym for?
8. What metal is used for the filament in a light bulb?
9. Who was the French soldier whose constant drilling made his name a byword for a strict disciplinarian?
10. Which poet laureate wrote the children's book *The Box of Delights*?

Answers on page 426

General Knowledge

30

1 In Scandinavian mythology, where did the gods live?

2 Which capital city is known to some of its citizens as Baile Atha Cliath?

3 After oxygen, what is the most abundant element in the Earth's crust?

4 Which state lies immediately west of Indiana?

5 Which English composer wrote a *Sea Symphony* and a *London Symphony*?

6 What did the astronomer Clyde Tombaugh discover in 1930?

7 Who was the Greek goddess of victory?

8 Who designed an analytical engine and a difference engine that were forerunners of modern computers?

9 In the Bible, who was the last king of Babylon, who saw his own death prophesied at a feast?

10 Which country is the world's largest consumer of champagne?

Answers on page 426

General Knowledge

31

1. Of which kind of computer program was VisiCalc the first?
2. Which former astronaut was elected senator for Ohio in 1974?
3. Which religion has five duties called the 'five pillars'?
4. Which bodily organ's functions can be taken by an artificial device called a haemodializer?
5. Which Brazilian dance became fashionable in Europe in 1989?
6. What is a fennec?
7. Whose last major painting was *A Bar at the Folies-Bergère*?
8. Which Norwegian's name has become a generic term for a traitor in war?
9. In semaphore, what letter is indicated by one flag held straight up and one flag held straight down?
10. Which African country has a land border with only one other country, Senegal?

Answers on page 427

General Knowledge
32

1 Which virus was identified, separately, by Robert Gallo and Luc Montagnier?
2 In Tibet, what are hard slabs of tea used as before being brewed?
3 Which real-life Elizabethan hero is satirized in Shakespeare's *Love's Labours Lost*?
4 What is the real first name of the tycoon Tiny Rowland?
5 In Japan, what is a koto?
6 Who won an Oscar for his performance in *Kiss of the Spider Woman* in 1985?
7 In which sport would you compete for Doggett's Coat and Badge?
8 Which island is known to the Greeks as Kérkira?
9 Who wrote the verse dramas *The Lady's Not for Burning* and *A Sleep of Prisoners*?
10 Who built the first jet aircraft?

Answers on page 427

General Knowledge

33

1. With which of the arts was Frederick Ashton involved?
2. With which philosophy is the French novelist Albert Camus associated?
3. In which country was Buddha born?
4. Who is the patron saint of painters?
5. Who was the king of the fairies in folklore?
6. The two main systems of which martial art are tomiki and uyeshiba?
7. Who was the first fashion designer to sell ready-to-wear collections to department stores?
8. What does Mohs' scale measure?
9. In which country is the world's oldest parliament?
10. How is the writer Jean-Baptiste Poquelin better known?

Answers on page 427

General Knowledge

34

1. Which founder member of the Royal Academy is famous for portraits of Mrs Siddons, David Garrick, and Dr Johnson?
2. Who is the Greek goddess of war?
3. In which city was Mussolini hanged with his mistress in a public square in 1945?
4. Which couple were played on television by Michael Crawford and Michelle Dotrice?
5. Which order of classical column has leaves in the capital?
6. What sort of religious building derives its name from the Latin word for 'seat'?
7. Who created the famous gardens at Sissinghurst?
8. What is a frogmouth?
9. Where is the Vincent van Gogh Museum?
10. Who built the first steam engine to run on rails?

Answers on page 427

MIXED BAG

Mixed Bag

True or False? 1

1. The mangelwurzel is a nickname for a scarecrow. True or false?
2. Bizet was a French composer. True or false?
3. Socrates, the great Greek philosopher, never wrote anything down. True or false?
4. The Arctic is one of the seven continents of the world. True or false?
5. All toadstools are mushrooms but not all mushrooms are toadstools. True or false?
6. The swastika was traditionally a symbol of good luck. True or false?
7. The chancellor of the Exchequer is the first lord of the Treasury. True or false?
8. Antarctica contains 70% of the world's fresh water. True or false?
9. Scorpions are eight-legged arachnids, like spiders. True or false?
10. King John signed the Magna Carta. True or false?

Answers on page 428

Mixed Bag

True or False? 2

1. The legendary female warriors called Amazons lived in the Amazon basin. True or false?
2. The word 'dinosaur' is derived from the Greek for 'terrible lizard'. True or false?
3. Richard the Lionheart spent all but six months of his ten-year reign in England. True or false?
4. Contestants in the Olympic Games of ancient Greece competed naked. True or false?
5. The American CIA is the equivalent organization of Britain's CID. True or false?
6. Titus and Philemon are two books of the New Testament. True or false?
7. Big Ben is the clock in the tower of the Houses of Parliament. True or false?
8. In computing, a kilobyte is 1,000 bytes. True or false?
9. The dogfish is actually a small shark. True or false?
10. The dingo, Australia's wild dog, cannot bark. True or false?

Answers on page 428

Mixed Bag

True or False? 3

1. Tomatoes and potatoes grow on plants belonging to the same family as deadly nightshade. True or false?

2. Jazz musician William Basie was better known as Duke. True or false?

3. Nicotine, in its pure form, is one of the most powerful poisons known. True or false?

4. Antarctica has less annual precipitation than the Sahara desert. True or false?

5. The Duke of Edinburgh's grandfather was King George I of Greece. True or false?

6. Prince is the real first name of 'the artist formerly known as Prince', the US pop star. True or false?

7. Anchorage is the capital of Alaska. True or false?

8. All century years such as 1700, 1800 and 1900 are leap years because they divide by four. True or false?

9. Caligula, the Roman emperor, gave a consulship to his horse, Incitatus. True or false?

10. All four feet of a beaver are webbed. True or false?

Answers on page 428

Mixed Bag

True or False? 4

1. An emu cannot fly. True or false?
2. A dowager is the widow of a peer or a baronet. True or false?
3. Julie Andrews was the original Eliza Doolittle in *My Fair Lady*. True or false?
4. Fleas are bloodsuckers. True or false?
5. Wyoming is on the Canadian border of the USA. True or false?
6. Two is a prime number. True or false?
7. 'Quaker' is another name for a Mormon. True or false?
8. Pythagoras shouted 'Eureka!' when he thought of his theorem. True or false?
9. Silly mid-on is a fielding position in cricket. True or false?
10. Spartacus was a great Roman general. True or false?

Answers on page 428

Mixed Bag

True or False? 5

1. The Roman emperor Hadrian was born in Italy. True or false?

2. In the Netherlands, all governments since 1945 have been coalitions. True or false?

3. The French eat an average of 5 kilos of snails per head per year. True or false?

4. The hands and feet contain almost half the bones in the human body. True or false?

5. There are three goals at each end in Australian Rules football. True or false?

6. A mudskipper fish often climbs out of the water, and skips away when alarmed. True or false?

7. British MPs have always received a salary. True or false?

8. P G Wodehouse collaborated with Kern and Gershwin to write Broadway musicals. True or false?

9. Giant worms over 3 metres long live at the bottom of the sea beside hydrothermal vents called smokers. True or false?

10. Washington, Jefferson, Lincoln, and Grant are the four Presidents' heads sculpted into Mount Rushmore. True or false?

Answers on page 428

Mixed Bag

True or False? 6

1. In Greek mythology, a Hydra had nine heads. True or false?

2. Bizet's opera *Carmen* was a hit when it was first performed. True or false?

3. Jean Muir was a fashion designer. True or false?

4. *Cosi fan tutte* means 'thus do all women'. True or false?

5. The name of the world's first nuclear-powered submarine is *Nautilus*. True or false?

6. President Lincoln was a Republican. True or false?

7. Raphael painted the *Birth of Venus*. True or false?

8. Dashiel Hammett created the detective Philip Marlowe. True or false?

9. Winston Churchill and his father were both chancellor of the Exchequer. True or false?

10. Canaries are found in the wild in the Canary Islands. True or false?

Answers on page 428

Mixed Bag

True or False? 7

1. Kinshasa used to be called Léopoldville. True or false?
2. The flag of Morocco shows a green star on a red background. True or false?
3. Henry Ford said 'History can teach us all we need to know'. True or false?
4. President Kennedy proposed the Four Noble Truths. True or false?
5. Manuel II succeeded Carlos I on the throne of Spain in 1908. True or false?
6. Baseball player Mickey Mantle batted both left- and right-handed. True or false?
7. Rudyard Kipling was born in India. True or false?
8. Haydn wrote more than 100 symphonies. True or false?
9. A chinook is a kind of reindeer. True or false?
10. U2 released their album *The Unforgiveable Fire* in 1984. True or false?

Answers on page 429

Mixed Bag

True or False? 8

1. Memphis was the name of an early capital of Egypt. True or false?
2. The laws of the United Kingdom are based on a written constitution kept at the Houses of Parliament. True or false?
3. William the Conqueror was the illegitimate son of Robert the Devil, Duke of Normandy. True or false?
4. Isaac Newton, the mathematician and physicist, was a Whig MP. True or false?
5. The South Orkneys is the name of a group of islands off the north coast of Scotland. True or false?
6. The numbat is a marsupial and rears its young in a pouch. True or false?
7. Stephenson's locomotive *Rocket* pulled the first public steam train from Stockton to Darlington in 1825. True or false?
8. An 'inferno' is a unit of heat equal to 1 billion K (about 1 billion°C). True or false?
9. Squirrels, beavers, chipmunks and porcupines are all rodents. True or false?
10. The group of long-established US universities known as the Ivy League is so named because each one had the emblem of an ivy leaf. True or false?

Answers on page 429

Mixed Bag

True or False? 9

1. The basic unit of currency in Egypt, Lebanon and Syria is the dinar. True or false?
2. The Russian parliament building in Moscow is called the White House. True or false?
3. The engine which powered the Sinclair C5 was a washing-machine motor. True or false?
4. Chinook, Sirocco, Harmattan and Mistral are all names of helicopters. True or false?
5. Tartans were banned after the Jacobite rebellion of 1745 until 1782. True or false?
6. The jackal-headed god Anubis guided the souls of the dead in ancient Egypt. True or false?
7. Roman soldiers were paid part of their salary in salt. True or false?
8. Only female wasps sting. True or false?
9. Kenneth MacAlpin united the kingdoms of Scotland in the 9th century. True or false?
10. Tokyo has a Disney theme park. True or false?

Answers on page 429

Mixed Bag

True or False? 10

1. Picasso said 'Art is a truth that lets us recognize a lie'. True or false?

2. IQ are the initials of the ratio between a person's mental age and actual age, multiplied by 100. True or false?

3. Zoetrope was the Greek goddess of flowers. True or false?

4. Sinn Féin means 'soldiers of destiny'. True or false?

5. A hellebore is a poisonous plant. True or false?

6. Utah is nicknamed 'the Waterfall State'. True or false?

7. A manometer measures the pressure of liquids. True or false?

8. Tex Avery unsuccessfully fought Joe Louis for the World Heavyweight Boxing championship. True or false?

9. Codeine suppresses a cough. True or false?

10. US Presidents William Henry Harrison and Benjamin Harrison were grandfather and grandson. True or false?

Answers on page 429

Mixed Bag

Choices 1

1. The colour of a polar bear's skin is: a) black b) pink c) white
2. Mother Teresa of Calcutta was born in: a) Afghanistan b) Albania c) India
3. In 1721 Britain's first prime minister took office. How many since then have been Labour prime ministers? a) six b) eight c) ten
4. What did the USA buy from the Russians for $7.2 million? a) The rights to the film of Lenin's life story b) Tchaikovsky's original manuscripts c) Alaska
5. The capybara is a South American rodent whose average weight is: a) 250 grams b) 3.5 kilos c) 50 kilos
6. The part of a sundial which casts a shadow to tell the time is called: a) an elfon b) a gnomon c) a pixion
7. The ice in the Antarctic reaches a depth of: a) 4.8 metres b) 487 metres c) 4876 metres
8. In 1953 Winston Churchill won a Nobel prize for: a) Peace b) Literature c) Economics
9. The basic currency unit of Vietnam is: a) the ding b) the deng c) the dong
10. Nelson lost an eye in 1794 and an arm in 1797; they were his: a) right arm/right eye b) right arm/left eye c) right eye/left arm

Answers on page 429

Mixed Bag

Choices 2

1. Gargoyles were often carved on Gothic churches as: a) frighteners to ward off the devil b) carvings done by apprentices to achieve skill c) embellished waterspouts
2. The *Laughing Cavalier* was painted by: a) Holbein b) Rembrandt c) Hals
3. Was the mythical centaur: a) half-man/half-bull b) half-man/half-horse c) half-man/half-goat?
4. No place in the UK is further from the sea than: a) $53\frac{1}{2}$ miles b) $74\frac{1}{2}$ miles c) $91\frac{1}{2}$ miles
5. Terry Waite's ordeal as a hostage in Lebanon lasted: a) 63 days b) 763 days c) 1,763 days
6. The president's wife who was the subject of a successful musical written in 1978 was: a) Imelda Marcos b) Eva Peron c) Jacqueline Kennedy
7. Which US writer moved to Europe, and took British citizenship the year before he died? a) Henry James b) T S Eliot c) W H Auden
8. The 'Great White Shark' is the nickname of the golfer: a) Jack Nicklaus b) Arnold Palmer c) Greg Norman
9. The approximate number of copies of Michael Jackson's best-selling album *Thriller* sold worldwide was: a) 20 million b) 40 million c) 60 million
10. The average adult human digestive tract measures: a) 75 cm b) 9 metres c) 27 metres

Answers on page 429

Mixed Bag

Choices 3

1. The stage name of the American film star Issur Danielovitch is: a) Richard Widmark b) Burt Lancaster c) Kirk Douglas

2. Bonnie Prince Charlie, the Young Pretender, was born in: a) Italy b) Ireland c) France

3. Which country has the largest Muslim population in the world? a) Indonesia b) India c) Iran

4. Chatsworth House, seat of the Duke of Devonshire, is in the county of: a) Derbyshire b) Dorset c) Devon

5. The heat at the centre of the Sun is: a) 27,000,000°C b) 80,000°C c) 15,000,000°C

6. The Dead Sea is below sea level by: a) 397 metres b) 699 metres c) 1003 metres

7. In Japan, the Shinkansen is: a) a religious rite b) a type of tea c) a fast railway network

8. Up to how many times its own height can a flea jump? a) 30 b) 130 c) 330

9. Hurricane Gilbert, which hit the Caribbean in 1988, had winds gusting over: a) 100 mph b) 150 mph c) 200 mph

10. The official language of the Pyrenean country of Andorra is: a) Catalan b) French c) Spanish

Answers on page 430

Mixed Bag

Choices 4

1. When did Canberra become the Australian capital? a) 1878 b) 1908 c) 1928
2. The Japanese word meaning 'empty hand' is: a) kungfu b) karate c) kendo
3. The approximate distance in miles between the Earth and the Sun is: a) 9,000,000 b) 90,000,000 c) 900,000,000
4. The last king of Albania was called: a) King Xog b) King Yog c) King Zog
5. The human body contains: a) 106 bones b) 156 bones c) 206 bones
6. Moscow's underground system, the Metro, carries approximately how many passengers per day? a) 1,500,000 b) 6,500,000 c) 16,500,000
7. According to the Old Testament, how old was Methuselah when he died? a) 696 yrs b) 969 yrs c) 996 yrs
8. Which sport had its first set of rules drawn up in 1848; its Association founded in 1863; and its League formed in 1888? a) rugby b) cricket c) football
9. Mount Ararat is in present-day: a) Turkey b) Israel c) Syria
10. In helping Bonnie Prince Charlie escape to France, Flora Macdonald disguised him as: a) her sister b) her tutor c) her maid

Answers on page 430

Mixed Bag

Choices 5

1. What creatures do wild bananas depend on for pollination? a) bats b) humming birds c) butterflies

2. Maurice Micklewhite is the real name of the film actor: a) Terence Stamp b) Bob Hoskins c) Michael Caine

3. The first British Open Golf Championship was held in: a) 1860 b) 1880 c) 1900

4. The loganberry was named after: a) Mount Logan in Canada where it was found b) The US judge James H Logan who grew it c) Logan Farm in Scotland, where it was cultivated

5. Karaoke is the Japanese word meaning: a) plain singing b) empty orchestra c) backing music

6. What bird family does the peacock belong to? a) pheasant b) kingfisher c) bird of paradise

7. The maximum diameter of a hockey stick is: a) 2.5 cm b) 5 cm c) 7.5 cm

8. The worldwide total of nuclear weapons in 1990 was: a) 5,000 b) 15,000 c) 50,000

9. The world's largest producer of wine is: a) Italy b) Bulgaria c) France

10. How many bicycles are said to be used in the world today? a) 800 million b) 8 billion c) 8 trillion

Answers on page 430

Mixed Bag

Choices 6

1 The largest known swarm of locusts covered an area of: a) 400 sq yd b) 400 sq km c) 400 sq mi

2 Domenikos Theotokopoulos is better known as: a) Zorba the Greek b) Demis Roussos c) El Greco

3 In 1991 in the UK smoking-related diseases killed: a) 13,000 b) 113,000 c) 213,000

4 A merino is: a) a Spanish sailor b) an Italian sculptor c) an Australian sheep

5 Wykehamists are old pupils of: a) Rugby School b) Marlborough College c) Winchester College

6 The poet laureate receives a yearly stipend of: a) £70 b) £700 c) £7,000

7 In which equestrian sport is a 'sulky' an essential piece of equipment? a) dressage b) harness racing c) polo

8 The actor Richard Burton's real Welsh surname was: a) Jenkins b) Jones c) Davies

9 Which English city did the Romans call Eboracum? a) Chester b) Bath c) York

10 The area of Russia is so large that the UK would fit into it: a) 40 times b) 70 times c) 100 times

Answers on page 430

Mixed Bag

1, 2, 3... 1

1. What is the alternative name for a one-humped camel?
2. Who wrote the play *Two Gentlemen of Verona*?
3. Who wrote *Three Men in a Boat*?
4. Which Italian-born US actor had his first starring role in *The Four Horsemen of the Apocalypse* in 1921?
5. What is the name of the five-sided office housing the US Department of Defence?
6. Italian playwright Pirandello wrote of *Six Characters in search of...* what?
7. Which of the Seven Wonders of the World was at Babylon?
8. What is the name for a distance of eight white notes on a piano keyboard?
9. Which composer born in 1770 wrote nine symphonies?
10. Which detective novelist wrote *Ten Little Indians*?

Answers on page 430

Mixed Bag

1, 2, 3... 2

1. Which number code system is based on the digits 1 and 0?
2. Who was the American U-2 pilot shot down over the USSR in 1960?
3. Who wrote *The Three Sisters*?
4. How many gold medals, in total, did Carl Lewis win in the Olympic Games of 1984 and 1988?
5. A pilgrimage to which city is stipulated in the five pillars of Islam?
6. Which king introduced the Six Articles Act to settle disputes over dogma in the English church?
7. Which of the seven deadly sins begins with the letter 'g'?
8. Who commanded the 8th Army at the Second Battle of El Alamein?
9. Who were the nine daughters of Zeus and Mnemosyne who inspired the creative arts?
10. On how many tablets of stone were the Ten Commandments engraved?

Answers on page 430

MIXED BAG

1, 2, 3... 3

1. Which gas has the atomic number 1?
2. In which country is K2?
3. Who wrote the music for *The Threepenny Opera*?
4. Who wrote *The Four Quartets*?
5. What is the Greek (and Christian) name for the first five books of the Bible?
6. Which cricketer established a record with six 6s in one over?
7. Who directed *The Seven Samurai*?
8. What does the ringing of eight bells mean on board a ship?
9. The ninth president of the USA shared his surname with the 23rd. What was it?
10. What was the name of Boccaccio's collection of stories told by ten young people fleeing plague-stricken Florence?

Answers on page 431

Mixed Bag

Colours 1

1 What name was given to Chinese students active during the revolution of the 1960s?

2 What is the name for an area around a city preserved as open space?

3 Which forest lies on the banks of the Rhine in Baden-Württemberg in Germany?

4 What is the English name for China's Huang He river?

5 Which folktale character murdered six wives who disobeyed his command not to enter a locked room?

6 In which London street does the Cenotaph stand?

7 Who was queen of England for nine days in 1553?

8 What is the Scottish village made famous as a venue for runaway marriages?

9 What was the badge of the House of York during the Wars of the Roses?

10 Which period of Picasso's creative life preceded his Rose Period?

Answers on page 431

Mixed Bag

Colours 2

1. What part of a redshank is red?
2. What is the better-known name for quicksilver?
3. Which grain crop comes in white, red, brown and black varieties?
4. What colour is the central strip on the French flag?
5. Who does Alice follow down a hole into Wonderland?
6. Who made the albums *The Dark Side of the Moon* and *The Wall*?
7. Who composed the waltz 'The Blue Danube'?
8. Which pop group provided the voices for the cartoon *Yellow Submarine*?
9. Which canal joins the Red Sea and the Mediterranean?
10. Of which country was Greenland a colony until 1981?

Answers on page 431

Mixed Bag

Colours 3

1. The royal family of Holland gained its name from which small town in France?
2. Who is the record six times winner at the Badminton Horse Trials?
3. Which British rock band formed in 1965 had Syd Barrett among its founders?
4. What is the popular name for the flower of the genus *Kniphofia* which has a flame-coloured spike of flowers?
5. What was the nickname of Edward, Prince of Wales, son of Edward III of England?
6. Which famous gardener, first name Lancelot, helped landscape Blenheim, Stowe and Petworth?
7. Which great epidemic of bubonic plague ravaged Europe in the 14th century?
8. What colour is the riband of the Order of the Garter?
9. On which gulf of the Arctic Ocean does Archangel stand?
10. What was Ghana's former name?

Answers on page 431

Mixed Bag

Colours 4

1 Which film gained Paul Newman an Oscar in 1986?
2 What colour are salmon's eggs?
3 How many does the blue ball score in snooker?
4 What are red giants?
5 Which celebrated actress and courtesan started her career as an orange seller?
6 Who wrote the jazz classic *Rhapsody in Blue*?
7 Whose World Series Cricket introduced coloured uniforms to the game?
8 What colourful new name did Francis Drake give his ship the *Pelican*?
9 What happened on Black Thursday, 29 October 1929?
10 Which world-famous tourist attraction is in Orange County, California?

Answers on page 431

Mixed Bag

Colours 5

1. Where is the USA's National Radio Astronomy Observatory?
2. What is the USA's earliest military award for distinguished service beyond the call of duty?
3. What is the capital of Canada's North West Territories?
4. What colour is the cross on the Greek flag?
5. Who was English prime minister from 1830–4?
6. A battle fought near Milan in 1859 is commemorated in the name of which dye?
7. In which Wilkie Collins novel does the fat villain Count Fosco appear?
8. From what colour rock is the Jordanian city of Petra carved?
9. What colour is the widely-banned liqueur absinthe?
10. Which two colours are mixed in a television to produce the effect of yellow?

Answers on page 431

Mixed Bag

Colours 6

1. Who wrote *The Scarlet Letter*?
2. What was the birthplace of naturalist Gilbert White, immortalized in his best-known book?
3. *Tom Brown's Schooldays* provided a fictionalized portrait of the headmaster of which great English public school?
4. What colour are halides, the light-sensitive compounds used to coat photographic film?
5. What kind of creature is a green darner?
6. What colour shirts were worn by the followers of Garibaldi?
7. Which king of England was nicknamed 'the Red'?
8. Which English composer wrote *A Colour Symphony* in 1922?
9. What is the red dye cochineal obtained from?
10. Who is the father of Lady Rose Windsor, born in 1980?

Answers on page 432

Mixed Bag

Colours in Science

1 What colour is chlorophyll?
2 What colour is haemoglobin?
3 What colour is the surface of Mars?
4 What colour is the planet Neptune when viewed from Earth?
5 What colour is the longest wavelength of visible light?
6 The dye indigo can be obtained naturally from which kind of organism?
7 What colour is the mineral lazurite?
8 In which branch of science is the 'red shift' important?
9 When our Sun runs out of fuel it will briefly pour out which colour of light?
10 What name is given to the blue-green coating that forms as a natural patina on copper, bronze, and brass?

Answers on page 432

MIXED BAG

Time

1. How many seconds are there in an hour?
2. Which device uses the Sun to tell the time?
3. Which crystal keeps time inside today's mass-produced watches?
4. What type of clocks are the most accurate timekeepers?
5. How many electronic pips does the British Broadcasting Corporation broadcast on the hour?
6. From a building in which London borough are all time zones calculated?
7. Who wrote *The Time Machine*?
8. Which device is used to keep time in music?
9. What is the main scientific time unit from which all others are calculated?
10. Where was the first known public clock located?

Answers on page 432

Mixed Bag

Money

1. Is the currency unit of Ecuador the sol, the quarani or the sucre?
2. Where was the Royal Mint for centuries until 1810?
3. What was the notional value of a guinea, used in billing professional fees in Britain until 1971?
4. What is San Marino's currency?
5. The anchor for the European monetary system was moved to which currency after the depreciation of the dollar?
6. Did Britain abandon the gold standard in 1911, 1931 or 1951?
7. What is pennyroyal?
8. Who directed *A Fistful of Dollars*?
9. What is the currency of the British colony of Bermuda?
10. How is a country's trade helped by devaluation?

Answers on page 432

Mixed Bag

Who, What, or Where? 1

1 Who lives in the Vatican?
2 Who was the youngest person to be elected president of the USA?
3 Who wrote a famous diary about her life in hiding from the Nazis in Amsterdam?
4 Who 'singed the king of Spain's beard' in 1587?
5 Where are the British crown jewels kept?
6 What was the name of Ho Chi Minh City before 1976?
7 Who ruled Rome in a triumvirate with Octavian and Lepidus?
8 What are shown every year at Crufts?
9 Where was St Paul converted by a vision?
10 What is the largest fast-food chain in the world?

Answers on page 432

Mixed Bag

Who, What, or Where? 2

1. Who told of his running and jumping exploits in 1990 in *Inside Track*?
2. What is numismatics?
3. Who patented the telephone in 1876?
4. Who was the wife of King Arthur?
5. What is a Bombay duck?
6. Where does Alice meet the Cheshire Cat and the Mad Hatter?
7. Who was assassinated on the Ides of March, 44BC?
8. What game is played for the Davis Cup?
9. Where is the cathedral of Nôtre Dame?
10. Who founded the Scout movement?

Answers on page 432

Mixed Bag

Who, What, or Where? 3

1. Who was the first English woman to qualify in medicine?
2. Where were 153 Sioux massacred by the US army two weeks after Sitting Bull was killed?
3. What is Bora-Bora?
4. Who co-wrote the *Liverpool Oratorio* with Carl Davis in 1991?
5. What is the least spoken official language in Switzerland?
6. Where did Livingstone and Stanley meet in 1871?
7. Who translated the Greek New Testament in 1516 and exposed the Vulgate as a second-hand document?
8. What is the capital of Sardinia?
9. Where was the treaty signed which ended the Crimean War?
10. Who painted *The Awakening Conscience* and *The Light of the World*?

Answers on page 433

Mixed Bag

Crime

1 Which area of London did Jack the Ripper terrorize in 1888?

2 For what offence was Al Capone imprisoned from 1931–39?

3 Who killed Billy the Kid in 1881?

4 The kidnap and murder of whose child horrified America in 1932?

5 Which brothers led the Quantrill raiders of US bank and train robbers?

6 Who shot Abraham Lincoln?

7 Which Belgian crimewriter created the detective Maigret?

8 Who was the convicted robber who was released by Pilate at Passover to appease a mob?

9 Which organization has bosses called *capos*?

10 Which secret society reputedly involved in organized crime allegedly has its headquarters in Hong Kong?

Answers on page 433

Mixed Bag

Catastrophes and Disasters

1. In which year did the space shuttle *Challenger* explode, killing all seven people on board?
2. The eruption of which Indonesian volcano caused 36,000 deaths in 1883?
3. Which country has seen the two worst earthquakes, in terms of numbers killed, this century?
4. What is the proper name for a tidal wave?
5. In which year did the *Titanic* sink?
6. In which thoroughfare did the Great Fire of London begin?
7. Which airship exploded in New Jersey in 1937?
8. Where did methyl isocyanate cause 2,600 deaths in 1984?
9. Who wrote unintentionally bad verse about the Tay Bridge disaster of 1879?
10. What did an announcement by US treasury secretary James Baker prompt in October 1987?

Answers on page 433

Mixed Bag

Fashion

1 Photographer Cecil Beaton won Oscars for his designs for *Gigi* and which other film?

2 Who made an impact with the 'New Look' after establishing a Paris salon in 1947?

3 Who was the first French women's clothes designer to show a collection for men?

4 How did the bikini gain its name?

5 Who gained international recognition with 'Pirate' and 'New Romantic' looks?

6 Which London thoroughfare is noted for its high quality tailors?

7 What was the trade name of American designer Roy Frowick, who died in 1990?

8 Under what label does Georgio Armani design for young men and women?

9 What was the name of Mary Quant's boutique which revolutionized fashion in the 1960s?

10 Who was the American pioneer of 'rational dress'?

Answers on page 433

Mixed Bag

Language

1. What is the official language of Iran?
2. What language did Jesus speak?
3. What kind of language are COBOL and ALGOL?
4. Which body ensures the purity of the French language?
5. RP is the standard form of English pronunciation – what do the letters stand for?
6. Who first translated the whole of the Bible into English?
7. From which language does Yiddish derive?
8. Pidgin English originally evolved for trade between Britain and which country?
9. Which Irish dramatist was an unsuccessful advocate of spelling reform?
10. Louis Braille invented a system of writing for the blind – was he blind himself?

Answers on page 433

Mixed Bag

Water, Water, Everywhere 1

1. What is the chemical symbol for water?
2. What is the better known name for the fatal disease hydrophobia whose sufferers have convulsions at the sight of water?
3. Which is the world's largest ocean?
4. Who wrote the *Water Music*?
5. Why are fluoride salts added to some drinking water?
6. Which star sign depicts a man pouring water from a jar?
7. What is the name of the geyser in Yellowstone National Park, USA, which erupts predictably?
8. Complete the title of Charles Kingsley's classic novel *The Water-* ...
9. What is the name for small rivers which join a major one along its length?
10. *Flatford Mill* was painted by John Constable. In which English county is this Flatford?

Answers on page 433

Mixed Bag

Water, Water, Everywhere 2

1 Which warship's wreck was raised in 1982, 437 years after it had sunk?
2 In which country is lake Baikal?
3 Which capital city is close to Waterloo?
4 What percentage of the human body is made up of water?
5 Who wrote *Watership Down*?
6 In which country is Lake Guatavita, the source of the legend of 'El Dorado'?
7 How many players are in the water at one time in a water polo match?
8 The male of which species of whale, found only in the Arctic Ocean, possesses a spiral tusk up to 2.7 metres long?
9 For what product is the Irish town of Waterford famous?
10 Which is the second largest of the Great Lakes?

Answers on page 434

Mixed Bag

Archeology

1. The existence of which legendary civilization was proved by Arthur Evans's excavations on Crete?
2. Did Howard Carter and Lord Carnarvon discover Tutankhamen's tomb in 1916, 1922 or 1934?
3. What did Charles Dawson 'discover' in 1913 that was proved a fake 40 years later?
4. What is dendrochronology, a useful discipline in some archaeological work?
5. What type of burial mounds date from the later Mesolithic peoples of the early Bronze Age?
6. Which well-known English archaeologist uncovered the Indus Valley civilization?
7. In which country were the skeletons of Cro-Magnon man found in 1868?
8. Systematic excavation of which major site began in 1763 and still continues?
9. What was the old Roman capital of England?
10. Excavation of the tombs of which civilization uncovered high-spirited paintings showing feasting, dancing and swimming?

Answers on page 434

Mixed Bag

Economics

1 After which international conference in 1944 was the International Monetary Fund set up?

2 Which English economist and cleric wrote *Essay on the Principle of Population*?

3 Whose law stated that income distribution remained constant whatever efforts were made to change it?

4 What does the Greek word 'economics' mean?

5 Who wrote *The General Theory of Employment, Interest and Money* in 1936?

6 In which year was the European Economic Community established?

7 Who wrote *The Wealth of Nations*?

8 Which English economist sat as a Radical in Parliament from 1865–68 and urged votes for women?

9 What nationality was the Nobel prize-winning economist Ragnar Frisch?

10 Which Russian economist produced the theory that decentralization of decisions in a planned economy could only be made with a rational price system?

Answers on page 434

Mixed Bag

Cats and Dogs 1

1. Who played Inspector Clouseau in five *Pink Panther* films?
2. Which breed of dog was kept by monks to find lost travellers in the Alps?
3. Which detective figures in the novel *The Hound of the Baskervilles*?
4. In which continent do jaguars live?
5. What was the name of the crew's pet cat in the original *Alien!* film?
6. Which general of World War II was nicknamed 'the Desert Fox'?
7. In astrology, which two months are in the star sign Leo?
8. What is unusual about a Manx cat?
9. Which dogs used to walk beside carriages to fend off highwaymen?
10. Which is the largest of the great cats?

Answers on page 434

Mixed Bag

Cats and Dogs 2

1. How many canine teeth does a human have?
2. What is another name for a mountain lion?
3. Who was the female star of the 1965 film *Cat Ballou*?
4. Which snow leopard has a name which suggests a unit of weight?
5. Which great cat is nearing extinction in Sumatra, due to poachers?
6. Which variety of dog originating in America cannot be imported, bred, or sold in Britain under laws passed in 1989 and 1991?
7. Who wrote the music for *Cats*?
8. What is a fox's den called?
9. A famous George Stubbs painting shows which animal attacking a horse?
10. How many heads did Cerberus, the dog who guarded Hades, have?

Answers on page 434

Mixed Bag

Cats and Dogs 3

1. Who directed the 1963 film *The Leopard*?
2. Who wrote the 1974 thriller *The Dogs of War*?
3. Which cartoon cat was the first to make the crossing from screen to comic strip?
4. What group of British political campaigners were affected by the Cat and Mouse Act?
5. Who collaborated with Christopher Isherwood on the verse drama *The Dog Beneath the Skin*?
6. Which make of car is built at Wolfsburg?
7. Who was called 'the Lion of Judah'?
8. Which size of poodle comes between standard and toy?
9. Which dog's name means 'badger-dog' in German?
10. Which jazzman recorded *Bitches' Brew* in 1970?

Answers on page 434

Mixed Bag

Name the Year 1

1. In which year did Wall Street crash and Herbert Hoover become president of the USA?
2. Which year saw Nicolae Ceauşescu overthrown in Romania and Jack Nicholson appearing in *Batman*?
3. Which year saw popes John Paul I and II elected and Princess Margaret divorced from Lord Snowdon?
4. In which year did England win soccer's World Cup and Bob Dylan release *Blonde on Blonde*?
5. In which year did the Allies mount the D-day invasion and Humphrey Bogart star in *To Have and Have Not*?
6. Which year saw the deaths of Pope John XXIII and John F Kennedy, and the flight of the first woman in space?
7. Which year saw an abortive coup against President Gorbachev, and Robert Maxwell found dead at sea?
8. In which year did Jesse Owens dominate the Berlin Olympics and Edward VIII abdicate?
9. In which year did Leonid Brezhnev die and Argentina and Britain fight a war over the Falkland Islands?
10. In which year did man first walk on the Moon and Georges Pompidou succeed Charles de Gaulle as president of France?

Answers on page 435

Mixed Bag

Name the Year 2

1. In which year did *Sputnik I* become the first artificial satellite, and Harold Macmillan become British prime minister?
2. Which year saw Scott of the Antarctic's last expedition and the sinking of the *Titanic*?
3. In which year was the wreck of the *Titanic* found and the Greenpeace ship *Rainbow Warrior* sunk?
4. In which year did Mao Zedong found the People's Republic of China and the USSR lift the Berlin blockade?
5. In which year did Richard Nixon resign as US president and Tom Stoppard's *Travesties* appear?
6. In which year did Fidel Castro overthrow the Batista regime in Cuba and Buddy Holly die in a plane crash?
7. Which year saw Margaret Thatcher elected leader of the Conservative party and Arthur Ashe win Wimbledon?
8. In which year was Prohibition lifted and Hitler appointed chancellor of Germany?
9. In which year did the Rolling Stones release 'Satisfaction' and Aleksei Leonov make the first space walk?
10. In which year did Jimmy Carter lose a presidential election and Bjorn Borg win his fifth and last Wimbledon title?

Answers on page 435

Mixed Bag

What's in a Name? 1

1. Which name was shared by three of Henry VIII's wives?
2. Thomas Newcomen called his invention a 'fire engine', but what do we call it?
3. Who gave his name to the SI unit of electrical current?
4. What was the name of the ferry that capsized off Zeebrugge in 1987?
5. What name is given to the wild pansy?
6. What was the boxer Muhammad Ali's former name?
7. What is the modern name of the city once called Byzantium?
8. What is the American rocket launch site, once called Cape Kennedy, now called?
9. What was the assumed name of Jean François Gravelet, who crossed Niagara Falls on a tightrope?
10. Which famous Apache chief became a Christian and a farmer?

Answers on page 435

Mixed Bag

What's in a Name? 2

1. What was the name of the Black Prince?
2. What adjective connects 24 September 1869, 29 October 1929, and 19 October 1987?
3. What was the first name of the children's writer E Nesbit?
4. What is the highest decoration awarded for bravery by the British armed forces?
5. What name was given to armed Russians fighting behind the French lines in 1812?
6. Which poet's middle name was Bysshe?
7. Who was known as Hollywood's 'Love Goddess' in the 1940s?
8. What does the F in John F Kennedy stand for?
9. What nickname was given to Arthur Harris of the RAF in World War II?
10. Who was the female star of the 1993 film *In the Name of the Father*?

Answers on page 435

Mixed Bag

What's in a Name? 3

1. What is blue john?
2. What stage name did the French actress and dancer Jeanne Bourgeois take?
3. What does the K in Jerome K Jerome stand for?
4. What was the name of the jet-powered car that took Richard Noble to the land-speed record in 1983?
5. Which planet has a moon named after a Shakespearean queen of the fairies?
6. Which Italian author wrote *The Name of the Rose*?
7. What was the name of the spacecraft that carried Yuri Gagarin on the first manned flight?
8. What is the common name of Risso's dolphin?
9. What name is given to a baseball player who bats both left- and right-handed?
10. Which film star started his career in 1927 under the name Duke Morrison?

Answers on page 435

ENTERTAINMENT

ENTERTAINMENT

General 1

1 Which of Bob Kane's strip-cartoon characters has the secret identity of millionaire playboy Bruce Wayne?

2 What is the pen-name of James Wight, whose books about his experiences as a Yorkshire vet were made into several television series?

3 By which collective name would you identify the group whose first names begin with J, P, G, and R?

4 Which cockney actor is famous for his part in the film *Alfie*?

5 Which type of music developed from the spirituals sung in the Baptist churches of the southern USA?

6 Who are the two characters, a dim-witted socialite and his urbane manservant, created by P G Wodehouse?

7 Which film starring Anthony Hopkins won the 1991 Academy Award for Best Picture?

8 Which writer of children's books also wrote *Tales of the Unexpected* for television and the screenplay for the film *You Only Live Twice*?

9 Which group of Jim Henson puppets first appeared on American television in *Sesame Street*?

10 What is the title of the Andrew Lloyd Webber musical based on a collection of animal poems by T S Eliot?

Answers on page 436

Entertainment

General 2

1 Which American pioneer of modern dance died when her long scarf caught in the wheel of a car?

2 What was the name of the American showman who established 'The Greatest Show on Earth' in 1871?

3 Who wrote the opera *Rigoletto*?

4 Which Swiss lakeside resort has an annual television festival whose top award is the Golden Rose?

5 Who appeared in the Oxford revue *Beyond The Fringe* and went on to open a satirical nightclub called the Establishment?

6 What was the screen name of Lee Yuen Kam?

7 Who wrote the lyrics for Leonard Bernstein's musical *West Side Story*?

8 Which London theatre began life as the Coburg, but should really be known as the Royal Victoria Hall?

9 Which playwright wrote the controversial television play *Brimstone and Treacle* in 1976, but found it banned from transmission until 1987?

10 Which German-born naturalist's work with wildlife in Kenya was portrayed in the film *Born Free*?

Answers on page 436

Entertainment

General 3

1. What is known in the USA as 'off-off Broadway'?
2. What was the nickname of the Marx brother who left the zany group before any films were made?
3. In which type of Japanese drama do men take all the parts, in the interests of propriety?
4. Who co-founded the Renaissance Theatre Company with David Parfitt in 1987?
5. Who wrote *The Beggar's Opera* in 1728?
6. Whose book *The Wonderful Wizard of Oz* was made into the film starring Judy Garland?
7. Which entertainer began his career as dancing partner to Mistinguett at the Folies-Bergère?
8. Which Scottish music-hall singer started out as an 'Irish' comedian?
9. Who was the jazz clarinettist nicknamed the 'King of Swing'?
10. Which two people were *Waiting for Godot*, in the play by Samuel Beckett?

Answers on page 436

ENTERTAINMENT

Music 1

1. Which Baroque composer wrote *The Four Seasons*?
2. Beethoven, Dvořák and Vaughan Williams all wrote the same number of symphonies. How many?
3. On which instrument was Frédéric Chopin a virtuoso?
4. What is the name of the guitar-like Russian stringed instrument with a triangular body?
5. Which Viennese composer left his eighth symphony unfinished?
6. How many valves does a trumpet have?
7. Which opera did Bizet write just before his death in 1875?
8. Of what kind of dance did Johann Strauss become 'king' in the late 19th century?
9. Which female singing voice lies between soprano and contralto?
10. Which instrument does Nigel Kennedy play?

Answers on page 436

ENTERTAINMENT

Music 2

1. Who was the youngest Beatle?
2. Who wrote the music for *West Side Story*?
3. Which composer's works are known by K-numbers?
4. Who had a 1966 hit with 'Good Vibrations'?
5. What style of composition are Haydn's *The Creation* and Handel's *Messiah*?
6. Which jazz musician was known as Yardbird, or Bird?
7. To what section of the orchestra do the bassoon and clarinet belong?
8. Which guitar maker produced the Stratocaster?
9. Who wrote the *Brandenburg Concertos*?
10. How is singer Paul Hewson better known?

Answers on page 436

Entertainment

Music 3

1 Which instrument's name translates literally as 'soft loud'?
2 What are performed at La Scala, Milan and at the auditorium in Covent Garden, London?
3 What is the name for the annual summer series of concerts held at the Royal Albert Hall, London, in which the audience originally walked about?
4 What were the surnames of Thomas and Arthur who collaborated to write 'the Savoy operas'?
5 What was the nationality of Bartók, Kodály and Liszt?
6 Which instrument is a pocket-sized reed-organ invented by Charles Wheatstone in 1829?
7 Why didn't Gustav Holst include Pluto in his 1918 orchestral suite *The Planets*?
8 Which instrument has 47 strings and seven pedals, and was introduced into the orchestra in the 19th century?
9 Which composer wrote 27 piano concertos, 23 string quartets, 35 violin sonatas and more than 50 symphonies?
10 Which instrument is a keyboard reed-organ, powered by foot pedals and used in American churches during the 1800s?

Answers on page 436

Entertainment

Music 4

1. On which instrument was Franz Liszt an inspired performer?
2. Who wrote *Porgy and Bess*?
3. By what name is Robert Zimmerman better known?
4. What was Madonna's first hit?
5. What nationality was Dvořák?
6. Who was Richard Rodgers's collaborator on *Oklahoma!*?
7. Whose albums include 'Beggar's Banquet' and 'Exile on Main Street'?
8. Which jazz trumpeter recorded the albums *Bitches' Brew* and *Birth of the Cool*?
9. Who wrote the opera *Cunning Little Vixen*?
10. Which teacher of Mozart and Beethoven wrote more than 100 symphonies?

Answers on page 437

Entertainment

Music 5

1. Who became conductor of the Birmingham Symphony Orchestra at the age of 25 in 1980?
2. Which instrument did Bartolommeo Cristofori invent in 1704?
3. What nationality was the composer Jean Sibelius?
4. Which Russian composer wrote *Peter and the Wolf*?
5. Which conductor said 'The English may not like music, but they absolutely love the noise it makes'?
6. Who wrote Italian and Scottish symphonies?
7. Who turned his score for the film *Scott of the Antarctic* into his *Sinfonia Antarctica*?
8. Which play by the French dramatist de Beaumarchais did Rossini turn into an opera?
9. Who wrote the *Moonlight* and *Appassionata* among his 32 piano sonatas?
10. Who wrote *Prélude à l'Après-midi d'un Faune*?

Answers on page 437

ENTERTAINMENT

Music 6

1. Which Borodin opera was completed by Rimsky-Korsakov and Glazunov after the composer's death?
2. Which country home and opera house hosts an annual summer festival established by John Christie in 1934?
3. What are the 5-note pentatonic, the 6-note whole-tone, the 7-note diatonic and the 13-note chromatic?
4. For which British king did Handel compose the *Water Music* in 1717?
5. What was used to conduct the orchestra before the baton was introduced in the early 19th century?
6. Which instrument do you associate with John Williams, Julian Bream and Andrès Segovia?
7. What are *Peter Grimes* and *Billy Budd*?
8. Which Irish flautist was a member of the Berlin Philharmonic 1969-75 before pursuing a solo career?
9. What is the title of Beethoven's only opera?
10. Which symphony did Dvořák write during his time as director of the National Conservatory in New York?

Answers on page 437

Entertainment

Music 7

1. Who composed the opera *Idomeneo*?
2. Which US gospel singer, famed for her version of 'Move On Up', was invited to sing at the presidential inauguration of John F Kennedy?
3. Which was Richard Wagner's last opera?
4. Where was Handel's *Messiah* first performed?
5. Which American composer wrote the march 'Stars and Stripes Forever!' and invented a bass tuba?
6. What did Cecil Sharp collect?
7. Which modern composer composed the operas *Punch and Judy*, *The Mask of Orpheus*, and *Gawain*?
8. Which useful musical device was invented by Johann Maelzel in 1814?
9. Who composed *Danse macabre* and *Carnival of the Animals*?
10. What kind of songs did Charles Wesley write?

Answers on page 437

Entertainment

Music 8

1. Which instrument did the theologian Albert Schweitzer play?
2. For which king was Lully the court composer?
3. In which year did Elvis Presley have hits with 'Heartbreak Hotel', 'Hound Dog', and 'Love Me Tender'?
4. Who developed the 12-tone system of composition?
5. Disc jockey Alan Freed popularized and helped to name which type of music from 1951?
6. Which modern composer's works include the operas *Einstein on the Beach* and *Akhnaten*?
7. Whose first album was titled *Are You Experienced*?
8. What nationality was Adolphe Sax, inventor of the saxophone?
9. What nationality is the pianist Alfred Brendel?
10. Whose first solo hit was 'Got to Be There'?

Answers on page 437

Entertainment

Music 9

1. Which composer held the office of prime minister in Poland in 1919?
2. What was the name of the Italian village renowned for its violin-making familes of Amati, Guarneri and Stradivari?
3. Which composer transcribed birdsong and incorporated it into much of his work?
4. What technique was used by guitarist Les Paul, and also describes the sound made by overloading circuits between guitar and amplifier?
5. Which legendary magician was the inspiration for musical works by Busoni, Berlioz, Gounod and Schumann?
6. To which family of instruments does the double bass belong?
7. Which Australian composer, pianist and organist has held the post of Master of the Queen's Music since 1975?
8. Who wrote the song 'Beautiful Dreamer'?
9. Which composer was kapellmeister to Prince Esterhazy 1761-90?
10. The German composer of *Almira* later became a British subject. Who was he?

Answers on page 437

Entertainment

Jazz

1. Which American jazz singer is particularly noted for her interpretations of songs by Gershwin and Cole Porter?
2. What style of music was pioneered by Charlie Parker and Dizzy Gillespie?
3. Which instrument did Lionel Hampton introduce to jazz?
4. In whose quintet did John Coltrane come to prominence in the 1950s?
5. Which jazzman said 'There are only two kinds of music: good and bad'?
6. Who is credited with describing the 1920s as the Jazz Age?
7. Who composed 'One O'Clock Jump'?
8. Whose 'Maple Leaf Rag' was the first instrumental sheet music to sell a million?
9. Who is credited with the invention of scat singing?
10. Who was the 'Empress of the Blues'?

Answers on page 438

Entertainment

Popular Music 1

1. Who was *Singin' in the Rain* in 1952?
2. Who was backed by the Shadows?
3. Which group's hits include 'Surfin' USA' and 'Good Vibrations'?
4. Which singer and songwriter had a successful partnership with Art Garfunkel?
5. Which destructive English rock band made the rock operas *Tommy* and *Quadrophenia*?
6. Which bandleader disappeared on a flight from England to France in 1944?
7. Which soul singer had a posthumous hit with '(Sittin' on the) Dock of the Bay'?
8. Who sang about *1999* in 1982?
9. Which singer became a star in *Funny Girl*?
10. Which band started their notorious career with 'Anarchy in the UK'?

Answers on page 438

Entertainment

Popular Music 2

1. Who is particularly associated with the song 'My Way'?
2. What was the title of Chris de Burgh's 1986 number 1 hit?
3. Who wrote *The Sound of Music*?
4. Which guitarist was in the Yardbirds, Cream and Derek and the Dominoes?
5. Which record company signed the Four Tops, the Temptations and Marvin Gaye?
6. Which record producer created the 'wall of sound' for the Crystals and the Ronettes?
7. Which of Michael Jackson's albums sold 41 million copies?
8. Which great rock-and-roller died in a plane crash in 1959 at the age of 22?
9. What was the first free rock festival, held in New York state in 1969?
10. Who was bass guitarist in the Beatles?

Answers on page 438

Entertainment

Popular Music 3

1. Which popular singer was born in Tupelo, Mississippi, and died in Memphis, Tennessee?
2. What is the stage name of the rock singer Reg Dwight?
3. What was Louis Armstrong's nickname?
4. For which rock group was Charlie Watts the drummer?
5. What was the name of the best-selling British female group of the 1980s?
6. Which British singer has had a string of hits including 'In the Air Tonight' in 1981, and 'Groovy Kind of Love' in 1988?
7. Who is the connection between the Boomtown Rats and Band Aid?
8. Which rock and soul singer's real name is Annie Mae Bullock?
9. Where did hip-hop music originate: New York, Detroit, or London?
10. Which US pioneer of rock and roll played with the Comets?

Answers on page 438

Entertainment

Popular Music 4

1. Which guitarist burned his guitar at the Monterey festival in 1967?
2. Which singer won an Oscar for acting in *From Here to Eternity*?
3. What instrument was played by jazzman Django Reinhardt?
4. Which country singer recorded an album at Folsom Prison in 1968?
5. Which rock star led Tin Machine?
6. Which jazz singer was nicknamed 'Lady Day'?
7. Which song did the Tweets take to number 2 in the charts in 1981?
8. Which group was been fronted by guitarists Jerry Garcia and Bob Weir for three decades?
9. Which composer had long-standing partnerships with Lorenz Hart and Oscar Hammerstein II?
10. Who was the 'Forces' Sweetheart' of World War II?

Answers on page 438

ENTERTAINMENT

Popular Music 5

1. Which Canadian singer/songwriter recorded the albums *Blue* and *Hejira*?
2. Who had a hit in 1965 with the song 'In the Midnight Hour'?
3. Who was *Born to Run* in 1975, and *Born in the USA* in 1984?
4. Which group of brothers had their first US hit with 'I Want You Back' in 1969?
5. Which guitarist formed the rock group whose album, *Brothers in Arms,* has sold over 20 million copies?
6. Who collaborated with Andrew Lloyd Webber to write *Joseph and the Amazing Technicolor Dreamcoat*?
7. What was the name of the hard-rock group formed by David Bowie in the late 1980s?
8. Which type of music developed from the folk music of English, Irish and Scottish settlers in the USA?
9. Who wrote the song 'White Christmas' in 1942?
10. What was the title of the theme song used for the film *The Blackboard Jungle*?

Answers on page 438

Entertainment

Popular Music 6

1. Who collaborated with Elvis Costello on his recording of 'Back on my Feet', and with Michael Jackson on 'Say, Say, Say'?

2. What was the title of Brecht's adaptation of *The Beggar's Opera*, which included the song 'Mac the Knife'?

3. Who founded Motown Records?

4. What is the better-known name of the drummer Richard Starkey?

5. Which song was a number 1 hit for Esther and Abi Ofarim?

6. Who created the character of Ziggy Stardust in his glam-rock period of the 1970s?

7. Which coarse-voiced Texan was the lead singer with the San Francisco group Big Brother and the Holding Company?

8. What is the specialist instrument of Wynton Marsalis, the jazz musician?

9. What is the name for a record label that is completely separate from the large conglomerate companies?

10. What is the syncopated music in 2/4 time, usually played on the piano?

Answers on page 439

Entertainment

Popular Music 7

1. What was Bing Crosby's real first name?
2. Who released the album *Natty Dread* in 1975?
3. Which Memphis label recorded both Elvis Presley and Johnny Cash?
4. Which rock group's original pianist Ian Stewart died in 1985?
5. Who wrote the atmospheric scores for such films as *A Fistful of Dollars* and *The Good, the Bad and the Ugly*?
6. Which pop group once consisted of Sarah Dallin, Keren Woodward and Jackie O'Sullivan?
7. Which 1965 Beatles song was covered by 1,186 performers in ten years?
8. In which American state were both Buddy Holly and Janis Joplin born?
9. Who made the jazz albums *Birth of the Cool* and *Sketches of Spain*?
10. What stage name was taken by the rapper Stanley Kirk Burrell?

Answers on page 439

Entertainment

Musical Instruments

1. What is a bass xylophone called?
2. Which is the only straight member of the saxophone family in common use?
3. What is the name of the metal discs set in the rim of a tambourine?
4. Which metal-keyed electric percussion instrument resembles a xylophone?
5. Alto, tenor, bass, and contra-bass are all sizes of which brass instrument?
6. What is the name of a bass tuba that wraps round the person playing it?
7. What was the electric tone-wheel organ invented in 1934?
8. How many reeds does an oboe have?
9. Which modern instrument was developed from the sackbut?
10. Which group had Keith Moon on drums?

Answers on page 439

Entertainment

Cinema and TV 1

1. Who was noted for his cameo walk-ons in his own films?
2. What was Arnold Schwarzenegger's original nationality?
3. Which film star, who played Rhett Butler in *Gone With the Wind*, starred in more than 90 films over 30 years?
4. Which actor won Oscars for his performances in *Kramer vs Kramer* and *Rain Man*?
5. Who was the cartoon character married to Jessica in a film starring Bob Hoskins?
6. Which television show is presented by Jim Bowen?
7. What was the surname shared by the actresses who starred in *My Fair Lady* and *The African Queen*?
8. Why did *The Jazz Singer*, starring Al Jolson, make history in 1927?
9. Which film actor shot to fame in 1976 with his portrayal of the boxer Rocky Balboa?
10. Which film, released by the Disney studios in 1938, was the first feature-length animated film?

Answers on page 439

Entertainment

Cinema and TV 2

1. In which television series did Roger Moore star from 1962 to 1970?
2. Who was the film director responsible for popularizing 'spaghetti' westerns?
3. What was the Beatles' first film?
4. Who introduced the Betamax video cassette system?
5. Who starred in *Desperately Seeking Susan* and *Dick Tracy*?
6. Which former reform school boy starred in *Bullitt* and *The Magnificent Seven*?
7. Who won a 1993 Oscar for Best Actress in *The Piano*?
8. Who starred in *The Elephant Man* and *The Silence of the Lambs*?
9. Who was the female star of the film *A Fish Called Wanda*?
10. Which star of the television show *Eastenders* sang the 1962 number 1 hit 'Come Outside'?

Answers on page 439

ENTERTAINMENT

Cinema and TV 3

1. In the Stephen King novel and film *Christine*, what was Christine?
2. The first US television show filmed before an audience was *I Love Lucy*. Who was its star?
3. Who directed *Jaws*, *Raiders of the Lost Ark* and *ET*?
4. Who played Douglas Bader in the film *Reach for the Sky*?
5. Who first played James Bond in the cinema?
6. Who played the title roles in the films *Henry V* (1944) and *Hamlet* (1948)?
7. Which Scottish engineer gave the first public demonstration of television in 1925?
8. In which 1964 film did Clint Eastwood first play 'The Man with No Name'?
9. What is Bugs Bunny's catchphrase?
10. Which three primary colours make up a colour television picture?

Answers on page 439

ENTERTAINMENT

Cinema and TV 4

1. Who played the monster in the 1931 film *Frankenstein*?

2. Which Ealing Studio film told the story of a scientist who developed a textile which never needed washing?

3. Which nuclear physicist was allegedly the model for the scientist in Stanley Kubrick's film *Dr Strangelove*?

4. Which US actor died at the age of 22 after collapsing outside a Hollywood nightclub in 1993?

5. Who made the 1902 science-fiction film *A trip to the Moon*?

6. Which Hollywood film maker produced a string of films in the 1950s and 1960s using animals as actors in a drama?

7. What is 'celluloid'?

8. Which film by Alfred Hitchcock is a study in animal behaviour?

9. Which television quiz/game show was hosted by Gordon Burns?

10. Which film by Steven Spielberg gives an unflattering account of *Carcharodon carcharias*?

Answers on page 440

Entertainment

Cinema and TV 5

1. In which film of the 1980s did Dudley Moore play the part of an elf?
2. Which silent film comedian was nicknamed the 'Great Stone Face'?
3. Which film star's real name is Allen Stewart Konigsberg?
4. Which satellite successfully transmitted television signals across the Atlantic in 1962?
5. Which former child star was appointed US ambassador to Czechoslovakia in 1989?
6. What kind of vacuum tube is an essential component of a television set?
7. Who wrote the theme music for Charlie Chaplin's film *Limelight*?
8. Which Oscar-winning actress married Laurence Olivier in 1940?
9. How did James Dean die?
10. Made in 1958, which was the first of the *Carry On* films?

Answers on page 440

Entertainment

Cinema and TV 6

1. Which world-famous cartoon cat was created in 1920 by Pat Sullivan?
2. By what name is Bernard Schwartz better known?
3. Which film did Barbra Streisand direct in 1983?
4. To whom is Mae West popularly (but wrongly) supposed to have said 'Come up and see me some time' in *She Done Him Wrong*?
5. Which 1987 film earned an Academy Award for Bernardo Bertolucci?
6. In which year was Channel 4 launched in Britain?
7. Which film studio was originally opened in 1912 as the Famous Players Film Company?
8. Why was Ingrid Bergman ostracized by Hollywood for many years?
9. Who wrote the screenplay for the film *A Private Function*?
10. Which pop star appeared in Nicholas Roeg's film *The Man Who Fell to Earth*?

Answers on page 440

Entertainment

Cinema and TV 7

1. Which character made his debut in the silent film *Plane Crazy* in 1928?
2. By which names were Virginia McMath and Frederick Austerlitz better known?
3. Which film actress starred in *Taxi Driver* and *Bugsy Malone* when she was only 14?
4. What was the stage name of Arthur Stanley Jefferson, the British comic, who made his name as half of a famous duo?
5. Whose use of 'Method acting' made him one of the cinema's most distinctive stars?
6. Which American directed the controversial 1988 film *The Last Temptation of Christ*?
7. Which Japanese director introduced Japanese cinema to Western audiences with his film *Seven Samurai*?
8. Who co-starred with Elizabeth Taylor in *Cleopatra*?
9. What is the name of the spoof reporter played on television by Steve Coogan?
10. Which author wrote the books on which the films *2001: A Space Odyssey* and *2010: Space Odyssey 2* were based?

Answers on page 440

ENTERTAINMENT

Cinema and TV 8

1. Which film star did the Canadian Gladys Mary Smith grow up to be?
2. Who directed *The Godfather* in 1972 and its two sequels in 1974 and 1990?
3. What was the title of the film in which Charlie Chaplin spoke for the first time?
4. Which television sci-fi show of the late 1970s and early 1980s starred Joanna Lumley and David McCallum as two of the 115 'elements'?
5. What were the animals in the title of the film which won an Oscar for Best Picture in the 1990 Academy Awards?
6. Who played the part of Spike in the television comedy show *Hi-di-Hi*?
7. Which film director is said to have invented montage in his films *Alexander Nevsky* and *Battleship Potemkin*?
8. Which actor did Mae West choose as her co-star for the film *She Done Him Wrong*?
9. What was the title of the big box-office flop that almost caused the collapse of United Artists in 1980?
10. Who played Bonnie Parker opposite Warren Beatty's Clyde Barrow in the 1967 film *Bonnie and Clyde*?

Answers on page 440

Entertainment

Cinema and TV 9

1. Which early screen idol was known as 'the Profile'?
2. Native life in which part of India is the subject of Satyajit Ray's great trilogy of films beginning with *Pather Panchali*?
3. Which director's films include *Witness* and *The Mosquito Coast*?
4. Who wrote the screenplay for the Bond film *You Only Live Twice*?
5. Where is the main centre of Dutch broadcasting?
6. Which actress's first 'talkie' was *Anna Christie*?
7. Which Hollywood legend's career spanned *Way Down East* in 1920 and *The Whales of August* in 1987?
8. Which 1971 film won Jane Fonda the first of her Oscars?
9. Which American playwright wrote the television film *Playing For Time* in 1980?
10. What was Sam Goldwyn's real name?

Answers on page 440

Entertainment

Cinema and TV 10

1. Which was the second of the *Star Wars* films?
2. In a standard cine film, how many frames are shown each second?
3. Which actress made her debut opposite Humphrey Bogart in *To Have and Have Not*, and later married him?
4. Name two dwarfs beginning with 'D' from *Snow White and the Seven Dwarfs*.
5. What does HDTV stand for?
6. Who were the French brothers who patented their cinematograph in 1895?
7. For which film did John Wayne win his only Academy Award?
8. Which French filmmaker made *The 400 Blows*, *Jules et Jim* and *Day for Night*?
9. In how many films did James Dean appear?
10. Whose first film as a director was *Ordinary People*?

Answers on page 441

ENTERTAINMENT

On the Stage 1

1 What is odd about the principal boy and the dame in a pantomime?

2 Which ventriloquist had a dummy called Lord Charles?

3 Was Macbeth a real person?

4 What kind of comic play shows stereotyped characters in complex and improbable situations, often involving extramarital relationships?

5 Which Agatha Christie play opened in London in 1952 and became the longest running show in the world?

6 A US singer/dancer of the 1930s with the real first name of Ethel, she appeared in musicals such as *Dames* and *42nd Street*. Who was she?

7 Of which art is Marcel Marceau a leading exponent?

8 Which character in *The Mikado* was Lord High Everything Else?

9 The first national theatre was founded in Paris by Louis XIV in 1680. What is its name?

10 In which country are Nō and Kabuki traditional types of drama?

Answers on page 441

ENTERTAINMENT

On the Stage 2

1. Where was William Shakespeare born?
2. What was the title of George Bernard Shaw's play about Joan of Arc?
3. Where in Germany was the Wagner theatre established in 1876?
4. Who is behind the character of Dame Edna Everage?
5. Who wrote and starred in *Hay Fever, Private Lives* and *Blithe Spirit*?
6. Who created the role of Archie Rice in *The Entertainer* and later had a London theatre named after him?
7. What is the subtitle of *Peter Pan*?
8. In which type of play is St George a major character?
9. Which traditional British form of entertainment combined harlequinade and burlesque?
10. In the Shakespeare play *Twelfth Night*, what is the name of Olivia's hard-drinking uncle?

Answers on page 441

ENTERTAINMENT

On the Stage 3

1. Which dramatist's works include *Arms and the Man*, *Man and Superman* and *St Joan*?
2. Which British actress was leading lady to Henry Irving in 1878?
3. Which playwright and poet wrote *Peer Gynt* and *Ghosts* while in exile from his native Norway?
4. In which of Shakespeare's plays do the 'rude mechanicals' perform the legend of Pyramus and Thisbe?
5. Which was the first 'rock' musical?
6. Which play of marital strife by Edward Albee was filmed with Elizabeth Taylor and Richard Burton?
7. What is the Latin expression used for the list of characters in a play?
8. Which great actor was the first director of Britain's National Theatre company?
9. Which English ballet dancer was born Margaret Hookham in 1919?
10. Which prolific comic playwright wrote the trilogy *The Norman Conquests*?

Answers on page 441

Entertainment

On the Stage 4

1. What was the stage name of Margarita Carmen Cansino?
2. Whose shows included *Gay's the Word* and *Glamorous Night*?
3. In which Gilbert and Sullivan operetta was Oscar Wilde's dandyism parodied?
4. Where can a theatre named after Gracie Fields be found?
5. Name the 17th century octagonal theatre recently reconstructed in Southwark?
6. Which famous actor was a pupil of Dr Johnson?
7. Which show contains the song 'Ol' Man River'?
8. Which playwright's first successful novel, *The Good Companions*, was about a travelling theatre company?
9. What is the nickname of Broadway, New York?
10. Which contemporary playwright acted in the films *The Right Stuff* and *Steel Magnolias*?

Answers on page 441

Entertainment

On the Stage 5

1. Which of Eugene O'Neill's plays was first seen 15 years after it was written and after he had died?
2. Who is the actor thought to have first played the parts of Hamlet, King Lear, and Othello?
3. Which Oscar-winning actor starred in the 1984 Broadway revival of *Death of a Salesman*?
4. On which real-life person was Terence Rattigan's *Ross* based?
5. Around the altar of which god were the earliest Greek dramas performed?
6. Which monarch protected Molière from attacks caused by his satires?
7. Which English actor shared the management of the Old Vic with Laurence Olivier from 1944 to 1950?
8. In which other field did the playwright John Vanbrugh make his mark?
9. The brother of which British prime minister wrote *Lloyd George Knew My Father* and *The Chiltern Hundreds*?
10. What is the name of the title character in *The Merchant of Venice*?

Answers on page 441

Entertainment

On the Stage 6

1. What is the American equivalent of the British music hall?
2. Which English actress, formerly a child performer in her parent's music-hall act, starred in films *10* and *Victor/Victoria*?
3. Who wrote the poetic drama *Murder in the Cathedral*?
4. Which play by J M Synge caused riots when it was first performed at the Abbey Theatre, Dublin, in 1907?
5. In which of Aristophanes' plays do the women of Athens refuse to make love to their husbands until a war is over?
6. Which Italian opera composer said 'In the theatre the public will stand for anything except boredom'?
7. In which country was the British playwright Tom Stoppard born?
8. Which US playwright wrote *Barefoot in the Park* and *The Odd Couple*?
9. Which American composer is renowned for '4 minutes 33 seconds' in which the audience is left waiting for a single note to be played?
10. Which Caryl Churchill play of 1987 satirized London's brash young financial brokers?

Answers on page 442

Entertainment

Comedians and Clowns 1

1. Who made the film *The Life of Brian*?
2. What was the name of Tony Hancock's radio show?
3. Who played the part of Sergeant Major Williams in the television comedy series *It Ain't Half Hot Mum*?
4. What was the title of Walt Disney's 1940 feature-length 'Silly Symphony'?
5. Which comic pair starred in such films as *The Road to Morocco* and *The Road to Singapore*?
6. To which race does the comic character Astérix belong?
7. In Jerome K Jerome's book, how many men were in a boat?
8. Who starred in the hit comedies *10* and *Arthur*?
9. Who was the presenter of the children's television show *TISWAS*, who also went on to present its adult equivalent, *OTT*?
10. Who is Punch's wife?

Answers on page 442

Entertainment

Comedians and Clowns 2

1. Which comic-strip hero was created by Jerome Siegel and Joseph Shuster in 1938?

2. Which playwright said in a 1960 revue 'Life is rather like a tin of sardines – we're all of us looking for the key'?

3. How were Peter Sellers, Harry Secombe and Spike Milligan collectively known?

4. Who was the original clown called 'Joey'?

5. What were the first names of Laurel and Hardy?

6. Which playwright wrote the black comedies *Loot* and *What the Butler Saw*?

7. Which studio produced such comedies as *Passport to Pimlico* and *Kind Hearts and Coronets*?

8. Who sang the comic songs 'Mr Wu' and 'Cleaning Windows'?

9. Which bespectacled silent-film comedian was famous for his cliff-hanging stunts?

10. Which school was created by the cartoonist Ronald Searle?

Answers on page 442

Entertainment

Comedians and Clowns 3

1. Which comedian of silent films was ruined in 1921 by a sex scandal?
2. Under what stage name did Maxwell George Lister do his funny walk?
3. Which magazine carried the ghoulish cartoons of Charles Addams, featuring the Addams family?
4. Who in the 1920s wrote such Aldwych farces as *A Cuckoo in the Nest* and *Rookery Nook*?
5. Which humorist wrote 'The Secret Life of Walter Mitty'?
6. Which master of slapstick created the Keystone Cops?
7. Which long-running British humorous magazine was founded in 1841?
8. Which cartoon strip is drawn by Garry Trudeau?
9. Which of the Marx Brothers was really named Arthur?
10. Which cartoon character is actually a *Geococcyx californianus*?

Answers on page 442

Sport and Leisure

SPORT AND LEISURE

Sport 1

1. Who was the bearded doctor from Bristol who became the best batsman in England in the late 19th century?

2. Which athletic event commemorates Pheidippides, who carried to Athens news of a Greek victory over the Persians?

3. How long is a game of association football?

4. Which runner broke the world record for the 100 metres at the 1988 Olympic games, but was disqualified for using drugs?

5. There are four strokes in competitive swimming: freestyle, butterfly, backstroke, and which other?

6. Which pair of brothers played in the England football team that won the World Cup in 1966?

7. What is the name of the event where skiers have to swerve in and out between flags?

8. How many players make up a Rugby League team?

9. Who became the first man to run a mile in under four minutes at Oxford in 1954?

10. What is the object that badminton players hit back and forth?

Answers on page 443

Sport and Leisure

Sport 2

1 Which footballer famously wept when he was booked in a World Cup semi-final?

2 What is the style of Japanese wrestling where very large men fight in a circular ring?

3 In lawn tennis, what name is given to a score of 40–40?

4 What is the name of the competition for teams of professional male golfers from the USA and Europe?

5 How many points are scored for a touchdown in American football?

6 In golf, what is the name of the grassed area between the tee and the green?

7 Which town in Sarthe, France, has an annual 24-hour car race?

8 Which football club defeated Arsenal in the final of the 1972 FA Cup and were themselves beaten in the final the following year?

9 Which sport featured in many of the Beach Boys' earliest hits?

10 Which football club did Kenny Dalglish manage to the Premiership title in 1995?

Answers on page 443

Sport and Leisure

Sport 3

1. Which stroke is totally disallowed in table tennis but must be every stroke in badminton?
2. Where would you see the events of calf roping, bull riding, steer wrestling and bronco busting contested?
3. In which sport would you use a puck instead of a ball?
4. Which world champion heavyweight boxer's middle name was originally Marcellus?
5. What is the third ball to be potted in the sequence of colours in snooker?
6. What is a version of the Gaelic word for 'pole' indicating an object tossed in the Highland Games?
7. Which equestrian sport tests the all-round ability of the horse and rider?
8. What is an alternative name for the sport of free falling?
9. Which city played host to the 1992 Summer Olympics?
10. Which swimming stroke propels the body through the water at the greatest speed?

Answers on page 443

SPORT AND LEISURE

Sport 4

1. Which national sport originated as a religious ritual performed in Shinto shrines?
2. Which team sport has periods of play called 'chukkas'?
3. Which four events constitute the Grand Slam in tennis?
4. Which US basketball team tours the world playing only exhibition matches?
5. What is the multi-discipline event in women's international athletics in which contestants compete over a two-day period?
6. How many of the drivers who finish a Formula One Grand Prix win points?
7. What is the name of the Berkshire village where Queen Anne established a famous racecourse on the heath?
8. Which Australian city has a cricket ground called the Oval?
9. Which national Scottish game is played on ice, with stones?
10. What is to American football as 'diamond' is to baseball?

Answers on page 443

Sport and Leisure

Sport 5

1 Who was voted the best footballer of the 1980s by the world's press?

2 Who was the youngest ever winner of a singles title at Wimbledon?

3 Who won three British Open golf championships during the 1980s?

4 Which British racing driver was never world champion, but was runner-up every year from 1955 to 1958?

5 Who had a record reign of more than eleven years as world heavyweight boxing champion?

6 Who won Wimbledon every year from 1976 to 1980?

7 Which Grand Prix team's world champions have included Emerson Fittipaldi, Niki Lauda, Alain Prost and Ayrton Senna?

8 What is the name of the method of training a horse to carry out a set routine of movements?

9 In which country is the Belmont Stakes horse race run?

10 In angling, what name is given to the revolving lures used to catch salmon and trout?

Answers on page 443

Sport and Leisure

Sport 6

1. Which sport was first played at a Christmas party in Wales in 1873 under the name 'Sphairistike'?

2. Who was the New York Yankees baseball player who married Marilyn Monroe?

3. Which card game has two forms called auction and contract?

4. Which West Indian cricketer made a test record score of 365 not out, and later hit six 6s in one over?

5. Who was the American swimmer who won seven gold medals in the 1972 Olympics, all in world record times?

6. Who won the first Rugby Union World Cup, held in 1987?

7. On which circuit is motor racing's Grand Prix d'Endurance run?

8. Which horse did Lester Pigott ride to victory in the 1984 St Leger?

9. What colour jersey is worn by the leader during the Tour de France?

10. Why were women forbidden to watch the Olympic Games in ancient Greece?

Answers on page 443

SPORT AND LEISURE

Sport 7

1. How long, exactly, is a marathon?
2. In which city is the Wanderers' cricket ground?
3. What are the two standard lifts in international weightlifting competitions?
4. Of what would you find types called Finn, Tornado and Windglider?
5. In which country did chess originate?
6. Which sport was started by James Plympton in Newport, Rhode Island, in 1866?
7. Which England cricketer scored a record 456 runs in a test match in 1990?
8. Why was Muhammad Ali stripped of his world heavyweight boxing title in 1967?
9. Which sport was originally called Mintonette?
10. Which was the earliest of the English classic horse races?

Answers on page 444

Sport and Leisure

Sport 8

1. Which British athlete won two sprinting medals at the Moscow Olympics in 1980?
2. Which sport's classic text was written by Izaak Walton in 1653?
3. In cricket, who is the fielder who patrols the boundary behind the slips?
4. Which Englishman has been British squash champion six times?
5. Which Norwegian Olympic skating champion went on to make many films in Hollywood in the 1930s?
6. How many players are there in a baseball team?
7. Which sport is started with a 'push-back'?
8. Who, in 1988, became the first boxer to win world titles at five officially recognized weights?
9. Which sport has two main international styles, called freestyle and Greco-Roman?
10. Which game takes place in an area 78 feet long and 36 feet wide?

Answers on page 444

SPORT AND LEISURE

Sport 9

1. Which two sports use mallets?
2. Which English League soccer club had Ian Botham on its books from 1979 to 1984?
3. What is the name of the most famous Highland Games held in a village near Balmoral Castle?
4. In American football, what do AFC and NFC stand for?
5. Name one of the two types of canoe used in competitive canoeing.
6. Which two sports are played on oval pitches?
7. How many innings are allowed for each team in baseball?
8. In which sport is the Webb Ellis Cup presented to the winners of the World Cup?
9. How many laps are completed in a heat of a speedway race?
10. What has no brakes, no steering mechanism, and is used in a sport contested in the winter Olympics?

Answers on page 444

Sport and Leisure

Food and Drink 1

1. Which drink did Dom Perignon invent?
2. What are dried plums called?
3. Which spirit is fermented and distilled from sugar cane?
4. What gives green pasta its colour?
5. What is a third name for a ground nut or monkey nut?
6. What is the salted roe of a sturgeon called?
7. Who was the Roman god of wine?
8. What is the name for a person who will eat no food of animal origin?
9. What is the only cereal grown standing in water?
10. Of what fish are skipjack and bonito varieties?

Answers on page 444

Sport and Leisure

Food and Drink 2

1 What cocktail consists of Tia Maria, vodka and coke?

2 What's the name of Popeye's girlfriend?

3 What is made from chicle, the milky-white fluid made into a popular American confection?

4 Which variety of hard green-skinned apple is named after an Australian woman who died in 1870?

5 What is another name for the dietary fibre which provides food bulk to aid digestion?

6 Which traditional dish is made from a sheep's heart, liver and lungs, minced with oatmeal and seasoning, and boiled in the sheep's stomach?

7 What is the purple fruit of the eggplant which is used as a vegetable?

8 Which tree of the laurel family produces a pear-shaped fruit used as a vegetable and usually eaten raw?

9 Which young French wine is released annually on the third Thursday in November?

10 What is eaten traditionally in the UK on the day before Ash Wednesday?

Answers on page 444

SPORT AND LEISURE

Food and Drink 3

1. Which edible bulb of the onion family is composed of small segments called cloves?
2. What two words guarantee the origin of French wine?
3. For which shellfish are Whitstable and Colchester famous?
4. Which opera singer is immortalized in the name of a fruit and ice cream dessert?
5. Which alcoholic drink is made from honey and yeast?
6. Who wrote *Cakes and Ale*?
7. Who reputedly introduced the potato to England in the 16th century?
8. What part of a cola tree is used to flavour drinks?
9. Which bean is the richest natural vegetable food?
10. In which century was tea first brought to Europe?

Answers on page 444

Sport and Leisure

Food and Drink 4

1 Which plant of the carrot family has stems that are crystallized and used in baking and cake decoration?

2 What is the salt solution used for curing meat and canning vegetables?

3 Which controversial process was introduced in the 1980s to prolong the life of foodstuffs?

4 What is the German word for 'store' and is the name we give to a light beer?

5 What does the abbreviation UHT stand for?

6 Which strong cheese, made from ewe's milk and stored in caves, is named after a village in France?

7 Which grain is said to be the staple food of more than one-third of the world's population?

8 What are the black fruits that produce monounsaturated oil when pressed?

9 What is the process that rids food, especially milk, of bacteria?

10 Which berries are used to give gin its flavour?

Answers on page 445

Sport and Leisure

Food and Drink 5

1. Which milk pudding is made from starch extracted from the pith of a palm tree?
2. Which vegetable is a green variety of banana, used as a staple food in the tropics?
3. Which cereal is used to make 'black' breads?
4. Which cheese is traditionally made around Melton Mowbray, and gets its name from the village where the cheeses were taken for transporting to London?
5. What accurately describes drinks with no C_2H_5OH content?
6. What is the secondary covering of a nutmeg?
7. For what are thaumatin, aspartame and manitol used as substitutes?
8. What sort of high-gluten flour is used for making pasta?
9. What type of flowers produce vanilla pods?
10. What are the dried stigmas of crocus flowers, used as a flavouring and colouring?

Answers on page 445

Sport and Leisure

Food and Drink 6

1. What plant-sucking insect caused huge disruption to the wine industry of Europe in the 19th century?
2. Which Italian region is the source of Marsala?
3. What do fennel leaves taste of?
4. Which is the largest species of flatfish?
5. Which member of the ginger family is used to colour curries?
6. Where were the first European coffee houses opened?
7. Henry I of England is reputed to have died through eating a surfeit of this eel-like fish. What is it?
8. For which edible fungus is Perigord, France, famous?
9. What is the name for food permissible under Moslem dietary laws?
10. Who was the fur trader who pioneered frozen food in the USA?

Answers on page 445

Sport and Leisure

Games and Pastimes

1. Which is the biggest participant sport in Britain?
2. How many counters are there on a backgammon board when play starts?
3. Why is the advantage with the banker at roulette?
4. In which country did stamp-collecting start?
5. What is the name for the art of making decorative lacework with knotted threads?
6. Where did chess originate in the 2nd century?
7. What number is the neutral ball at pool?
8. Why did ninepin bowling become tenpin bowling in the USA?
9. Which card game devised by poet John Suckling involves players discarding in turn until a total of 31 is reached?
10. Which indoor game was invented by British army officers serving in India in 1875?

Answers on page 445

Art and Literature

Art and Literature

Literature 1

1. Who did Jane Eyre marry after working for him?
2. Which author created the sleuths Miss Jane Marple and Hercule Poirot?
3. Who was the author of *The Wind in the Willows*, dramatized by A A Milne as *Toad of Toad Hall*?
4. Who is the narrator of Arthur Conan Doyle's Sherlock Holmes stories?
5. What was the pen-name of the Mississippi riverboat pilot who created the fictional characters of Tom Sawyer and Huckleberry Finn?
6. What is the name of Don Quixote's servant in the novel by Cervantes?
7. Which of Tolkien's fantasy characters inhabit the world of Middle Earth?
8. Which literary family lived at the parsonage in the village of Haworth on the Yorkshire Moors?
9. Which English author, who sometimes wrote under the name 'Boz', portrayed the social and economic ills of Victorian England in his novels?
10. Which fictional character is said to be based on Vlad the Impaler, a Transylvanian king of Wallachia?

Answers on page 446

Art and Literature

Literature 2

1. What was the title of Tolkien's sequel to *The Hobbit*?
2. Who wrote *Kidnapped*?
3. Where were Chaucer's pilgrims bound?
4. Whose works include *Howards End* and *A Passage to India*?
5. In which ocean was the island setting of *Lord of the Flies*?
6. As a creator of which type of novels was Zane Grey a pioneer?
7. Complete this Graham Greene novel title: *The Power and the ....*
8. Which English writer married Anne Hathaway?
9. Who wrote *The Book of Nonsense*?
10. Which science-fiction pioneer wrote *The Time Machine*?

Answers on page 446

Art and Literature

Literature 3

1. Who created the mischievous schoolboy hero William?
2. Who wrote *For Whom the Bell Tolls* and *The Old Man and the Sea*?
3. Which great book was started in Bedford Jail in 1675?
4. What animal story was Anna Sewell's only published work?
5. What sort of animals did Richard Adams write about in *Watership Down*?
6. Who hunted Moby-Dick?
7. Complete the title of Shakespeare's play: *The Two Gentlemen of* ...
8. What sort of factory did Roald Dahl write about?
9. How far under the sea were Jules Verne's explorers?
10. Which magic land did C S Lewis write of?

Answers on page 446

Art and Literature

Literature 4

1. What is Shakespeare's only play to have an English place name in its title?
2. Which annual British literary prize has been won by Salman Rushdie, Kingsley Amis and Anita Brookner?
3. What is a three-line, 17-syllable Japanese verse-form?
4. What is the title of Franz Kafka's short story in which the hero turns into an insect?
5. Which French author, the son of one of Napoleon's generals, spent 19 years exiled in Guernsey?
6. Which of Swift's novels is an allegorical tale describing travel to lands of giants, miniature people and intelligent horses?
7. What is the surname shared by the author of *Tom Brown's Schooldays* and the poet laureate appointed in 1984?
8. What was the name of the Onondaga chief about whom Longfellow wrote an epic poem?
9. Which novel was set in a bureaucratic totalitarian state, 35 years ahead of the book's publication date?
10. Which English poet was the spouse of the novelist who created Frankenstein?

Answers on page 446

Art and Literature

Literature 5

1. Which English poet became poet laureate in 1843?

2. What nationality is the novelist Gabriel García Márquez?

3. Which title is held by the character Edmund Dantes in a novel by Alexander Dumas?

4. Who wrote about a pig called the Empress of Blandings?

5. What was Oscar Wilde's only novel?

6. Who wrote the 1988 novel *Foucault's Pendulum*?

7. What nationality was the playwright Henrik Ibsen?

8. He was a physician and founder of the University of London. His book, first published in 1852, is still a popular reference work on the English language. What is its title?

9. Which medieval writer was brother-in-law to John of Gaunt?

10. Who wrote the 18th-century novels *The Adventures of Peregrine Pickle* and *The Adventures of Roderick Random*?

Answers on page 446

Art and Literature

Literature 6

1 What nationality was Nobel prizewinner Patrick White?
2 Who wrote *The Moonstone*?
3 Which Dickens novel was left unfinished at the time of his death?
4 Who wrote *Of Human Bondage*?
5 Who is the American author of *Couples* and *The Witches of Eastwick*?
6 Which English poet drowned while sailing off the coast of Italy in 1822?
7 Which English prime minister wrote *Coningsby* and *Sybil*?
8 Who wrote *The Divine Comedy*?
9 What was W H Auden's first name?
10 Whose fan did Oscar Wilde write of?

Answers on page 446

Art and Literature

Literature 7

1. Whose political philosophy is expounded in *The Republic* and *Laws*?
2. Which Roman writer was famous for his *Satires* and *Ars Poetica*?
3. For which work other than the *Odyssey* is Homer noted?
4. Who wrote the plays *The Wasps*, *The Birds* and *The Frogs*?
5. Who led the crew of the *Argo* in their search for the Golden Fleece?
6. Whose letters describe the eruption of Vesuvius and the death of his historian uncle?
7. From which mythical creatures was Odysseus protecting his sailors when he stuffed their ears with wax?
8. Whose work *Parallel Lives* inspired Shakespeare's Roman plays?
9. Who was banished to the Black Sea by the Emperor Augustus for his supposedly immoral *Ars Amatoria*?
10. Who is widely regarded as the founder of Greek tragedy?

Answers on page 447

Art and Literature

Literature 8

1 Which of Scott Fitzgerald's novels was unfinished at the time of his death?
2 Complete the Graham Greene novel title: *The Heart of ...*
3 Which Roman poet wrote *Metamorphoses*?
4 Complete the Beatrix Potter book title: *The Tailor of ...*
5 What relation to each other were Rabelais' giants Gargantua and Pantagruel?
6 Which English poet planned a Communist colony in America with Robert Southey?
7 Whose novels include *The Aunt's Story* and *The Tree of Man*?
8 Which American writer was court-martialled in 1830 for neglect of duty?
9 Who wrote *Boris Godunov*?
10 Complete the title of this Ionesco play: *The Bald ...*

Answers on page 447

Art and Literature

Literature 9

1. Who created the detective Father Brown?
2. Which French writer won the Nobel Prize in 1947?
3. Who wrote *In Memoriam*?
4. Which 18th century writer was Dean of St Patrick's, Dublin?
5. Who wrote *Schindler's Ark*?
6. Who recited 'The Gift Outright' at President Kennedy's inauguration?
7. Whose plays include *Anna Christie* and *Mourning Becomes Electra*?
8. Who wrote the trilogy *Childhood, Boyhood* and *Youth*?
9. Which famous writer was prime minister at the Weimar court from 1775–85?
10. Which Brontë sister lived longest?

Answers on page 447

Art and Literature

Literature 10

1. What is the title of the play that chronicles a day in the life of the small Welsh village of Llareggub?
2. Whose name is synonymous with *Le Grand dictionnaire universel du XIXème siècle*?
3. Which of King Lear's three daughters was murdered?
4. Which poet laureate wrote the biography *The Life of Nelson* in 1813?
5. What is the term applied to the unrhymed, iambic pentameter used by Shakespeare in all his plays?
6. Which English poet was the Latin secretary to Oliver Cromwell's Council of State during the Commonwealth period?
7. Which 16th-century English dramatist was imprisoned for murder, and was himself murdered in a tavern brawl?
8. Who wrote an elegy on Abraham Lincoln called 'When Lilacs Last in the Dooryard Bloom'd'?
9. Which phrase refers to the group of British writers that included Colin Wilson, Kingsley Amis, John Braine and Alan Sillitoe?
10. Which American dramatist and novelist wrote *A Streetcar Named Desire* in 1947?

Answers on page 447

Art and Literature

Literature 11

1. Which British psychologist wrote the book *The Use of Lateral Thinking*?
2. Which was the home planet for the aliens in H G Wells' *War of the Worlds*?
3. What was the last book written by Aldous Huxley?
4. Which book by Robert Louis Stevenson featured a doctor who experimented with drugs?
5. Who wrote *Journey to the Centre of the Earth*?
6. What happened one night to the central character of Kafka's *Metamorphosis*?
7. Which character in *Alice's Adventures in Wonderland* suffered from the mercury poisoning characteristic of his trade?
8. Who wrote *The Alchemist*?
9. Who described the gap between science and literature as 'the two cultures'?
10. Who wrote *A Brief History of Time*?

Answers on page 447

Art and Literature

Art and Artists 1

1 In which Italian town was the artist Leonardo born?

2 Who designed the largest Protestant church in England, St Paul's Cathedral?

3 Which Yorkshire sculptor, known for his reclining figures, was an official war artist in World War II?

4 Which French post-Impressionist artist spent eight years of his life painting in Tahiti?

5 Which animals, sculpted by Edward Landseer, stand at the four corners of Trafalgar Square?

6 In front of which French art gallery is there a large glass pyramid designed by I M Pei?

7 Which 16th-century Belgian artist painted scenes of peasant life?

8 Which style of architecture was used in England during the 11th and 12th centuries?

9 Which modern building in Sydney was designed by Joern Utzon?

10 Which English artist was famous for his industrial Lancashire townscapes filled with matchstick figures?

Answers on page 447

Art and Literature

Art and Artists 2

1. Who painted the *Mona Lisa*?
2. In which Italian city can Michelangelo's *David* be seen?
3. Which English monarch did Holbein paint in 1536?
4. In which country can you see the Sphinx?
5. Which pop artist predicted that everyone would be famous for 15 minutes?
6. Who painted *The Scream*?
7. Who painted the ceiling of the Sistine Chapel?
8. What nationality was Picasso?
9. Which English painter born in 1724 was famous for paintings of horses?
10. Which Dutch painter cut off part of his ear after a quarrel?

Answers on page 448

Art and Literature

Art and Artists 3

1. Which famous painter and sculptor was also an architect and engineer to Cesare Borgia?
2. Which artist made his name with paintings of soup cans and Coca-Cola bottles?
3. Which famous painting by Frans Hals is in the Wallace collection in London?
4. Which name, intended as an insult, was used to describe the style of Monet and other French painters of the 1870s?
5. Which famous portrait painter's sitters include Mrs Siddons, Dr Johnson, Sheridan, and royalty?
6. Who illustrated *Alice's Adventures in Wonderland*?
7. In which English resort would you find the oriental-style Royal Pavilion?
8. In which century did Rembrandt live?
9. Whose portrait of Winston Churchill was burned on Lady Churchill's orders?
10. Outside which building in Hollywood do film stars traditionally leave their hand and footprints?

Answers on page 448

Art and Literature

Art and Artists 4

1 Which Swiss painter taught at the Bauhaus school during the 1920s?
2 Who was the architect of the Guggenheim Museum in New York?
3 Of what type of artist is Kandinsky generally regarded as the first?
4 What style of English architecture is described as 'Early English', 'Decorated' and 'Perpendicular'?
5 How do we refer to the group of late 19th-century French artists who depicted real life, nature and light in their paintings?
6 Which artist became famous through his posters of Parisian entertainers and prostitutes?
7 Which painter was famous for his pictures of distorted bodies, limp watches, etc.?
8 What was the extravagant style of art and architecture that dominated Europe during most of the 17th century?
9 What is the title of the painting by Picasso inspired by the bombing of civilians in the Spanish Civil War?
10 Which American artist was a pioneer of Abstract Expressionism, and a leading exponent of action painting?

Answers on page 448

Art and Literature

Art and Artists 5

1 Which English landscape artist painted *The Fighting Téméraire* and *Rain, Steam and Speed*?
2 How many paintings did Van Gogh sell in his lifetime?
3 Which artist painted *St George and the Dragon*, which is in London's National Gallery?
4 What nationality was the painter Goya?
5 Which painting technique uses water-based paint on wet plaster?
6 Which 20th-century English poet was famous for his enthusiasm for Victorian and Edwardian architecture?
7 Who was the leading exponent of the 'kitchen sink' school of painters whose work in the 1950s concentrated on working-class domestic life?
8 What is Joseph Niepce's place in the history of visual arts?
9 Which artistic movement, founded by Tristan Tzara, later evolved into Surrealism?
10 In which Spanish city is Gaudi's still unfinished Church of the Holy Family?

Answers on page 448

Art and Literature

Art and Artists 6

1. Whose sculptures include *The Thinker*?
2. Where did the Renaissance begin in the 15th century?
3. Who painted *The Night Watch*?
4. Which Dutch artist painted *The Artist's Studio*?
5. Who painted *The Garden of Earthly Delights*?
6. Which artist was featured in the film *A Bigger Splash*?
7. Which French artist was court painter to Louis XIII from 1640–43?
8. Which Italian fresco painter is famous for his *Adoration of the Magi*?
9. What group comprised Millais, Holman Hunt and Rosetti?
10. Who became potter to King George III in 1806?

Answers on page 448

Art and Literature

Art and Artists 7

1. Which French Impressionist painter was famous for his studies of ballet, horse racing, and young women working?

2. Which English architect's masterpiece is the Banqueting House in Whitehall, London?

3. Which American National Park was the subject of many of Ansel Adams' greatest photographs?

4. Whose paintings *Raising of the Cross* and *Descent from the Cross* are in Antwerp Cathedral?

5. Which painter was given his nickname because his father was a dyer?

6. Who designed a tapestry for Coventry cathedral?

7. What is the acronym for using computers to create and edit design drawings?

8. Which European capital city has the Atomium, an iron model of an atom enlarged many billions of times?

9. Which children's stories are illustrated by E H Shepard?

10. Who was the Italian sculptor and goldsmith who produced the *Gates of Paradise* for the baptistry in Florence?

Answers on page 448

Art and Literature

Art and Artists 8

1. Who painted *The Persistence of Memory*?
2. Which oil painting technique developed by Seurat uses small dabs of pure colour laid side by side?
3. Where was Europe's first hard paste porcelain made?
4. Which American painter is famous for capturing the loneliness of city life in the thirties and forties?
5. Who converted the Louvre from a palace to an art gallery?
6. Which famous sculptor created the angel over the tomb of Oscar Wilde?
7. What painting medium uses powdered pigments bound together with egg yolk and water?
8. Which English sculptress exhibited her *Mother and Child* in 1930?
9. Which collection is exhibited at Hertford House, London?
10. How was the Paris-based American photographer Emmanuel Rudnitsky better known?

Answers on page 449

ART AND LITERATURE

Art and Artists 9

1. Which Dutch graphic artist painted pictures of visual paradoxes and optical illusions?
2. Which German architect founded the Bauhaus School in 1919?
3. What is the collective name for the three goddesses who are said to be the personifications of pleasure, charm and beauty?
4. Who designed the Cenotaph in Whitehall?
5. Which 17th-century artist painted more than 60 self-portraits?
6. Which family's art treasures became the basis of the collection at the Uffizi Gallery in Florence?
7. Which French artist painted *Napoleon Crossing the Alps* in 1800?
8. What was designed by the architect Sir Joseph Paxton to house the Great Exhibition of 1851?
9. Which French artist was best known for his streetscapes of Paris?
10. Which British artist painted a series of screaming popes based on a portrait of Innocent X by Velazquez?

Answers on page 449

Art and Literature

Art and Artists 10

1. Who drew a rhinoceros without ever seeing one?
2. Philip Glass wrote an opera about which scientist?
3. Which composer based an opera on the book *The man who mistook his wife for a hat*?
4. Which of Captain Scott's ships is now a London museum?
5. Sir Christopher Wren was a professor in which scientific field?
6. Which Italian artist included a picture of Halley's comet in a fresco of the Nativity story?
7. What name is given to the Italian technique of inlaying furniture with semi-precious stones?
8. In which field of medicine might Leonardo da Vinci be said to be especially expert?
9. Who painted *The anatomy lesson of Dr Tulp*?
10. Which early 20th century artistic movement eulogized the modern world of science and technology?

Answers on page 449

AROUND THE WORLD

AROUND THE WORLD

General 1

1. Which is the world's longest river?
2. Which two oceans does the Panama Canal connect?
3. On which river is Vienna situated?
4. What is the world's largest desert?
5. Which is the largest and deepest of the Great Lakes of North America?
6. Which continent contains 90 per cent of the world's ice?
7. In which country is the Great Barrier Reef?
8. In which country is the great port of Antwerp?
9. Of which American state is Boston the capital?
10. Which Sicilian volcano is the highest in Europe?

Answers on page 450

Around the World

General 2

1 Three-quarters of which continent lie within the tropics?

2 Which European capital was originally two places, separated by the River Danube, whose names have been joined to form the city's name?

3 Which weather system often results in clear, hot, sunny days in summer and fine, frosty days in winter?

4 Which river's waters, headwaters and tributaries drain half the continent of South America?

5 The equator passes through many countries; which one bears its Spanish name?

6 What is the name of the river of which the Niagara Falls are a part?

7 Which country is the second largest in the world, in area?

8 Of which European country do the Magyars make up 92% of the population?

9 Which is the largest city in the largest state of the USA?

10 Which is the only parallel to divide the Earth into hemispheres?

Answers on page 450

Around the World

General 3

1 Which country is bordered by the Czech Republic, Slovakia, Germany, Hungary, Italy, and Switzerland?
2 Of which Australian state is Melbourne the capital?
3 What is the largest island in Greece?
4 Which country has the world's largest merchant navy?
5 What is Pakistan's capital city?
6 On which river is Baton Rouge?
7 In which country are Bat-Yam and Holon?
8 Which strait links San Francisco Bay with the Pacific?
9 In which country of the Republic of Ireland is the town Naas?
10 Which city is the capital of the Italian region of Lombardy?

Answers on page 450

Around the World

General 4

1. Name the mountain that overlooks Cape Town.
2. Which populous country is over $3\frac{1}{2}$ million square miles in area, of which two-thirds is either mountains or desert?
3. What is the name of the marshy area of France formed by the Rhône delta and is famous for its white horses?
4. What is to Jordan as Beirut is to Lebanon and Damascus to Syria?
5. In which English county is the Cheddar Gorge?
6. Which Japanese industrial port was the target of the second atom bomb dropped in World War II?
7. Which Pacific state of the USA was called the Sandwich Islands by Captain Cook?
8. 42% of which European country is reclaimed land called polder?
9. What number five to make up New York City, and 32 plus the City to make up Greater London?
10. What flows from the Black Forest to the Black Sea and is the second longest river in Europe?

Answers on page 450

AROUND THE WORLD

General 5

1. What is the world's largest island?
2. What was the former name of Vanuatu?
3. Near which city is the Taj Mahal?
4. Where on the Pacific coast does the Trans-Siberian railway terminate?
5. Which is the largest island in the West Indies?
6. In which country does the Indus rise?
7. Where is Ellis Island?
8. Between which two rivers are the Jura mountains?
9. On which island is Sarawak?
10. What is the world's largest monolith, in Australia's Northern Territory?

Answers on page 450

Around the World

General 6

1 What is the name of the trench in the Pacific Ocean which is the lowest place on the Earth's surface?

2 In which African country is the town of Timbuktu?

3 Which group of South Atlantic Islands was named after a 17th-century treasurer of the British navy?

4 Which historic city is Italy's main port?

5 What is the collective name for the eastern region of the Mediterranean, consisting of the coastal regions of Syria, Lebanon, Israel, and Turkey?

6 In which American state are the sources of the Red river, St Lawrence river and the Mississippi river?

7 Which Russian seaport is the largest city within the Arctic Circle, with a population of 432,000?

8 In which country is the highest waterfall in the world, the Angel Falls, at 978 metres?

9 What is the name for the rocky debris eroded, carried along and deposited by glaciers?

10 Which country's capital is situated on a tributary of the Murrumbidgee river?

Answers on page 450

Around the World

UK 1

1. Which of the five original Cinque Ports has a name describing a snack?

2. Which English county was created in 1974 when Bristol was merged with parts of south Gloucestershire and north Somerset?

3. Which wooded area of Nottinghamshire was once a royal park and hunting ground?

4. In which county are England's largest lake and highest mountain situated?

5. Which English town is renowned for lace, pharmaceuticals, and tobacco?

6. Which motorway, the first in the UK, was opened as the Preston Bypass in 1958?

7. Where in the British Isles are Macgillycuddy's Reeks and the Giant's Causeway?

8. Which of the countries in the British Isles is said to have the highest density of sheep in the world?

9. Which mountain system is sometimes referred to as 'the backbone of England'?

10. What is the highest point in England's Peak District?

Answers on page 451

AROUND THE WORLD

UK 2

1. What is the name for the area of north Staffordshire where the Wedgwood and Minton factories are situated?
2. Which island and ferry port is connected to Anglesey by road and rail bridges?
3. Which is the largest lake in the British Isles?
4. Through which Yorkshire city does the river Don flow?
5. Which is the only English island county?
6. Which range of hills forms a natural border between England and Scotland?
7. Which city is the second largest in the UK?
8. What was the name of the Roman road that ran from London to Chester?
9. The Norfolk Broads are man-made. How were they created?
10. In which range of mountains is Aviemore, the Scottish winter sports centre, situated?

Answers on page 451

Around the World
UK 3

1 What is the county town of County Antrim?

2 Which Scottish waterway links the North Sea with the Atlantic Ocean?

3 Which strait separates Anglesey from the mainland?

4 Which Home County was absorbed into Greater London in the 1974 reorganization?

5 What is the common igneous rock that forms Fingal's Cave and Giant's Causeway?

6 What is the name of the bight where the River Mersey joins the Irish Sea?

7 Which new town in Berkshire is home to the Meteorological Office?

8 Which English county contains the area called the Dukeries?

9 The names of which two English towns, one in the heart of England and one in Kent, are prefixed by the word 'Royal'?

10 What is the name of the national park where the highest point is Kinder Scout?

Answers on page 451

AROUND THE WORLD

USA and Canada 1

1. What is the largest North American mountain range?
2. What is the capital city of Canada?
3. Which district in Los Angeles became the centre of the film industry from 1911?
4. Which party did John F Kennedy belong to?
5. How many states are in the United States of America?
6. Who was killed with all his men at the Battle of Little Bighorn in 1876?
7. Which state has the nickname of the 'Lone Star State'?
8. What is the city in Nevada known for its gambling casinos and nightclubs?
9. What is the nickname of Alaska?
10. Which president of the USA was elected for four terms of office?

Answers on page 451

Around the World

USA and Canada 2

1. Which is the North American member of the weasel family which emits a foul-smelling fluid in self-defence?
2. What city is the capital of the state of Utah?
3. In which state are the Everglades and Palm Beach?
4. What collective name is given to the states of Maine, Vermont, New Hampshire, Massachusetts, Rhode Island, and Connecticut?
5. Who was the female star of *Sleepless in Seattle*?
6. What kind of leaf appears on the Canadian flag?
7. Which US territory became a state in 1907 and was the subject of a Rodgers and Hammerstein musical in 1943?
8. On the site of which battle did Abraham Lincoln make a famous speech stressing the constitutional ideals of freedom, equality and democracy?
9. What is the capital of New York state?
10. Which Pacific naval base was attacked by the Japanese in 1941, an act which brought the USA into World War II?

Answers on page 451

Around the World

USA and Canada 3

1. Of the four American states whose names begin with 'A', which ends in a different letter?
2. What do people in the USA call a 5 cent coin?
3. What is the written statute containing all the fundamental laws of the USA?
4. What is the state capital of Ohio?
5. Which film actress, originally called Frances Gumm, had the theme song 'Over the Rainbow'?
6. Who was the director of the FBI from 1924 until his death in 1972?
7. Which American film actor was governor of California from 1966–74?
8. If all the US states were listed in alphabetical order, which would be last?
9. Which bandleader led the US Army Air Force Band in Europe and composed his own signature tune 'Moonlight Serenade'?
10. In which city is Graceland, Elvis Presley's home?

Answers on page 451

AROUND THE WORLD

USA and Canada 4

1. In which river would you find the Thousand Islands?
2. Which city was the first capital of the USA?
3. Which of the United States is bordered by California and New Mexico?
4. Which British general captured Québec in 1759, but died in the attempt?
5. Who was prime minister of Canada from 1968 to 1979 and from 1980 to 1984?
6. Who made history at Kitty Hawk, North Carolina, in 1903?
7. What did Captain Cook call Hawaii?
8. What was Abraham Lincoln doing when he was shot?
9. In which state is Yosemite National Park?
10. Which is the largest Canadian province in area?

Answers on page 452

Around the World

USA and Canada 5

1. What was the surname shared by two US presidents who took office as the result of assassination?
2. Which two Sioux Indian chiefs defeated General Custer at the Battle of Little Bighorn?
3. Which state is nicknamed the 'Sunflower State'?
4. The threat of which judicial procedure forced the resignation of President Richard Nixon in 1974?
5. Which oil magnate left his fortune to found a museum and art gallery in Malibu, California?
6. What was the 13-year period between the passing of the 18th and 21st Amendments, notorious for the rise of gangsters and organized crime, known as?
7. Which office was held in the 19th century by James K Polk, Rutherford B Hayes and Chester A Arthur?
8. Which political scandal resulted in the conviction of John Poindexter and Oliver North?
9. Who was the only president since World War II to hold office without ever being elected?
10. What is the title of the US government official responsible for foreign affairs?

Answers on page 452

Around the World

USA and Canada 6

1. Which Canadian city is, after Paris, the world's largest French-speaking city?
2. What name did Dutch settlers give their settlement on Manhattan in 1626?
3. Who rode from Boston to Lexington and Concord on the night of 18 April 1775, bringing news of the approach of British troops?
4. Which river runs through the Grand Canyon?
5. What is the geological fault that runs the length of California and causes periodic earthquakes?
6. Which state is nicknamed the 'Beehive State'?
7. On the shores of which lake does Toronto stand?
8. Which city, now the capital of Georgia, was burned by General Sherman during the American Civil War?
9. Which river forms the border between the USA and Mexico for 1,500 miles?
10. In the state of Minnesota, which city, together with St Paul, forms the Twin City area?

Answers on page 452

Around the World

USA and Canada 7

1. Who were the two explorers commissioned by president Jefferson to find a land route to the Pacific?
2. Who, at 42, was the youngest president of the United States?
3. In which battle were the British commander Wolfe and the French commander Montcalm both killed?
4. Which sport was invented by YMCA instructor Dr James Naismith at Springfield, Massachusetts in 1891?
5. What is the highest mountain in North America?
6. Which are the only two rectangular states of the USA?
7. Which Canadian territory was the destination of a gold rush starting in 1896?
8. Who was the only US president whose terms of office were not consecutive?
9. What was the name of D W Griffith's classic silent film about the aftermath of the American Civil War?
10. Which Canadian province has Alberta on its west and Manitoba on its east?

Answers on page 452

Around the World

USA and Canada 8

1. What is the mainland part of Newfoundland called?
2. What new name was given to Bedloe's Island in 1956?
3. Who is the head of state in Canada?
4. Where in Texas is the Alamo?
5. Who was the last Aztec king, killed in 1520 by the Spanish?
6. Which of the United States is nicknamed the 'First State'?
7. What was the name of the provisional government of the USA during the American Revolution?
8. Which is the smallest state of the USA?
9. Who wrote the song 'God Bless America' in 1939?
10. In which city did Berry Gordy set up his Motown record company in 1959?

Answers on page 452

Around the World

USA and Canada 9

1 Which state is known as 'The Land of Enchantment'?
2 What was the name of the commission set up to investigate the assassination of President Kennedy?
3 Which one of the five Great Lakes lies totally within the United States?
4 Who was president of the Screen Actors' Guild in America 1947-52?
5 What are collectively known as the Bill of Rights?
6 In which city is the University of California situated?
7 Which astronaut remained in the orbiting command module while Neil Armstrong first set foot on the moon?
8 What was transported from England in 1971 and has now become a big tourist attraction in Lake Havasu City, Arizona?
9 What was the codename for the development of the atom bomb in World War II?
10 Which president was actually impeached, but the Senate failed to convict him . . . by one vote?

Answers on page 452

AROUND THE WORLD

Africa 1

1. Which 100-mile long waterway links the Mediterranean and the Red Sea?
2. In which country is the Aswan Dam?
3. Who was Zambia's first president?
4. Afrikaans is a variety of which European language?
5. Which is the second longest river in Africa?
6. What is the former name of the People's Republic of Benin?
7. What does ANC stand for?
8. Where did Idi Amin rule from 1971–79?
9. In which country are Tangier and Casablanca?
10. Which country has the rand as its currency?

Answers on page 453

Around the World

Africa 2

1. Which country unilaterally declared independence in November 1965?
2. The flag of Libya is a plain rectangle of which colour?
3. Which country was called Upper Volta until 1984?
4. Who was the Egyptian king whose tomb and treasures were discovered in the Valley of the Kings in 1922?
5. Who was the Egyptian president who was assassinated in 1981?
6. Name the East African country which lies on the Equator.
7. Which volcano in Tanzania is the highest mountain in Africa?
8. Which narrow stretch of water separates North Africa from Spain?
9. What are the two main arms of the River Nile called?
10. Which country, bordering Zaire, takes its name from the former name of the Zaïre river?

Answers on page 453

AROUND THE WORLD

Africa 3

1. In which country did King Hassan II ascend the throne in 1961?
2. Which British general was killed at Khartoum in 1885?
3. On the border of which two countries is the Victoria Falls?
4. What is the name shared by the currency units of Algeria and Tunisia?
5. Which actor won an Academy Award for his performance in *The African Queen*?
6. From which European country did Angola achieve independence in 1975?
7. Who wrote the novel *Cry, the Beloved Country* about South Africa?
8. What is the capital of Kenya?
9. What is the name of the volcanic valley that runs from the Sinai peninsula to central Mozambique?
10. Which explorer was the first to reach the Cape of Good Hope?

Answers on page 453

Around the World

Africa 4

1. At which town in the Sudan do the White and Blue Niles join?
2. Mount Toubkal is the highest peak of which range of mountains?
3. What is Africa's largest country?
4. Which African country is bordered by Benin, Ghana, Ivory Coast, Niger, and Mali?
5. Which country mainly makes up the Horn of Africa?
6. Which country is the island of Zanzibar part of?
7. In which country were the Mau-Mau a secret guerrilla movement?
8. Who was the woman sentenced to six years in jail after the murder of Stompei Seipi?
9. In which country are the towns of Gweru and Kwekwe?
10. What is the capital of Sierra Leone?

Answers on page 453

Around the World

Africa 5

1. Which African explorer translated the *Arabian Nights*?
2. Of which African country is Niamey the capital?
3. Who was the Danish author of *Out of Africa*?
4. The Zambesi and which other river define the borders of Matabeleland?
5. Who was the founder of the Back to Africa movement who largely inspired Rastafarianism?
6. Which country has the ports of Oran and Bone?
7. Which country is the home of the Ashanti?
8. What is sorghum, exported by a number of African countries?
9. Which African country is sandwiched between Ghana and Benin?
10. In which country are the ruins of ancient Carthage?

Answers on page 453

Around the World

Africa 6

1. Which country includes the Yoruba, Ibo, and Hausa-Fulani peoples?
2. After which American president is the capital of Liberia named?
3. In which township were 69 demonstrators killed by South African police in March 1960?
4. In which country does the White Nile leave Lake Victoria?
5. Which country ruled Sudan from 1820 to 1881?
6. In and around which desert do the Bushmen live?
7. What appears in the middle of the Rwandan flag?
8. Which new city in Nigeria has been shaped like a crescent, and has replaced Lagos as capital?
9. Which is Africa's largest city?
10. Which South African politician won the Nobel Peace Prize in 1960?

Answers on page 453

Around the World

Asia 1

1. What is the name of the mountain pass which lies between Pakistan and Afghanistan?
2. By what name was Thailand known until 1939?
3. Which British soldier helped organize an Arab revolt against the Turks during World War I?
4. Which river runs 1,560 miles to the Bay of Bengal?
5. Of which country is Katmandu the capital?
6. Is the Great Wall of China 650, 1,450 or 2,050 miles long?
7. Which sheikhdom is the capital of the United Arab Emirates?
8. What kind of wild cattle with shaggy coats and upturned horns live in the mountains of Tibet?
9. What is the currency of India?
10. Which Asian city hosted the 1988 Olympic Games?

Answers on page 454

Around the World

Asia 2

1. What was the former name of Iran?
2. Which country is the world's largest producer of tea?
3. In which modern country are the ports of Sidon and Tyre?
4. With what is the Japanese art of bonsai concerned?
5. Which 13th-century Mongol warlord controlled probably a larger area than anyone in history, from the Yellow Sea to the Black Sea?
6. Where did the Gang of Four try to seize power in 1976?
7. Which native East Asian plant is the richest natural vegetable food?
8. The West Bank of which river has been occupied by Israel since 1967?
9. Which Asian island is the second largest island in the world?
10. What colour is the circle on the Japanese flag?

Answers on page 454

AROUND THE WORLD

Asia 3

1 Which 15th-century navigator discovered the sea route from Europe to India by the Cape of Good Hope?

2 Which major export of Bangladesh is used to make sacking?

3 Which country uses the ringgit as its currency?

4 Who was emperor of Japan during World War II?

5 What is the capital of Hong Kong?

6 Who was supposed to have told the *Arabian Nights* tales?

7 Which country was suspended from the Arab League for ten years from 1979?

8 Which sea lies between China and Korea?

9 What is the holy city of Sikhism?

10 Which country is bounded by Saudi Arabia, Oman, the Gulf of Aden, and the Red Sea?

Answers on page 454

Around the World

Asia 4

1. What is the capital of Saudi Arabia?
2. Who led the North Vietnamese in the Vietnam war?
3. Of which state in India is Lucknow the capital?
4. Which Syrian city is said to be the oldest continually inhabited city in the world?
5. What is the name of the group of 1,196 islands in the North Indian Ocean, none bigger than five square miles?
6. Which is the largest city in India?
7. In which square in Beijing did troops massacre more than 1,000 demonstrators in 1989?
8. Which two Middle-Eastern countries fought a war from 1980 to 1988?
9. Which Japanese company is the world's largest manufacturer of motorcycles?
10. What nationality are the Gurkhas, who have fought for the British and Indian armies since 1815?

Answers on page 454

Around the World

Asia 5

1. Who erected the Taj Mahal in memory of his wife?
2. Who was the Mongol ruler who conquered Persia, Azerbaijan, Armenia, and Georgia in the 14th Century?
3. Which is the principal island of Japan?
4. During which years was the Opium War between Britain and China: 1816–20, 1839–42, or 1860–67?
5. On which inland sea do the ports of Astrakhan and Baku lie?
6. Which Indian poet and philosopher was the first Asian to win the Nobel Prize for Literature?
7. What did Burma change its name to in 1989?
8. Who founded the modern republic of Turkey and, in 1934, took a name meaning 'Father of the Turks'?
9. In which 1954 battle did the Vietminh defeat the French and end their influence in Indochina?
10. In which country did polo originate?

Answers on page 454

Around the World

Asia 6

1. What distinguished the Japanese tanker *Shin-Aitoku-Maru*, launched in 1980?
2. Which country is made up of 13,677 islands?
3. A 25 km causeway, the longest in the world, links Saudi Arabia with which other country?
4. Which river with a vast delta to the South China Sea rises as the Za Qu in Tibet?
5. Isfahan is a major city in which country?
6. Beside which river are the Indian cities of Delhi and Agra?
7. What is the Japanese product kakiemon?
8. The dong is which country's currency unit?
9. What is the dominant classical language of the Indian subcontinent?
10. Of which country is Vientiane the capital?

Answers on page 454

AROUND THE WORLD

Australasia 1

1. In which kind of tree does a koala bear spend almost its entire life?
2. Papua New Guinea occupies the eastern part of the island of New Guinea. Which country occupies the western part?
3. Which Australian actor became an international star with the *Mad Max* films?
4. Which fuzzy, brown, egg-shaped fruit is grown on a large scale in New Zealand?
5. What was the name of the raft sailed across the Pacific by Thor Heyerdahl to show that South Americans could have reached Polynesia?
6. Which city is the capital of the State of Queensland?
7. Does the date go forward a day or back a day when you travel east across the International Date Line?
8. What is the name of the long chain of coral off the coast of Queensland that is believed to be the world's largest living organism?
9. Which city stands on the site of the original penal colony at Botany Bay?
10. Australian Capital Territory is enclosed by which state?

Answers on page 455

Around the World

Australasia 2

1. Who was Lord Melbourne, after whom the city of Melbourne is named?
2. Which Australian state has no land borders with any other state?
3. In which year did Melbourne host the Olympic Games?
4. Which famous song did the Australian journalist Banjo Paterson write?
5. Queen Alexandra's birdwing, found on Papua New Guinea, is the world's largest species of what?
6. By what name is the Solomon Sea better known?
7. What is Australia's largest state?
8. Rockhampton in Queensland lies on which geographical line?
9. What was the main purpose of James Cook's first voyage to the South Pacific?
10. In what type of fiction did New Zealand's Dame Ngaio Marsh specialize?

Answers on page 455

Around the World

Australasia 3

1. Who was the Australian-born star of *The Charge of the Light Brigade* and *The Master of Ballantrae*?
2. Which long-serving Australian prime minister was in office from 1949 to 1966?
3. What is a bandicoot?
4. How many times did Rod Laver win the Wimbledon men's singles championship?
5. What was the former name of Tasmania?
6. What does *Aotearoa*, the Maori name for New Zealand, mean?
7. Which Nobel prizewinner from New Zealand discovered alpha, beta, and gamma rays?
8. What shape is the pitch for Australian rules football?
9. Which Australian opera singer made her debut in England in 1952?
10. What is the name of the arid coastal plain between Western and South Australia?

Answers on page 455

AROUND THE WORLD

Australasia 4

1. What is the word for a baby kangaroo?
2. What was the name of the Greenpeace ship sunk by French agents in Auckland harbour in 1985?
3. What name was taken by the swash-buckling actor born in Australia as Leslie Thompson in 1909?
4. Which Dutch explorer was the first European to see New Zealand, Fiji and Tonga?
5. Who is the soprano from New Zealand who played her first important role at Covent Garden in 1971?
6. Who was Labor prime minister of Australia from 1983 to 1991?
7. What is the other name of the Friendly Islands?
8. Which strait separates the North and South Islands of New Zealand?
9. Which city stands near the mouth of the Yarra river?
10. In which country is the island of Guadalcanal?

Answers on page 455

Around the World
Australasia 5

1. What is the name of the Australian actress who starred in *My Brilliant Career*, *Who Dares Wins*, and *A Passage to India*?
2. Which two Australian explorers made the first south to north crossing of the country?
3. Which Australian-born author wrote *The Female Eunuch*?
4. Which river forms the boundary between New South Wales and Victoria, flowing into the sea at Encounter Bay?
5. Who, true to form, provoked a mutiny as governor of New South Wales in 1808?
6. Where in Australia was the world water speed record set in 1964?
7. Where was the America's Cup hosted in 1987?
8. Which city is the capital of Tasmania?
9. Which great aviator is thought to have died of thirst on Nikumaroro Island, southeast of Kiribati's main island group, after disappearing on a Pacific flight in 1937?
10. Which two Australian states never received transported convicts?

Answers on page 455

Around the World

Australasia 6

1. What kind of creature is a Tasmanian devil?
2. In Fiji, ethnic Fijians are outnumbered by people from which other country, who were brought in in the 19th century to work the sugar crop?
3. Which great Australian cricketer needed to score only four in his last test innings to average 100, but made a duck?
4. In which group of islands is Tahiti?
5. *Aurora borealis* is the name of the northern lights. What is the equivalent in the southern hemisphere?
6. Which New Zealand physicist succeeded in changing one element into another, and later had an element named after him?
7. Which public holiday in both countries commemorates the landing of Australian and New Zealand troops at Gallipoli, Turkey, in 1915?
8. Which Australian writer, the author of *The Tree of Man* and *Voss*, won the Nobel Prize for Literature in 1973?
9. Which port lies at the mouth of the Swan river?
10. What did the Englishman William Dampier name the island of New Guinea in 1700?

Answers on page 455

Around the World

Europe 1

1. What is the name of the bay between northern Spain and western France, known for its rough seas?
2. Which is the highest mountain in the Alps?
3. Which European country left the Commonwealth and declared itself a republic in 1949?
4. In which country was Pope John Paul II a cardinal before his election?
5. What is the principal language of Bulgaria?
6. Which city, linked by canal with Rotterdam and Amsterdam, is the seat of the Netherlands government?
7. Which is further north, Corsica or Sardinia?
8. What is the tiny principality in the Pyrenees on the border between Spain and France?
9. In which country was Adolf Hitler born?
10. Which is the largest island in the Mediterranean Sea?

Answers on page 456

Around the World

Europe 2

1. Which city was the capital of West Germany from 1949 to 1990?
2. The shamrock is the national badge of which country?
3. Which river runs through Budapest?
4. Which two countries have a border with Liechtenstein?
5. In which country is Legoland Park?
6. Which European country colonized Brazil?
7. Which French river flows into the sea at St Nazaire and is famous for its châteaux?
8. Which country is divided into cantons?
9. Which country has as its joint heads of state a Spaniard and a Frenchman?
10. From which city did Neville Chamberlain claim that he had brought back 'peace in our time'?

Answers on page 456

Around the World

Europe 3

1. Of which island is Valletta the capital?
2. In which city does the Council of Europe sit?
3. Which two colours appear on the flag of Denmark?
4. In which Polish city was the Solidarity union formed in 1980?
5. In which Italian city would you find Leonardo's *Last Supper*?
6. In which autonomous region of Spain are the cities of Cadiz and Córdoba?
7. With which power did Bulgaria side in World War II?
8. Into which country were Bohemia and Moravia incorporated after World War I?
9. From which country did Iceland become independent in 1944?
10. In which capital city were the treaties signed that established the European Economic Community?

Answers on page 456

Around the World

Europe 4

1. Which is Italy's longest river?
2. In which year were East and West Germany unified?
3. In which Cypriot town will you find the 'Tombs of the Kings'?
4. Which German city is known as Aix-la-Chapelle in French?
5. Who was king of France at the time of the French Revolution?
6. Which European country restored its monarchy in 1975?
7. Which is the most northerly capital city on the European continent?
8. In which capital city is the Tivoli amusement park?
9. Which two colours appear on the flag of Greece?
10. Which country was ruled for 40 years by the dictator Antonio Salazar?

Answers on page 456

Around the World

Europe 5

1. Which poet died while helping the Greeks fight for their independence?
2. Which country was defeated by the USSR in the 'Winter War' of 1939?
3. Which crusade was led by Philip II Augustus of France and Richard I of England?
4. In Norway, what are Hardanger and Sogne?
5. On which river does Prague stand?
6. What emblem appears on the flag of Albania?
7. In which country did Grand Duke Jean become head of state in 1964?
8. What nationality was the 16th-century poet and soldier Camoëns?
9. On which river does Verona stand?
10. On which of the Greek islands did Bacchus find Ariadne, according to legend?

Answers on page 456

Around the World

Europe 6

1. In which Netherlands city does the United Nations International Court of Justice sit?
2. What do the French call the English Channel?
3. What is the name of the cathedral in Red Square, Moscow?
4. Which country's parliament is called the Storting?
5. Of which Italian region is Turin the capital?
6. Which country is known to its people as *Suomen Tasavalta*?
7. Who was crowned the first Holy Roman Emperor in 800?
8. Which group had most seats in the European Parliament after the 1989 election – the left, the centre or the right?
9. Where did Roosevelt, Churchill and Stalin meet in 1945 to plan the final defeat of Germany?
10. In which country is the Eiger?

Answers on page 456

AROUND THE WORLD

South America and the Caribbean 1

1. What is the official language of Brazil?
2. What strait divides mainland South America from Tierra del Fuego?
3. The name of which city commemorates the arrival of Portuguese explorers on 1 Jan 1502?
4. What is the capital of Venezuela?
5. What is the name of the flat, treeless Argentine plains between the Andes and the Atlantic?
6. Is the approximate population of the Falkland Islands 2,000, 10,000 or 50,000?
7. What is the capital of Brazil?
8. Which Argentine tennis player became the youngest Wimbledon semi-finalist for 99 years in 1986?
9. What is the capital of the Republic of Haiti?
10. Which river flows for 1,500 miles through Venezuela and partly defines the border with Colombia?

Answers on page 457

AROUND THE WORLD

South America and the Caribbean 2

1. In which country is the region Patagonia?
2. Which islands were the subject of a war between Argentina and Britain in 1982?
3. What is the capital of Colombia?
4. With which other island does Trinidad form a republic?
5. On which island is Cape Horn?
6. Which two South American countries have no sea-coast?
7. Which central American country did the USA invade in December 1989?
8. Which mountain stands at the entrance of the harbour at Rio de Janeiro?
9. Which country was ruled by the Duvalier family from 1957 to 1986?
10. Which sea lies at the western end of the Panama Canal?

Answers on page 457

Around the World

South America and the Caribbean 3

1 Which South American leader was known as 'the Liberator'?
2 What is the meaning of Sendero Luminoso, the name of the Peruvian guerrilla group?
3 Of which European country was Surinam once a colony?
4 Which country shares the island of Hispaniola with Haiti?
5 Which two countries have shores on Lake Titicaca?
6 In which country has the city of Medellín become a centre for the drugs trade?
7 What was Evita Duarte's profession before she married Juan Perón?
8 Where in Cuba did the USA sponsor an abortive invasion in 1961?
9 In which country was Che Guevara born?
10 What is the capital of Guatemala?

Answers on page 457

Around the World

South America and the Caribbean 4

1. In which country was Simon Bolivar born?
2. Who was the star of the Hollywood musical *Down Argentine Way*, famous for her fruit headdresses?
3. What is the capital of Ecuador?
4. In which country does the Amazon rise?
5. What is the name of the notorious penal colony which lies off French Guiana?
6. In which year did Brazilian driver Ayrton Senna win his first world drivers' championship?
7. Which islands belonging to Ecuador inspired Darwin's theory of evolution?
8. Which two South American countries produce the most coffee?
9. Which country is the world's leading producer of copper?
10. What is the name of the rabbit-sized Andean rodent valued for its silver-grey fur?

Answers on page 457

Around the World

South America and the Caribbean 5

1. What is the most southerly point of the continent?
2. What is the capital of Nicaragua?
3. What is the world's highest capital city?
4. Who was the last emperor of the Incas?
5. Which Chilean port was occupied by Drake in 1578 and Hawkins 17 years later?
6. For what profession is the Brazilian Oscar Niemeyer famous?
7. How is the Brazilian Edson Arantes do Nascimento better known?
8. In what country is Aconcagua, the highest peak in the New World?
9. In which country are the towns of Salto and Paysandu?
10. Which country's currency is the guarani?

Answers on page 457

AROUND THE WORLD

South America and the Caribbean 6

1. Which is the oldest colonial city in the Americas, founded by Christopher Columbus's brother?
2. In which country did the Tupamaros urban guerrilla movement operate?
3. What is the name of the Barbadian dialect of English?
4. Who was the left-wing president of Chile who was killed during a coup by the army in 1973?
5. Of which country is La Ceiba the chief Atlantic port?
6. What nationality was the composer Heitor Villa-Lobos?
7. Which two Central American countries fought the 'soccer war' in 1969?
8. What are Peru's two official languages?
9. What colour is the middle stripe on the Argentine flag?
10. What is the meaning of the Indian word *Amossona*, which gives the River Amazon its name?

Answers on page 457

Around the World

Built World 1

1. What island in San Francisco Bay was the site of an almost escape-proof prison?
2. What is the remaining part of the Temple in Jerusalem, a place of pilgrimage and prayer for Jews?
3. Who designed the Lloyd's building in the City of London?
4. In which city is the Kaaba, the building containing the Black Stone, revered by Muslims?
5. In which London street is the Monument?
6. Where in Manhatten is the New York stock exchange located?
7. In which English county is the prime minister's country home, Chequers?
8. What is the Eiffel Tower made of?
9. Which city contains a palace called the Forbidden City?
10. What runs from Wallsend, Tyne and Wear, to Maryport, Cumbria?

Answers on page 458

Around the World

Built World 2

1. Which famous French engineer provided the iron skeleton for the Statue of Liberty which stands in New York harbour?
2. Who designed the Clore Gallery to house the Turner Collection of the Tate Gallery in London?
3. In which country is the Owen Falls dam, which creates the world's largest reservoir capacity?
4. What did the Romans build at Ostia, Boulogne, Ravenna and Dover?
5. Which British seaside resort boasts a tower 152 metres high?
6. Why was the White House painted white?
7. What is the other name for Paris's modern art gallery, the Beaubourg?
8. Where is the Topkapi Palace?
9. Sydney harbour bridge is an example of which kind of bridge construction?
10. The great cathedral of Nôtre Dame at Chartres is a masterpiece of which style of architecture?

Answers on page 458

Around the World

Built World 3

1. What is the name of the twin skyscrapers, 415 metres high, that are the tallest buildings in New York?
2. What was the ancient city, carved out of red rock in Jordan, that was forgotten by Europeans until the 19th century?
3. What was built in Hyde Park for the Great Exhibition of 1851, rebuilt at Sydenham Hill, and burned down in 1936?
4. What was the assumed name of the Swiss architect Charles-Édouard Jeanneret?
5. In which city would you find the Blue Mosque?
6. What name is given to a walled courtyard in a castle?
7. There are two Cleopatra's Needles; in which cities would you find them now?
8. Which of the Seven Wonders of the World was at Ephesus?
9. Which palace was built by Cardinal Wolsey and presented to Henry VIII?
10. What was the original purpose of the leaning tower of Pisa?

Answers on page 458

Around the World

Built World 4

1. In which city would you find the world's tallest free-standing structure, the CN Tower?
2. How was the Hoover Dam on the Colorado River known from 1933 to 1947?
3. Where in the world can you see two bridges linking one continent with another?
4. Who designed the city of New Delhi?
5. On which French river is the world's first successful tidal power station?
6. What world-famous landmark was built on Bedloe's Island?
7. What is the name of the great fortified Moorish palace that stands on a rocky hill in Granada, Spain?
8. Which famous author lived in Abbotsford, a farmhouse rebuilt into a baronial hall?
9. Which model village in north-west England was built in 1888 for workers at a Lever Brothers factory?
10. What kind of stepped brick pyramid was built in ancient Babylonia and Assyria as the base for a shrine?

Answers on page 458

Around the World

Built World 5

1. What was the former site of the two temples celebrating Ramses II and Nefertari, before they were moved because of flooding by the waters of the Aswan High Dam?
2. Who was joint architect with Vanbrugh at Castle Howard and Blenheim Palace?
3. Which Parisian church contains the remains of Napoleon?
4. In which American city is Harvard University located?
5. In which city is the world's largest medieval cathedral to be found?
6. Which countries are linked by the Karakoram Highway, completed in 1979?
7. In which American state is the 'planet in a bottle' test project, BioSphere 2?
8. What is the British monarch's official Scottish residence?
9. Which Venetian building is linked to the Doge's Palace by the Bridge of Sighs?
10. On which river is the Kariba dam?

Answers on page 458

HISTORY AND POLITICS

HISTORY AND POLITICS

History 1

1 With which animals did Hannibal cross the Alps to Rome?
2 In which Indian city did 43 people die in the notorious Black Hole?
3 Which countries fought the Hundred Years' War?
4 Who became president of South Africa in 1994?
5 Which British field marshall received the German surrender in 1945?
6 Who was the first president of the USA?
7 Which Soviet foreign minister gave his name to a petrol bomb?
8 What important position did Dick Whittington hold from 1397 to 1398?
9 Where was Napoleon exiled in 1814–15?
10 Of which country did the playwright Václav Havel become president in 1989?

Answers on page 459

HISTORY AND POLITICS

History 2

1. Who became leader of the Russian people after the October Revolution of 1917?
2. In which war did the Charge of the Light Brigade take place?
3. Who was queen of England for only nine days?
4. Which 17-year-old girl led the French army that raised the siege of Orléans in 1429?
5. Who was stabbed to death in the Senate house, Rome, on 15 March 44BC?
6. Marie Josèphe Rose Tascher de la Pagerie became empress of France. By what name was she better known?
7. Who overthrew the Batista regime in Cuba in 1959, at the third attempt?
8. From which French port were 337,131 Allied troops evacuated in May and June 1940?
9. Which queen led a revolt against the Romans and burned London, St Albans and Colchester?
10. Which Polish trade union did Lech Walesa found?

Answers on page 459

HISTORY AND POLITICS

History 3

1. What were the names of the royal first cousins who married in 1840 and had four sons and five daughters?
2. What was built from the Tyne to the Solway in AD 122–126 as the northern border of Roman Britain?
3. Name the 11th-century survey documented in two volumes and kept in London's Public Record Office.
4. What did Pope Pius V do to Elizabeth I and Pope Paul III do to Henry VIII?
5. What killed 100,000 of London's 400,000 population in 1665?
6. Whose exploration of the New World had its quincentenary in 1992?
7. Which two countries were joined in the Act of Union 1707?
8. Which war was fought over 'the Union' and the emancipation of slaves?
9. What was the name of the flag captain who attended mortally wounded Nelson at the Battle of Trafalgar?
10. Which war made Florence Nightingale famous?

Answers on page 459

HISTORY AND POLITICS

History 4

1. Who conquered Greece in 336 at the head of a vast Macedonian army?
2. Who was the father of Cleopatra's son, Ptolemy XV?
3. Who did Rome fight in the Punic Wars?
4. Which Scottish queen was executed in 1587?
5. Who was king of Egypt from 1936 to 1952, when he abdicated?
6. Which country did Xerxes rule?
7. Which temple stands on the Acropolis in Athens?
8. Who was the first Christian emperor of Rome and founder of Constantinople?
9. Which rival did Julius Caesar cross the Rubicon to fight?
10. Which religion was founded by Prince Gautama Siddhartha in the 6th century BC?

Answers on page 459

HISTORY AND POLITICS
History 5

1. In which Spanish port did Sir Francis Drake 'singe the King of Spain's beard'?
2. Who was the French army captain whose unjust imprisonment for espionage in 1894 divided the French people?
3. Which war started with the capture of Fort Sumter and ended with the surrender at Appomattox courthouse?
4. Could Attila the Hun have met Genghis Khan?
5. Which 15th century earl was known as 'the kingmaker'?
6. Which island was held by the Knights of St John of Jerusalem from 1530 to 1798?
7. Who was the former British diplomat and Irish nationalist knighted in 1911 and hanged for treason in 1916?
8. Which international agreement of 1864 regulated the treatment of those wounded in war?
9. Which English prime minister was known as 'the Great Commoner'?
10. Who married Josephine de Beauharnais and Princess Marie Louise of Austria?

Answers on page 459

History and Politics

History 6

1. In which year did Dublin's Easter Rising take place?
2. Which family ruled Florence for three centuries from 1434?
3. Which British monarch married Anne of Denmark?
4. What title did Charlemagne, already king of the Franks, acquire in 800?
5. What was the first permanent English settlement in the New World, now in ruins?
6. Who proclaimed the People's Republic of China in 1949?
7. Which country first tried unsuccessfully to build the Panama Canal?
8. In which industrial process was the inventor Joseph Arkwright responsible for an important breakthrough in 1768?
9. Who was the first president of independent Kenya?
10. Which country sold land including the present-day states of Louisiana, Arkansas, and Oklahoma to the USA in 1803?

Answers on page 459

History and Politics

History 7

1. Which US president was shot five days after the end of the American Civil War?
2. What is the name of the British political regime 1649-60 established by Oliver Cromwell?
3. Which country was ruled by the Romanov dynasty 1613-1917?
4. What was the name of the last battle of the Wars of the Roses, fought in 1485?
5. Who were the Celtic-speaking peoples living in France and Belgium during Roman times?
6. Which wife of Henry VIII had already married twice before she became queen, and married for a fourth time after Henry's death?
7. What was the name of the Austrian-born dictator who succeeded Hindenburg as Germany's head of state?
8. Which country's liberalization programme was halted by the invasion of 600,000 Soviet troops in 1968?
9. In which battle did Harold II, the last Saxon king, lose his life?
10. Which Axis Power changed sides during World War II, declaring war on Germany in October 1943?

Answers on page 460

HISTORY AND POLITICS

History 8

1 Which king of England had a mother and a son who were both beheaded?

2 What year saw the nationalization of British Railways?

3 Who was the prime minister of South Africa who was assassinated in 1966?

4 In which naval battle did Rome decisively defeat the forces of Antony and Cleopatra?

5 Which royal house consisted of Henry IV, Henry V and Henry VI?

6 Which new policy in 1958 was an attempt to achieve 'true communism' in China?

7 Who was the black educationist who was born a slave but became a leader in the search for civil rights in the early 1900s?

8 Who are the only two English sovereigns from whom Prince Charles is not descended?

9 In which Indian city did British troops open fire without warning on a crowd of 10,000 in 1919?

10 Which 17th-century king of Sweden was known as the 'Lion of the North'?

Answers on page 460

HISTORY AND POLITICS

History 9

1 Who succeeded the Roman emperor, Trajan?
2 In which war was the Battle of Ramillies?
3 Which people did Alaric lead in the capture of Rome in 410?
4 Which French revolutionary was nicknamed 'the Incorruptible'?
5 Where did George Washington's army endure the winter of 1777–78?
6 In which country is the castle that gives the Habsburg dynasty its name?
7 Whom did Charles V confront at the Diet of Worms in 1521?
8 Which battle of 1746 ended the Jacobite revolution?
9 Who was appointed successor to Hitler in 1939 but expelled from the Nazi party six years later?
10 Who was the first democratically elected Marxist head of state?

Answers on page 460

History and Politics

History 10

1. Where did Florence Nightingale establish a hospital to treat casualties of the Crimean War?
2. What was the name of the Libyan king deposed by Colonel Khaddhafi in 1969?
3. Who was the admiral of the French fleet defeated by Nelson at the Battle of Trafalgar?
4. What was ceded to Britain in 1713 as part of the settlement of the War of Spanish Succession?
5. Who was the queen of the British king, Charles I?
6. What was the name of the basalt slab that became the key for deciphering ancient Egyptian hieroglyphics?
7. Which US president ended his country's participation in the Vietnam War?
8. Which sultan of Egypt, who precipitated the third Crusade, subsequently made peace with Richard I?
9. What Soviet 'man of steel' was educated for the priesthood but was expelled from the seminary?
10. Who succeeded Henry I as king of England in 1135?

Answers on page 460

HISTORY AND POLITICS

History 11

1. Who were the victors of the Battle of Austerlitz?
2. What was the first considerable engagement in the American Revolution?
3. Which rebellion was effectively ended by the Battle of Culloden?
4. In which war was the Battle of Shiloh?
5. In which year did the Japanese attack Pearl Harbor?
6. In which year did Brunei gain independence from Britain?
7. Which treaty after World War I established the League of Nations?
8. During which war was the Battle of Blenheim?
9. In which year did the Korean War break out?
10. Which three states did the USA gain after the Mexican war?

Answers on page 460

History and Politics

Kings and Queens 1

1. How many kings of England have been named George?
2. Of which dynasty was Elizabeth I the last monarch?
3. Who became king of Spain on General Franco's death?
4. Which king of England was killed while hunting in the New Forest?
5. In which century did Cleopatra live?
6. What was the nickname of Louis XIV of France?
7. Who was Elizabeth I's mother?
8. Which country deposed King Constantine II in 1967?
9. Which English king defeated the French at Agincourt?
10. Which Shakespearean king gave shares of his kingdom to two of his daughters, but not to a third?

Answers on page 460

History and Politics

Kings and Queens 2

1 Who was King of England from 1016, of Denmark from 1018, and of Norway from 1028 until his death in 1035?

2 What did Louis XVIII of France call 'the politeness of kings'?

3 In which country did King Albert succeed his brother Baudouin in 1993?

4 Which king's lovers included Nell Gwyn, Lady Portsmouth and Lucy Walter?

5 Which English king was killed at the Battle of Bosworth?

6 Which country's king and queen financed Christopher Columbus' voyage of exploration in 1492?

7 Which English king suffered bouts of insanity, which became permanent in 1811?

8 In which country did Queen Juliana abdicate in favour of her daughter Beatrix in 1980?

9 Who did Queen Victoria succeed?

10 Who was emperor of Germany throughout the First World War?

Answers on page 461

HISTORY AND POLITICS

Kings and Queens 3

1. With which other king did Edmund Ironside share the monarchy of England?
2. On which island did Queen Victoria die?
3. 'Good King Wenceslas' was actually a duke, but of which country?
4. Which disease was known as the king's evil?
5. French kings nicknamed 'the Bald', 'the Simple', 'the Fair', and 'the Mad' shared which name?
6. Which queen of England was prevented from entering Westminster Abbey for her husband's coronation?
7. Which royal family ruled Austria from 1278 until 1918?
8. Which of Alexander the Great's generals became king of Egypt?
9. In which country did a communist-led coalition force King Michael to abdicate in 1947?
10. Which English kingdom was ruled by Offa from 757 to 796?

Answers on page 461

History and Politics

Politics 1

1. Who preceded Ronald Reagan as American president?
2. In which country did Pol Pot lead the feared Khmer Rouge?
3. Who was Italy's Fascist leader from 1925–43?
4. What is the official residence of the president of France?
5. Which British company was effectively the ruler of much of India until the India Act of 1858?
6. Israel was proclaimed an independent state in 1948. Who was its prime minister from then until 1963?
7. Which human-rights organization campaigns for the release of political prisoners worldwide?
8. Who set out his political ideas in *Mein Kampf*?
9. What offence was former Panamanian leader Manuel Noriega tried for in the USA?
10. How often are American presidential elections held?

Answers on page 461

History and Politics

Politics 2

1. Who did Margaret Thatcher succeed as leader of the Conservative Party?
2. Which are the two main political parties in the USA?
3. Which party was led by Adolf Hitler from 1921 to 1945?
4. Who said 'A week is a long time in politics'?
5. How old must you be to vote in a British parliamentary election?
6. What was the racial segregation policy practised by South Africa's National Party until 1994?
7. In which year was Ulster incorporated into the UK, under the Home Rule Act?
8. Which German Nazi was minister of propaganda in 1933?
9. What do the British call the person other countries might call minister of the interior?
10. What name is shared by the chairs of the UK House of Commons and the US House of Representatives?

Answers on page 461

History and Politics

Politics 3

1 Who was the youngest-ever leader of the Labour Party, elected in 1983?

2 Which is the lower house of the British parliament?

3 Who was the last foreign secretary to serve in Margaret Thatcher's cabinet, an MP who also contested the leadership after her resignation?

4 What is the name for the group of opposition spokesmen and spokeswomen who comment on the policies of government ministers?

5 In which parliament has the UK 87 seats for members who are elected for a five-year term?

6 Who were the two prime ministers of Britain during World War II?

7 Which publication documents all proceedings of the British parliament?

8 Which party leader was a Royal Marine commando?

9 How many readings does an act of Parliament have in the House of Commons before being given royal assent?

10 What was the British government forced to abolish in 1991, replacing it with the council tax?

Answers on page 461

History and Politics

Politics 4

1. In which city did Karl Marx write *Das Kapital*?
2. Which US president introduced the New Deal in 1933 to counter the depression?
3. Which British minister of health inaugurated the National Health Service?
4. What is the name of the Welsh nationalist party?
5. Of what electoral system are 'single transferable vote' and 'party list' forms?
6. In which year was the US Declaration of Independence made?
7. What name is given to the series of strikes in the winter of 1978–79 that led to the defeat of the Labour government?
8. What is the Swedish name of the official who acts for the private citizen in complaints against the government?
9. What was the former name of the British Green Party?
10. Who was Britain's first ever Labour prime minister in 1924?

Answers on page 461

History and Politics

Politics 5

1 Which British prime minister fell from office because of his repeal of the Corn Laws?

2 Who was the first president of France's Fifth Republic?

3 Which party did F W de Klerk represent as South African president?

4 In which year did Saddam Hussein's forces invade Kuwait?

5 Who was the USA's vice president in 1990?

6 What is the Irish house of representatives called?

7 Which government post did Winston Churchill hold from 1924 to 1929?

8 Which Elizabethan politician, philosopher and essayist was fined £40,000 for taking bribes?

9 Mario Soares became the first socialist president of which country in 1986?

10 Which politician has been referred to as 'Red Ken'?

Answers on page 462

History and Politics

Politics 6

1. Which Conservative MP was a middle-distance runner who won two Olympic gold medals and set eleven world records during the 1970s and 1980s?
2. How many countries are there in the British Commonwealth?
3. Which prime minister took Britain into the European Community in 1973?
4. What became known as 'the F-word' at the 1991 Maastricht summit, where Britain wanted it removed from the treaty?
5. Which document was drawn up and unveiled by John Major in 1991 in an effort to raise standards for consumers and improve public services?
6. Who succeeded Clement Attlee as Labour Party leader in 1955?
7. What is the title of the presiding officer who keeps order in the House of Commons?
8. Which British actress won the Hampstead and Highgate seat for Labour in the 1992 General Election?
9. What is the term used when a sitting MP is removed as the candidate for a forthcoming election?
10. Which political commentator has presented both *Weekend World* and *A Week in Politics*?

Answers on page 462

History and Politics

Politics 7

1. Whose book *Sexual Politics* was a landmark in feminist thinking?

2. Who played the part of Piers Fletcher Dervish, personal assistant to MP Alan B'stard, in the television comedy series *The New Statesman*?

3. Of which party is Benazir Bhutto the leader?

4. Which policy helped Pierre Trudeau to a landslide victory in the Canadian presidential election of 1980?

5. Which publication was the vehicle for John Wilkes's attacks on the Tories for which he was imprisoned in 1768?

6. Who was dismissed from office as Australian prime minister in 1975 after refusing to call a general election?

7. Whose book *Inside No 10* described Harold Wilson's Downing Street years?

8. Which American president extended the New Deal into the Fair Deal?

9. In which year did Mikhail Gorbachev resign as Soviet president?

10. Which event prompted Anthony Eden to resign as prime minister in 1957?

Answers on page 462

History and Politics

Politics 8

1. How did the suffragette Emily Davison meet her death in 1913?
2. Which word, meaning 'I forbid' in Latin, means the right to prevent a law being enacted or an action being taken?
3. Who wrote *The Rights of Man*?
4. What is the name of the indirect system by which the president and vice-president of the USA are elected?
5. Which government office was held successively by Geoffrey Howe, Nigel Lawson, and John Major?
6. What name was given to processions of unemployed people who marched to London in the interwar years?
7. Which American economist is the foremost advocate of monetarism?
8. What word for unthinking patriotism is derived from the name of one of Napoleon's admirers?
9. What is the more common name of the 'simple plurality' system of voting?
10. What collective name is given to the first ten amendments to the US constitution?

Answers on page 462

History and Politics

Politics 9

1 What is the title of the member of the upper house equivalent to that of the Speaker in the lower house?
2 What is the collective name of the international agreements signed by all the member states of the European Community?
3 Which MP entered Parliament as a Tory in 1833, but became Liberal prime minister in 1868?
4 Who preceded Norman Lamont as chancellor of the Exchequer?
5 What is the other post held by the minister who is also chancellor of the Duchy of Lancaster in a Conservative cabinet?
6 Who was the first party leader in British politics to be elected by party members who were not MPs?
7 What was enforced by Parliament in 1379 and was the trigger that caused the Peasants' Revolt?
8 In what year did the Representation of the People Act give the vote to all women over 21?
9 Which county has a Tinners' Parliament called the Stannary, whose rights have never been rescinded by Westminster?
10 The secretary of state for which government ministry has responsibility for the council tax?

Answers on page 462

PEOPLE

People

General 1

1. Which author had the real name Charles Dodgson?
2. For what purpose did Melvil Dewey devise his decimal system in 1876?
3. Who was Sherlock Holmes' assistant?
4. Who was pope for only 33 days in 1978?
5. What are the indigenous people of New Zealand called?
6. Who was the 'king of rock 'n' roll'?
7. What term is used for an official count of the population?
8. Who was lead singer with the group Queen?
9. Who was the film star who married Prince Rainier III of Monaco?
10. Who introduced the potato and tobacco to Europe?

Answers on page 463

People

General 2

1. Who was the Lord Chancellor beheaded for refusing to recognize Henry VIII as head of the church?
2. In which city do people travel in water-buses called *vaporetti*?
3. What was the first name of the politician Gladstone, the composer Walton, and the reformer Wilberforce?
4. In which of the arts did Vaslav Nijinsky and Margot Fonteyn excel?
5. Which religious group migrated westward to the Great Salt Lake, Utah, in 1847?
6. Of which tribe was Goliath the champion?
7. How many people traditionally sing in a barbershop group?
8. Who led the Free French forces during World War II?
9. Which 18th-century dictionary compiler defined himself as a 'harmless drudge'?
10. Where does a troglodyte live?

Answers on page 463

People

General 3

1. Who was president of the USSR from 1985–91?
2. Which building is the official residence of Queen Elizabeth the Queen Mother?
3. Which battle of 1876 was Custer's last stand?
4. Which English king abdicated and became Duke of Windsor?
5. What was the nickname of the French singer Edith Piaf?
6. Which English potter originated the 'willow pattern' design?
7. Which actor, comedian and singer was born David Daniel Kaminski?
8. What was the name of the Thracian slave who led an ultimately unsuccessful gladiator revolt against Rome in 73 BC?
9. Who was the first man in space in 1961?
10. What nickname was given to General Thomas Jackson because of his stern defence at the battle of Bull Run?

Answers on page 463

People

General 4

1. Who said: 'We're not a family; we're a firm'?
2. Which admiral's mistress was Emma Hamilton?
3. Whose birthday is celebrated by a public holiday on the third Monday in January in the USA?
4. Who was the American politician who made wild claims of communist infiltration in the 1950s?
5. Which actress starred opposite Alan Ladd in the film *The Blue Dahlia*?
6. Which builder of steam engines formed a successful partnership with Matthew Boulton?
7. Of which country was de Valera the prime minister, and later the president?
8. What nationality was the spy Mata Hari?
9. What did Herbert Austin begin manufacturing at Northfield, Birmingham in 1905?
10. Which British historian wrote *The Origins of the Second World War*?

Answers on page 463

People

General 5

1. Where was Samuel Johnson born?
2. Who said: 'The customer is always right'?
3. Whose influential book on baby and child care was published in 1946?
4. Which French fashion designer created the 'little black dress'?
5. What invention made the fortune of Alfred Nobel, founder of the Nobel prize?
6. Who circumnavigated the world alone in *Gipsy Moth IV* in 1966–67?
7. Which Christian martyr was first bishop of Rome?
8. What, in a word, are Franciscans, Dominicans, and Cistercians?
9. What nationality was Everest's first conqueror Tenzing Norgay?
10. Who invented lightning conductors after flying a kite in a storm?

Answers on page 463

People

General 6

1 Who was the most famous of English lexicographers?

2 Over which part of Captain Robert Jenkins were Britain and Spain at war in 1739?

3 Who was the French tightrope walker famous for repeated crossings above Niagara Falls from 1859?

4 Which Russian goldsmith became famous for his jewelled eggs?

5 Who was the first criminal captured by radio after a message to a ship?

6 What did Thomas Blood try to steal in London in 1671?

7 Whose circus did General Tom Thumb join at the age of five in 1843?

8 Which British dandy introduced long trousers as conventional wear for men?

9 After which philanthropist was New York's Music Hall renamed in 1898?

10 Which film mogul was famous for illogical sayings, such as 'include me out'?

Answers on page 463

PEOPLE

General 7

1. Which language is spoken by about one-third of Algerians and nearly two-thirds of Moroccans?
2. Who was Peter Abelard's secret lover?
3. The holder of which office is responsible for organizing major British state occasions?
4. Who was the unsuccessful Democratic candidate for the US presidency in both 1952 and 1956?
5. In which of the arts has Richard Avedon distinguished himself?
6. What was Lewis Carroll's hobby?
7. In which city was Maria Callas born?
8. What was the real first name of the couturier Coco Chanel?
9. What pen name was used by the Spanish orator Dolores Ibarruri, who said 'It is better to die on your feet than to live on your knees'?
10. Who stated that populations increase in geometric ratio and food only in arithmetic ratio?

Answers on page 464

People

Murders and Assassinations 1

1. Who was assassinated in Dallas on 22 November 1963?
2. Which playwright was murdered in a Deptford tavern in 1593?
3. Which country's prime minister was Olof Palme, who was assassinated in 1986?
4. Who murdered at least five women in Whitechapel in 1888, but was never caught?
5. Who had seven members of a rival gang killed on St Valentine's Day 1929?
6. Who wrote *The Murder of Roger Ackroyd*?
7. Which rock singer was shot dead by a fan in 1980?
8. Which Shakespearean character is haunted by the ghost of his murdered father?
9. What method of execution was used during the French Revolution?
10. In which city was Archduke Franz Ferdinand of Austria assassinated in 1914?

Answers on page 464

People

Murders and Assassinations 2

1. What was Jean Paul Marat doing when he was stabbed by Charlotte Corday?
2. What weapon was used to kill Leon Trotsky?
3. Who was killed by a bomb at an election rally near Madras?
4. In which country was Benigno Aquino assassinated at the airport on his return from exile in 1983?
5. Which country's royal family was killed at Ekaterinburg?
6. According to the Bible, who committed the world's first murder?
7. Which English Jesuit and Roman Catholic martyr was hanged, drawn and quartered in the Tower of London in 1581?
8. Who did Claus von Stauffenberg try to kill in 1944?
9. Which king did Guy Fawkes try to blow up?
10. What was the profession of John Wilkes Booth, the assassin of Abraham Lincoln?

Answers on page 464

People

Murders and Assassinations 3

1 Who was poisoned, then shot, then dumped in the river Neva in 1916?

2 Who was Irish head of state for 10 days until he was killed in an ambush?

3 Who was assassinated by members of her own bodyguard in 1984?

4 Which British prime minister was shot dead in the lobby of the House of Commons?

5 Which US president had been in office only four months when he was assassinated?

6 Who was the black nationalist leader assassinated by Black Muslims in Harlem in 1965?

7 Which pre-Norman English king was murdered at Corfe Castle?

8 Where in Rome was Julius Caesar assassinated?

9 What was the name of the surviving daughter of the murdered Romanov family?

10 On which religious festival did Catherine de' Medici have thousands of Huguenots killed in Paris in 1572?

Answers on page 464

People

Conquerors and Explorers 1

1. In which year did Julius Caesar first visit Britain?

2. Who led the second expedition to reach the North Pole and the first to the South Pole?

3. Which Norweigian explorer reached the South Pole before Scott?

4. Where was Napoleon I exiled after his defeat at Waterloo?

5. Which leader of the Huns was known as the 'Scourge of God'?

6. Which French general and emperor was forced to retreat from Moscow in 1812?

7. What phrase was used to describe the German empire under Hitler?

8. What is the Spanish word for 'conqueror' used for explorers of South and Central America?

9. What new name did Francis Drake give his ship the *Pelican* during his circumnavigation of the world?

10. Which Venetian explorer served the emperor Kublai Khan?

Answers on page 464

People

Conquerors and Explorers 2

1. Which Germanic people sacked Rome in 410, bringing the Roman Empire to an end?
2. After which navigator is America named?
3. What did the aviator James Angel discover in 1935 that now bears his name?
4. On which day in 1066 was William the Conqueror crowned king of England?
5. What were the names of the three ships on Columbus' first voyage?
6. Which mountain was first climbed by Edward Whymper in 1865?
7. Which tsar of Russia conquered Kazan, Astrakhan and Siberia in the 16th century?
8. Who, with only 180 followers, conquered Peru in 1531?
9. Who was the Norse explorer who landed in North America and named it Vinland?
10. Where was Captain Cook killed?

Answers on page 464

PEOPLE

Partners

1 Who was Franklin D Roosevelt's wife, who helped draw up the Declaration of Human Rights in 1945?

2 Who was Stan Laurel's comic partner?

3 Who was Louis XVI's wife, guillotined in 1793?

4 What were the Montgolfier brothers known for?

5 Who was Othello's wife in Shakespeare's play?

6 Which pair make up the constellation Gemini?

7 Who was closely associated with Dr Jekyll in Robert Louis Stevenson's classic novel?

8 According to legend, which two brothers founded Rome?

9 Who shared the 1993 Nobel Peace Prize?

10 Who were the sons of Adam and Eve?

Answers on page 465

People

Who Said It? 1

1. Who said: 'Remember that time is money'?
2. Who said in 1966: 'We are more popular than Jesus now'?
3. Which footballer scored in the 1986 World Cup by 'the hand of God'?
4. Who came to regret saying 'Read my lips – no new taxes'?
5. Which poet wrote of a 'verray, parfit gentle knyght'?
6. Who claimed she had been thought of as a 'one act disco dolly who was just going to pop in and pop out'?
7. Whom did Walt Disney love more than 'any woman I've ever known'?
8. Which book contains the words: 'All for one and one for all'?
9. Who said in 1973: 'There can be no whitewash at the White House'?
10. 'Tomorrow is another day' ends which novel?

Answers on page 465

People

Who Said It? 2

1. 'A park, a policeman, a pretty girl' were whose ingredients for comedy?
2. Who claimed he transformed Elvis Presley from having a million dollars' worth of talent to having a million dollars?
3. Who told his followers: 'A Scout smiles and whistles under all circumstances'?
4. Who boasted: 'When you are as great as I am, it's hard to be humble'?
5. Who first urged Beethoven to 'roll over' in 1956?
6. Which great film director said: 'There is no terror in a bang, only in the suspense'?
7. Who preferred '50,000 rifles to 50,000 votes'?
8. Who first talked of 'natural selection'?
9. Who addressed a mouse as a 'sleekit, cow'rin', tim'rous beastie'?
10. Who predicted in 1865 that the 'star spangled banner of the United States' would be planted on the Moon?

Answers on page 465

People

Who Said It? 3

1. Who said 'Anyone who hates small dogs and children can't be all bad'?
2. In which children's story does a carpenter find 'a piece of wood that laughed and cried like a child'?
3. What did Henry Ford say was 'more or less bunk'?
4. Who said 'We are not amused'?
5. Which film star told reporters 'I want to be alone'?
6. Whose 1963 speech began 'I have a dream …'?
7. What did Alexander Pope think was 'a dangerous thing'?
8. Of which battle did Winston Churchill say 'Before … we never had a victory; after … we never had a defeat'?
9. Who telephoned Mr Watson and said 'come here; I want you' on 7 March 1876?
10. Which children's writer said that breakfast cereal is 'made of all those little curly wooden shavings you find in pencil sharpeners'?

Answers on page 465

People

Who Said It? 4

1. Which explorer's last words were 'I am just going outside, and may be some time'?
2. What did Le Corbusier call 'a machine for living in'?
3. What did James Bryce describe in 1912 as 'the greatest liberty that Man has ever taken with Nature'?
4. What did Elbert Hubbard call 'just one damned thing after another'?
5. Who said 'If one tells the truth, one is sure, sooner or later, to be found out'?
6. What did Marshall McLuhan call 'the greatest art form of the twentieth century'?
7. Complete Henry Thoreau's quote: 'The mass of men lead lives of quiet ...'
8. Who said 'No man is good enough to govern another without that other's consent'?
9. Which document declares 'To no man will we sell, or deny, or delay, right or justice'?
10. What philosphy's first principle, according to one of its chief exponents, is 'Man is nothing else but what he makes of himself'?

Answers on page 465

People

Who Said It? 5

1. Who said there are 'lies, damned lies and statistics'?
2. Which song writer got 'no kick from champagne'?
3. Which great explorer's last words were: 'I have not told half of what I saw'?
4. What was Queen Victoria first 'not amused' by?
5. Which comedian said that a bank will lend money to those who can prove they don't need it?
6. Who said: 'I used to be Snow White, but I drifted'?
7. Where, according to Dante, was the inscription: 'Abandon hope all ye who enter here!'?
8. Who penned the famous introductory remark: 'Me Tarzan, you Jane'?
9. On crossing which river did Julius Caesar say 'The die is cast'?
10. Who said: 'A Rose is a rose is a rose is a rose'?

Answers on page 465

IDEAS AND BELIEFS

IDEAS AND BELIEFS

General 1

1. Which of Jesus' disciples was the treasurer?
2. Who was the pacifist who led India's struggle for independence?
3. What name was given to members of the 'flower power' movement?
4. Which religion supports the caste system?
5. What is the name of the day before Good Friday?
6. Whose teachings were used as a basis for the government of China for more than 2,000 years until 1912?
7. Who is the Roman counterpart of the Greek god Zeus?
8. In which book did Charles Darwin expound the idea of evolution?
9. Which book of the Bible describes the end of the world and the Last Judgement?
10. How many Noble Truths does Buddhism recognize?

Answers on page 466

Ideas and Beliefs
General 2

1 To which religion is the Ganges the most sacred river?
2 Who is the exiled spiritual leader of Tibet?
3 What nationality was Sigmund Freud?
4 Which German church reformer is regarded as the instigator of protestantism?
5 Which great philosopher was a pupil of Socrates and a teacher of Aristotle?
6 What is the alternative name of the Church of Jesus Christ of Latter-day Saints?
7 Which Anglican archbishop of Cape Town was awarded the Nobel Peace Prize in 1984?
8 Who propounded the theory of relativity?
9 What is the name for the slender tower from which Moslems are called to prayer?
10 The Babylonian and the Palestinian *Talmuds* are the sacred texts of which religion?

Answers on page 466

IDEAS AND BELIEFS

General 3

1. In which religion do men take the last name 'Singh' and women 'Kaur'?

2. What, in the Christian church, occurs 49 days before Whit Sunday and 40 days after Shrove Tuesday?

3. In which religion must adherents visit Mecca at least once in a lifetime?

4. The followers of which religion observe the Sabbath from sunset on Friday to sunset on Saturday?

5. Who was the first emperor of the Holy Roman Empire?

6. Which members of the Christian Church believe that Christ will make a second appearance on Earth?

7. In which religion are the gods Brahma, Vishnu and Siva worshipped?

8. What is the name of the established Church of Scotland which follows a Calvinistic doctrine?

9. The members of which Christian sect have no ministers or priests, and gather for worship in a Meeting House?

10. In Buddhism, what is the name for the attainment of perfect serenity, achieved when all desires are eradicated?

Answers on page 466

IDEAS AND BELIEFS

General 4

1. Who founded the Christian Science movement?
2. Who was the Egyptian god of the underworld?
3. Members of which persecuted religious group founded Pennsylvania?
4. In Eastern systems of teaching what is the opposite principle of nature to Yin?
5. Which building is used for the election of a pope?
6. Which 19th century English philosopher wrote *Utilitarianism*?
7. In which Christian creed is the orthodox doctrine of the Trinity spelt out?
8. Members of which secret society refer to God as 'the Great Architect of the Universe'?
9. In which Far Eastern country was the Unification Church (Moonies) founded in 1954?
10. Where was Mohammed born?

Answers on page 466

IDEAS AND BELIEFS

General 5

1 Which ancient Greek philosopher thought that knowledge emerges through dialogue and systematic questioning?

2 Which Christian festival celebrates the coming of the Magi?

3 What is the highest title in the Shi'ite sect of Islam?

4 Which astronomer said 'Finally we shall place the Sun himself at the centre of the Universe'?

5 How many lines make up each of the 64 patterns in the I Ching?

6 What Protestant sect was founded by the Reverend John Nelson Darby?

7 What is the stage before full sainthood?

8 In which century did Roman Catholics declare the Pope infallible?

9 Which emperor disavowed his divinity in 1946?

10 What, in Hinduism, is the sum of a person's actions, which affects his or her fate in their next life?

Answers on page 466

IDEAS AND BELIEFS

General 6

1. What was the name of the prophet on whose book Joseph Smith founded the Church of Latter-day Saints?
2. The name of which religion translates as 'submission'?
3. Where did St Bernadette experience a vision of the Virgin Mary in 1858?
4. Which colourful festival is celebrated on and named after Shrove Tuesday, the day before the Lenten fast?
5. In Greek mythology, who was the nymph who pined away until only her voice remained?
6. Which movement within the Christian Church is working towards its eventual reunification?
7. Which parasite of trees was used in Druidism?
8. What name is given to the dish or cup used by Jesus at the Last Supper, and purported to have contained his blood?
9. Which Christian religious order was founded by Ignatius Loyola?
10. What is the indigenous religion of Japan?

Answers on page 466

IDEAS AND BELIEFS

General 7

1. Which philosopher invented 'the Superman'?
2. Which American politician defined the Four Freedoms?
3. Who put forward the theory of the 'collective unconscious'?
4. Who believe that 144,000 chosen will reign with Christ after Armageddon?
5. Which leading British occultist wrote *Diary of a Drug Fiend*?
6. Who is the foremost exponent of monetarism?
7. Which religious movement honours the Guru Maharaj Ji?
8. To which Anglican movement did Newman, Pusey and Keble belong?
9. In the Old Testament, who married his cousins Leah and Rachel?
10. The Digambaras and the Swetambaras are the main sects of which religion?

Answers on page 467

Ideas and Beliefs

General 8

1. Which philosophical system was founded by the Chinese philosopher Lao Zi?
2. Which Christian theory sees Christ as freeing the poor from oppression?
3. Which 17th-century radical Christian sect was headed by Gerrard Winstanley?
4. In which religion did the sect the Digambaras originally go about naked?
5. Which communist leader expounded the concept of permanent revolution?
6. Who is known as the 'Black Pope'?
7. Which Greek mythological hero and inventor of writing was stoned to death by the Greek army?
8. What do we now call the Christian Revival Association?
9. Which doctrine regards all reality as divine, and God as present in all of nature?
10. Who published his laws of planetary motion in 1609 and 1619?

Answers on page 467

Ideas and Beliefs

General 9

1. What event does the Jewish festival Hanukkah celebrate?
2. In Greek mythology, who was the goddess of retribution?
3. What is the title of either of the two epic Hindu poems written in Sanskrit?
4. What was originally a religious inscription, but is now a short, witty, and pithy saying?
5. What is the name of the process, culminating in a ceremony at St Peter's basilica in Rome, by which a member of the Catholic church achieves full sainthood?
6. Which archbishop holds the official title 'Primate of England'?
7. What is the meaning of the name 'Christ'?
8. In Greek mythology, who was transformed by Zeus into a heifer?
9. Which is the ninth month of the Muslim calendar?
10. Which French declaration gave religious freedom to the Huguenots?

Answers on page 467

IDEAS AND BELIEFS

Bible 1

1. Whose wife was turned into a pillar of salt?
2. Whose favourite son was sold into Egypt by his jealous half-brothers?
3. Who killed Goliath with a sling and a stone?
4. What was the source of Samson's strength?
5. What is the alternative name for the Authorized Version of the Bible?
6. Who was the first to meet the risen Jesus?
7. Who was the Roman procurator who confirmed the sentence of death on Christ?
8. What profession did St Luke supposedly follow?
9. As a reward for which skill did Salome demand the gift of John the Baptist's head?
10. Where was Daniel imprisoned according to the Bible?

Answers on page 467

Ideas and Beliefs

Bible 2

1 What is the title shared by four books of the New Testament?
2 Who was the brother of Martha, raised from the dead by Jesus?
3 Who made the Golden Calf for the Hebrews to worship while Moses was on Mount Sinai?
4 Where was Jesus arrested?
5 Which book of the Old Testament is a collection of moral and ethical maxims?
6 Which book of the Bible contains the story of the Great Flood?
7 Which was the Canaanite town whose walls fell at the blast of Joshua's trumpets?
8 Who committed suicide after receiving 30 pieces of silver as payment for betraying his master?
9 What are the 150 sacred poems and songs of praise said to have been written by David?
10 Who was formed from the dust by God, then given the breath of life, to become the progenitor of the human race?

Answers on page 467

Ideas and Beliefs

Bible 3

1. What comprise the Decalogue?
2. Which two priceless resins were brought by the Magi to the infant Jesus?
3. What were the names of Noah's three sons?
4. Which of the New Testament gospels is not synoptic?
5. Who was the son of Jesse, father of Solomon and second king of Israel?
6. Who is the false god, representing greed and wealth, cited in the New Testament?
7. Which biblical son of King David was caught by his hair in a tree while fleeing on a mule?
8. Which five books of the Old Testament make up the Pentateuch?
9. What is the collective word for the writers of the four Gospels?
10. In what did the prophet Jonah spend three days and three nights?

Answers on page 467

IDEAS AND BELIEFS

Bible 4

1. Which of the gospel writers also wrote the Acts of the Apostles?
2. What was the language spoken 2,000 years ago in Palestine?
3. Who was John the Baptist's mother?
4. Which section of the Bible was written in Greek during the 1st and 2nd centuries?
5. To which race of non-Semitic people did Delilah belong?
6. The reigns of which two kings are chronicled in the two books of Samuel?
7. What was the name of Naomi's daughter-in-law?
8. Which prophetess of the Old Testament led an army of Israelites to victory over the Canaanites?
9. What was the clerical office held by John when he wrote his three New Testament epistles?
10. Which two books of the Old Testament have female names as titles?

Answers on page 468

IDEAS AND BELIEFS

Mythology 1

1. What was the name of King Arthur's seat?
2. What is the name of the winged horse in Greek mythology?
3. What magic object did Mozart write about in his opera?
4. Which tiny boy, immortalized by the Grimm brothers, later lent his name to a circus performer?
5. Who wrote the novel *Dracula*?
6. In Greek mythology, who flew too close to the Sun?
7. Who was the Norse god of thunder?
8. Which Shakespearean title character committed murder after a prophecy by three witches?
9. What date is Hallowe'en?
10. In which city is the statue of Hans Christian Andersen's 'Little Mermaid'?

Answers on page 468

IDEAS AND BELIEFS

Mythology 2

1. What happens to Pinocchio every time he tells a lie?
2. Who was the Roman god of war?
3. Who was the legendary magician at the court of King Arthur?
4. Which character created by Washington Irving fell asleep for 20 years?
5. Which English outlaw is said to have lived in Sherwood Forest during the reign of Richard I?
6. What is the name for an undead corpse that sleeps by day and sucks the blood of the living by night?
7. In Norse mythology, where do the souls of heroes killed in battle go?
8. What name is given to magic used with evil intent?
9. What was the Greek hero Achilles' only vulnerable part?
10. In which story does the heroine Dorothy make a journey along a yellow brick road?

Answers on page 468

Ideas and Beliefs

Mythology 3

1. The Pilgrim's Way can be traced for most of its length between which two cities in Britain?
2. What did Daedalus construct for King Minos so that he could keep the Minotaur there?
3. Who was the ancient Egyptian redeemer god, husband of Isis?
4. What is the collective name for the three sisters who had wings, talons, huge teeth and snakes for hair?
5. In which fairy tale do two children find a cottage made of gingerbread?
6. Who spurned Echo's love and was punished by being made to fall in love with his own reflection?
7. Which mountain in Thessaly did the ancient Greeks believe to be home of the gods?
8. Where did Odin feast with the souls of dead heroes?
9. What sort of mythical creature is identified with the constellation Sagittarius?
10. Who left Ithaca on a ten-year voyage, leaving behind his wife Penelope and son Telemachus?

Answers on page 468

IDEAS AND BELIEFS

Mythology 4

1 What are magic bullets?
2 Whom did Orpheus try to rescue from the realm of the dead?
3 What would be your zodiac sign if you were born on New Year's Day?
4 What creature's head did Anubis, the Egyptian god of the dead, have?
5 What was the name of a one-eyed Sicilian giant in Greek mythology?
6 Which sign of the zodiac is represented by the scales of justice?
7 To which British monarch was *The Faerie Queene* dedicated?
8 In which river does the Lorelei lure sailors onto a rock?
9 In Greek mythology, who was fated to make true prophecies that were never believed?
10 Which poem tells of a sailor cursed for shooting an albatross?

Answers on page 468

Ideas and Beliefs

Mythology 5

1. Which pair of German brothers collected such stories as 'Hansel and Gretel'?
2. Which sign of the zodiac is represented by a ram?
3. What was the Holy Grail sought by the Knights of King Arthur?
4. Which set of magical beliefs and practices is adhered to by 4% of the people of Haiti?
5. Which mythical monster has the body, tail and hind legs of a lion, and the head, forelegs and wings of an eagle?
6. Who was Electra's brother?
7. What was the fabled city of gold that some 16th century Europeans believed existed in South America?
8. In Norse mythology, who are the female attendants of Odin?
9. In which much-told legend does a magician sell his soul to the Devil?
10. Who was the beautiful youth loved by the Greek goddess Aphrodite?

Answers on page 468

Ideas and Beliefs

Mythology 6

1. Who were the guardian spirits of nature in Greek mythology?
2. What was left as a consolation inside Pandora's box?
3. What was the name of the 'river of hate' that flowed round the Underworld?
4. Which animals are thought to have given rise to the belief in mermaids?
5. Which Trojan fell in love with Dido?
6. Which Cornish village is said to be the birthplace of King Arthur?
7. Who was Persephone's mother?
8. What was the food of the gods, said to give eternal life to those who ate it?
9. Who was the Roman goddess of peace?
10. Which handsome god was killed by a twig of mistletoe in Norse mythology?

Answers on page 469

Ideas and Beliefs

Mythology 7

1. In Greek mythology, which god was the twin brother of Artemis?
2. Which British occultist designed a tarot pack that bears his name?
3. Whose collection of fairy tales published in 1697 included 'Little Red Riding Hood' and 'Sleeping Beauty'?
4. Who wrote the Arthurian romance *Le Morte d'Arthur*?
5. How were the goddesses Aglaia, Euphrosyne, and Thalia collectively known?
6. Which Massachusetts town was the scene of witch trials in 1692 which led to 19 executions?
7. When is Walpurgis Night, noted for witches' sabbaths?
8. Which British writer, noted for a series of novels dealing with black magic and occultism, also wrote *Murder off Miami*?
9. Who in Greek mythology was seduced by Zeus disguised as a swan?
10. In the mythology of which ancient people was Marduk the creator of Earth and humans?

Answers on page 469

IDEAS AND BELIEFS

Mythology 8

1. Which legendary hero of an Anglo-Saxon epic poem defeated the water-demon Grendel?
2. Which month is named after the Roman god who has two faces, one looking forwards and one back?
3. Which 18th-century German soldier was famous for his exaggerated accounts of his adventures?
4. In folklore, who is the king of the elves and fairies?
5. Who were the heroes who accompanied Jason in his search for the Golden Fleece?
6. Which civilization originated the myth of the phoenix, which rose from its own ashes?
7. Which American escapologist and conjuror campaigned against fraudulent mindreaders and mediums?
8. Who was the mythical Greek hunter after whom a constellation is named?
9. How many cards are there in a tarot pack?
10. What mystical word, whose Greek letters are equivalent to 365 in numbers, was used as a superstitious charm?

Answers on page 469

Ideas and Beliefs

Mythology 9

1. Who, in Hindu mythology, is the wife of Siva and the goddess of death and destruction?
2. From which sun goddess did all Japanese emperors claim to be descended?
3. What was the name of Zeus's shield?
4. Where were unicorns said to live?
5. Who fell in love with a statue he had carved?
6. What is the collective name for the three goddesses Clotho, Lachesis and Atropos who controlled human destiny according to the ancient Greeks?
7. In Norse mythology, where is the home of the gods, reached by crossing the rainbow bridge?
8. Which nymphs in Greek mythology were the guardian spirits of the sea?
9. Who is the Chinese and Japanese mother goddess, whose attributes are compassion and mercy, and who is a form of the bodhisattva Avalokitesvara?
10. What was the name for the 'Islands of the Blessed' where heroes were sent by the Greek gods to enjoy a life after death?

Answers on page 469

SCIENCE

SCIENCE

General 1

1. What type of coal is brown and fibrous?
2. What raw material is used for making glass?
3. Which flower has the same name as a diaphragm in the eye?
4. What is the sticky wax obtained from sheep?
5. What is the strong inelastic material found in a human tendon?
6. What is the name of the strong material found in plant cell walls?
7. What is the trade name for the non-stick material used for coating cooking pans?
8. What material forms the hard outermost layer of a human tooth?
9. Snowflakes are symmetrical. How many sides do they have?
10. What name is given to the brittle kind of iron used for making engine blocks and manhole covers?

Answers on page 470

SCIENCE

General 2

1. Which scientific unit gives a measure of loudness?
2. Which animals are arthropods and have eight legs?
3. What name is given to an atomic particle carrying a negative charge?
4. Which is the modern scientific unit of work and energy?
5. The behaviour of sound in rooms and concert halls is a separate science. What is its name?
6. Chlorine, fluorine and bromine belong to which family of elements?
7. DNA is found in which part of the cell?
8. What name is given to the change of state from liquid to gas?
9. What kind of an animal is an iguana?
10. By which name is the drug acetylsalicyclic acid better known?

Answers on page 470

SCIENCE

General 3

1. How many legs has an insect?
2. What is oncology?
3. Who pioneered the airship?
4. Camera film bears an ISO number. What does ISO stand for?
5. What kind of an organism is a truffle?
6. What is the boiling point of water?
7. What is the name given to the molten rock beneath the surface of the Earth?
8. Which was the first antibiotic to be discovered?
9. Ascorbic acid is which vitamin?
10. Where in the body does a cataract form?

Answers on page 470

SCIENCE

General 4

1. What, specifically, are the metals amalgam, solder, pewter and steel?
2. Which branch of science has four fundamental principles: addition, subtraction, multiplication, and division?
3. What is the name given to the longest side of a right-angled triangle?
4. Which disease is spread in minute water drops?
5. In which area of science are the terms CPU, PC and VDU used?
6. What, in genetics, is the term denoting the transmission of traits and characteristics from parents to offspring?
7. What are classified by their measurement in degrees as 'right', 'reflex', 'obtuse' or 'acute'?
8. What is the most abundant element in the universe?
9. What kind of elements are found in a pure state in nature?
10. What is the generic term for the mechanical, electrical and electronic components of a computer?

Answers on page 470

SCIENCE

General 5

1. Which scientist won the Nobel Prize for Chemistry *and* the Nobel Peace Prize?

2. Whose research on X-ray diffraction of DNA crystals helped Crick and Watson during the race to discover the structure of DNA?

3. Who persuaded Einstein to write to President F D Roosevelt of the USA, warning him of the power of atomic fission?

4. Which scientist discovered the neutron?

5. Who was the first scientist to win Nobel Prizes for Physics *and* Chemistry?

6. Einstein left Germany to work at which American university?

7. Heisenberg is most associated with which branch of physics?

8. Stephen Jay Gould developed which evolutionary theory?

9. What did Heike Kamerlingh-Onnes discover?

10. Which scientist wrote the science-fiction novel *The Black Cloud*?

Answers on page 470

SCIENCE

General 6

1 Who was the first Englishman to put a dinosaur on show?
2 Who, referring to the principle of leverage, said, 'Give me the place to stand and I will move the earth'?
3 What is 'Lamarckism'?
4 Which field of learning attracted the attention of the ancient Greek Galen?
5 What science is the study of missiles in motion?
6 Robert Oppenheimer is remembered for his work on which invention?
7 Which metaphysician developed the theory of calculus at the same time as did Newton?
8 Who developed the modern system of classifying plants and animals?
9 Who discovered X-rays?
10 Which radioactive element is named after the progenitor of the periodic table?

Answers on page 470

Science

General 7

1. Which nebula is contained in the constellation Taurus?
2. Who was captain of Darwin's ship *HMS Beagle*, and subsequently became governor of New Zealand?
3. Which of Einstein's theories of relativity, the general or the special, was published first?
4. What name is given to the medieval practices which tried to turn lead into silver and gold?
5. Who lived in Pisa, discovered that freely falling bodies have an identical acceleration, and died under house arrest?
6. Who suggested that 'necessity is the mother of invention'?
7. What is the name of the process of freezing bodies at the moment of death, with the aim of resuscitation later?
8. Which scientist proposed that atoms are the smallest unit of matter?
9. Who shared a Nobel Prize for Physics with his son?
10. Who was director of the Natural History Museum during Darwin's lifetime, and one of his strongest opponents?

Answers on page 471

SCIENCE

General 8

1. What are the four fundamental forces of nature?
2. What is the branch of science concerning the study of bodies in motion?
3. What is divided into genera in plant and animal classification?
4. What is the name for a three-dimensional curve generated by a line encircling a cylinder at a constant angle?
5. What is the word which means either the strength of an earthquake or the brightness of a star?
6. What is the more common name for oil of vitriol?
7. What term is given to creatures such as earthworms which are both male and female?
8. What is another name for a rhombus whose internal angles are equal?
9. What is measured by a hygrometer and a hygroscope?
10. What is a device in a machine which allows free movement, especially of a rotating shaft in a housing?

Answers on page 471

SCIENCE

General 9

1. Who first proposed that the geological processes occurring now can be used to understand the changes of the past?

2. Who proposed that in searching for an explanation one should reduce assumptions to a minimum?

3. Which philosopher of science made popular the term 'paradigm'?

4. Who developed a general electrochemical theory as well as effective ways of poisoning people?

5. Which branch of philosophy emphasizes the importance of sense experience?

6. Which branch of philosophy rejects as meaningless everything except logic, mathematics, science, and observation?

7. Who claimed that the sciences and the arts were divided by a gaping chasm?

8. Which philosopher of science wrote *Against Method*?

9. Who said 'the physicists have known sin; and this is a knowledge which they cannot lose'?

10. Which problem ensures that no scientific statement can ever be 'true'?

Answers on page 471

Science

General 10

1. What was the first synthetic plastic?
2. What kind of a material is 'Quorn'?
3. Rusting produces which material?
4. Tungsten gets its name from the words 'heavy stone'. But in which language?
5. Camphor is what type of chemical?
6. Which material is produced by the Haber process?
7. What is the name of the material found inside living cells but outside the nucleus?
8. The first florin, minted in 1252, was composed of which material?
9. Which metallic element, with the atomic number 83, is used to soothe gastric ulcers?
10. American designer Louis Comfort Tiffany is famous for his work in which material?

Answers on page 471

SCIENCE

General 11

1. What name is given to the study of very low temperatures?
2. Who founded the science of electromagnetism?
3. Which protein forms the main constituent of an insect's exoskeleton?
4. Corundum is a mineral oxide of which metal?
5. Where would you find a Golgi body?
6. Ornithophily is what?
7. How many moons has Mars?
8. What name is given to the development of the individual?
9. Potassium belongs to which group of elements?
10. What is *Solanum tuberosum*?

Answers on page 471

SCIENCE

General 12

1 What discovery, made by Alec Jeffreys in the mid-1980s, is now used as a means of identification?

2 What is the study of electronic systems that can perform the functions of living beings?

3 Which Russian chemist devised the first form of the periodic table in 1869?

4 Which English naturalist, concurrently and independently, arrived at a theory of evolution similar to that of Darwin?

5 What natural organism is used to obtain litmus dye, used as an indicator in chemistry?

6 What describes a triangle whose three sides are all of different lengths?

7 What is the prefix denoting 'multiplied by 10 to the power 6'?

8 What is said to have been invented by Charles Babbage when he designed his 'analytical engine' in 1833?

9 What is the major ore of uranium?

10 Which French chemist gave oxygen its name and proved that water was a compound of oxygen and hydrogen?

Answers on page 471

SCIENCE

General 13

1. How many pecks are there in a bushel?
2. What is the earliest known unit of length?
3. What name is given to the series of international units used by scientists?
4. What is a fathom?
5. How many metres are there in a kilometre?
6. What is the Hertz?
7. How many kilos are there in a tonne?
8. How many pints are there in a gallon?
9. How many yards are there in a mile?
10. What unit is used in measuring the height of a horse?

Answers on page 472

SCIENCE

Physics 1

1. The discovery of which law provoked the surprised cry 'Eureka!'?
2. What name is given to the very serious chain of events which can follow the failure of the cooling system in a nuclear reactor?
3. In Britain, how many lines make up the picture on a TV screen?
4. Which Swedish scientist had a temperature scale named after him?
5. Which electronic device magnifies the strength of a signal?
6. What diverges rays of light, if it is concave?
7. What is any material that allows the passage of electricity and heat called?
8. How many colours are there in the spectrum when white light is separated?
9. What was the name of the unit of heat now replaced by the joule?
10. What is the term used to denote the tendency of an object to remain in a state of rest until acted upon by an external force?

Answers on page 472

SCIENCE

Physics 2

1. What is an unchanging position in which forces cancel each other out?
2. What does c represent in the equation $e = mc^2$?
3. What can be expressed as the number of cycles of a vibration occurring per unit of time?
4. What is measured by the SI unit called a 'henry'?
5. What does the abbreviation STP stand for?
6. What is commonly used in a rectifier to convert alternating current to direct current?
7. What is the product of the mass of a body and its linear velocity?
8. What is the force that opposes the relative motion of two bodies that are in contact?
9. What is a cylindrical coil of wire in which a magnetic field is created when an electric current is passed through it?
10. What is the study and use of frequencies above 20 khz?

Answers on page 472

SCIENCE

Physics 3

1. Which quantity has direction as well as magnitude?
2. Which physicist's law states that equal volumes of all gases, measured at the same temperature and pressure, contain the same number of molecules?
3. What describes a substance that exists in more than one form, differing in physical rather than chemical properties?
4. What is the ability of fluids to offer resistance to flow?
5. What is studied in the science of cryogenics?
6. Whose 'unified field theory' tried to explain the four fundamental forces in terms of a single, unified force?
7. What is the SI unit of magnetic flux density, named after a Croatian electrical engineer?
8. What was invented by Dennis Gabor in 1947, winning him a Nobel prize in 1971?
9. What does the acronym maser stand for?
10. What is described as an ionized gas with approximately equal numbers of positive and negative charges?

Answers on page 472

SCIENCE

Chemistry 1

1. What is used as the lead in pencils?
2. Which gas, produced by rotting vegetation, causes the phenomenon known as will o' the wisp?
3. What name is given to calcite deposits suspended from cave roofs?
4. What are the three states of matter?
5. Which common mineral is used to make casts, moulds, blackboard chalk and plaster of Paris?
6. What metal is an alloy of copper and tin?
7. Which element is used as a disinfectant, as a bleaching agent and to purify water?
8. What is the mixture of potassium nitrate, charcoal and sulphur which constitutes the explosive used in fireworks?
9. What is a very hard, transparent form of carbon, whose crystals are octahedral in shape?
10. From which country did fireworks originate?

Answers on page 472

SCIENCE

Chemistry 2

1. Which toxic, crystalline metalloid has the chemical symbol As?
2. What is alloyed with lead to make pewter?
3. What is the scale of hardness on which talc registers one and diamond ten?
4. Which substance, used in medicine, photography and making dyes, gives off a violet vapour when heated?
5. What aptly describes all transuranic elements?
6. What is the common name for solid carbon dioxide?
7. What is the process in which a solid changes to a vapour without passing through the liquid stage?
8. Which metal is produced from the ores limonite, hematite and magnetite?
9. What is the collective name for the five elements which make up Group VII of the periodic table?
10. Amino acids are mainly composed of four elements – carbon, oxygen, hydrogen, and one other. Name this other element?

Answers on page 472

SCIENCE

Chemistry 3

1 Which oxide expands by one-eleventh of its volume when frozen?

2 What is a very hard, naturally-occurring mineral, of which ruby and sapphire are gem-quality varieties?

3 Which element has the highest melting point of any metal at 3,410°C?

4 What are formed by the condensation reaction of dibasic acids and polyhydric alcohols?

5 Which is the densest known gas?

6 Which metal of the platinum group is twice as heavy as lead?

7 What is the chief ore of mercury?

8 What does the abbreviation PVC stand for?

9 What is the technique of analytical chemistry for finding the concentration of a dissolved compound by using a reagent?

10 What has a molecule of six carbon atoms formed into the shape of a ring, with six hydrogen atoms attached?

Answers on page 473

SCIENCE

Elements 1

1 Which is the lightest of all the elements?
2 What is the most common element in the universe?
3 Which element is used in the manufacture of computer microprocessors?
4 What element is found in bones, teeth, and shells?
5 Which element is mixed with copper to make brass?
6 Which lightweight metal is used in the manufacture of aircraft, cars and ships?
7 What is another name for lanthanide?
8 Which element was found in Greenland in 1989?
9 Which element is used to treat indigestion and stomach acidity?
10 Which element is used to make the rod found inside an ordinary electric battery?

Answers on page 473

SCIENCE

Elements 2

1. Which element ignites spontaneously in normal air?
2. Which element was discovered to have a link with Alzheimer's disease?
3. Which metallic element is an important constituent of haemoglobin?
4. Which element has the symbol Au?
5. Which poisonous yellow gas is commonly used in refrigerants?
6. Bauxite is the ore of which element?
7. Which is the most reactive halogen?
8. Which element is used in vulcanizing rubber?
9. Which element, used to make brass in the Bronze Age, was not recognized as a separate metal until 1746?
10. Which metal is the best conductor of electricity?

Answers on page 473

SCIENCE

Elements 3

1. Argon, helium, krypton, neon, radon, and xenon are the six inert gases. What is another name for this group?
2. Pitchblende is an important source of which element?
3. What isotope of hydrogen is combined with oxygen to make 'heavy water'?
4. What is the element basic to all organic chemistry?
5. What is the atomic number of magnesium?
6. Which element gains its symbol from the Latin word *plumbum*?
7. Which element is the most toxic substance known?
8. What metallic element is found in fool's gold?
9. Which element is used in the preparation of the light-sensitive layer of photographic film?
10. What is the third most abundant metal in the world?

Answers on page 473

SCIENCE

Energy 1

1. From where do green plants get their energy?
2. Which gas is essential for combustion?
3. Sunburn is caused by which type of electromagnetic radiation?
4. Which molecule is the source of energy for the body?
5. Which kind of energy is possessed by a stretched spring?
6. In degrees kelvin, what is absolute zero?
7. The sun's energy is produced by which type of nuclear reaction?
8. Which English physicist made the first dynamite?
9. Which type of radiation is screened out by the Earth's ozone layer?
10. What kind of energy does a moving object possess?

Answers on page 473

SCIENCE

Energy 2

1. What does 'm' stand for in Einstein's equation $E=mc^2$?
2. Which law would be violated by a perpetual motion machine?
3. What is the name of the process by which the body burns food molecules?
4. What is the ultimate source of energy for most renewable energy systems?
5. What name is given to a quantum of light?
6. What is the term for the production of light by living organisms?
7. In the electromagnetic spectrum, which radiation has the shortest wavelength?
8. What form of energy is produced by an electric motor?
9. What gas is needed by plants for photosynthesis to occur?
10. What is the scientific term for the emission of electrons from a substance when illuminated?

Answers on page 473

SCIENCE

Energy 3

1. Which organelles provide the cell with energy?
2. What does 'ATP' stand for?
3. What device converts chemical energy into electrical energy?
4. What is the temperature at the surface of the sun?
5. What is the name given to the fraction of incoming energy reflected by a body such as a planet?
6. Who first used a hypocaust heating system?
7. Where are the energy-sensitive cells of the eye's retina most concentrated?
8. Which capital city is heated by volcanic springs?
9. What kind of coolant is used in a fast reactor?
10. What type of energy is carried round the human body by blood?

Answers on page 474

SCIENCE

Instruments and Techniques of Science 1

1. What does a potometer measure?
2. What fuel is used by a bunsen burner?
3. What does a micrometer gauge measure?
4. What kind of electron microscope would be used for examining a surface?
5. Which instrument allowed Galileo to make his discovery that the Moon has mountains and craters?
6. Which plants did Gregor Mendel use for his experiments on genetics?
7. How are the beams of an electron microscope focused?
8. What technique is often used for identifying substances or for checking their purity?
9. What information does the technique of carbon dating aim to provide?
10. Which instrument is used to detect radioactivity?

Answers on page 474

SCIENCE

Instruments and Techniques of Science 2

1. What is the name given to the technique of measuring at a distance?
2. What device would be used to explore the depths of an ocean?
3. In what field is magnetic resonance imaging used?
4. What is an astrolabe?
5. What is the most accurate clock available?
6. In what field is electron spin resonance used?
7. How would a biologist use the technique of electrophoresis?
8. What is the term given to the precise measurement of the position of stars and other celestial bodies?
9. What is an electroscope used for?
10. Which technique consists of a mobile phase and a stationary phase?

Answers on page 474

SCIENCE

Animals and Plants 1

1. What is the name of the protective outer layer of trees?
2. How long is a giraffe's neck, approximately?
3. Why do fish have gills?
4. What liquid do plants need for photosynthesis?
5. Which animal can run at 70 mph?
6. What is the favourite food of the giant panda?
7. In the Bible, who tasted the forbidden fruit?
8. What is the fastest animal on two legs?
9. Which animal can move by jet propulsion?
10. What leaves does a silkworm prefer to eat?

Answers on page 474

SCIENCE

Animals and Plants 2

1. What name is given to animals that eat both flesh and plant material?
2. What is the green pigment used by plants to trap sunlight?
3. Which acid is produced in large quantities by lemon trees?
4. What kind of an animal is a marmoset?
5. What name is given to the microscopic plants found in great numbers in rivers, lakes, and oceans?
6. What are the young of bats called?
7. What is the name given to the study of birds?
8. Which plant has flowers but no proper leaves?
9. Which European tree lives the longest?
10. Socrates was poisoned by a potion made from which plant?

Answers on page 474

SCIENCE

Animals and Plants 3

1 Which flightless marine birds of the southern hemisphere live in rookeries?
2 What is the larva of a toad called?
3 Which bird feeds with its head upside-down and its beak held horizontally beneath the water?
4 Of which reptile are there only two species, one living in the Mississippi and the other in China?
5 Which birds of prey have acute hearing, binocular vision and heads which can turn 180°?
6 Which species of decapod has varieties called 'fiddler', 'spider' and 'hermit'?
7 What is a beaver's home called?
8 Which microscopic organisms form the basis of marine and freshwater food chains?
9 Which bird, a member of the cuckoo family, is often seen dashing along the highways of the southern USA and Mexico . . . hence its name?
10 What is the name of the seasonal journey undertaken by many animals to distant feeding and breeding grounds?

Answers on page 474

Science

Animals and Plants 4

1. Which family of insects has species named 'drivers', 'weavers' and even individuals called 'soldiers'?
2. Which digestive organ is well-developed in grass-eating herbivores, but is only vestigial in humans?
3. What are the nocturnal, herding herbivores of Australia, Tasmania, and New Guinea?
4. Which insects' larvae secrete blobs of froth called 'cuckoo spit'?
5. Which are the only birds able to fly backwards?
6. Which rodent rears its young, called kittens, in a nest called a drey?
7. What is the most abundant substance in the plant kingdom, which no mammal produces the enzyme to digest?
8. Which South American vulture can have a wing span of up to 3 metres and a body weight of up to 13 kilos?
9. What grow as parasites and saprotrophs, contain no chlorophyll, and reproduce by means of spores?
10. What type of seaweed grows up to 100 metres in length, and is farmed for its alginates?

Answers on page 475

Science

Animals and Plants 5

1. Which tissue carries sugary sap around the plant?
2. Which Hindu god is represented as elephant-headed?
3. What name is given to the study of animal behaviour?
4. Photosynthesis is carried out in which part of the cell?
5. Which part of a beetle's body is a skeleton?
6. Where in an animal would you find a mandible?
7. Which sub-division of plants is named after their practice of forming 'naked seeds'?
8. What kind of a creature is a scorpion?
9. Which vertebrates have a skeleton of cartilage rather than bone?
10. What is the name of the food storage organ found in many birds?

Answers on page 475

SCIENCE

Animals and Plants 6

1. What do baleen whales eat?
2. Mosses are classified as belonging to which part of the plant kingdom?
3. Which cells form the middle layer of plant leaves?
4. In what state is a 'sessile' animal likely to be?
5. Which part of a plant may be sinuate?
6. The maidenhair tree is the sole survivor of which class of plant?
7. How long is the gestation period of a duck-billed platypus?
8. Which part of the common valerian is used to make a sedative?
9. What is the name of the structures which allow leaves to breathe?
10. What is the name of the structures which allow stems to breathe?

Answers on page 475

SCIENCE

Animals and Plants 7

1. What has a central vein called a midrib?
2. What kind of a tongue does the okapi have?
3. What is the name of the lustrous substance that forms pearl and mother-of-pearl?
4. Which acid is contained in rhubarb leaves, making them poisonous to eat?
5. What do amoebas do by binary fission?
6. What is the Latin word for 'liquid' which we use to mean the fluid produced by the tree *Ficus elastica*?
7. Which antipodean bird is the largest member of the kingfisher family?
8. What is the generic word for plants that grow in water or water-logged conditions?
9. What is the state of inactivity through the dry, summer season, as hibernation is the dormancy of the winter months?
10. Which mammal constructs a lodge in which to store food, rear young and pass the winter?

Answers on page 475

SCIENCE

Animals and Plants 8

1. What is a tragopan?
2. Which step in photosynthesis is responsible for splitting water molecules?
3. What is the main use of the tree *Citrus bergamia*?
4. Where in a vertebrate would you find the protein myoglobin?
5. Machiavelli used which plant's name as the title of one of his books?
6. Which physician developed a type of remedy involving wild flowers?
7. What is a hackney?
8. What kind of an organism causes a 'rust' attack on plants?
9. The best longbows were constructed from which wood?
10. Which beautiful youth from mythology has a plant named after him?

Answers on page 475

Science

Animals and Plants 9

1. Which is the dominant generation in the ferns?
2. What kind of specialist would study storm petrels?
3. Which kind of organisms are likely to show a 'taxis'?
4. Which is the biggest flower in the world?
5. What is the name of the evolutionary theory suggesting that evolution has an uneven pace?
6. What is the name of the so-called 'first bird'?
7. Aphids insert their mouthparts into which part of a plant?
8. In animal classification, how are the phyla subdivided?
9. How many species of domestic dog are found today?
10. What kind of creature is a barnacle?

Answers on page 475

Science

Human Body 1

1. What is the scapula?
2. What is the scientific name for the kneecap?
3. Which part of the brain regulates physiological stability in the body?
4. Which is the most acidic part of the digestive system?
5. What is protected by the cranium?
6. Which organ is responsible for regulating the blood sugar level?
7. What is the name of the large muscle just beneath the lungs?
8. Which organ makes urine?
9. Where in the body is the thyroid?
10. What is the scientific name for the human 'tail'?

Answers on page 476

SCIENCE

Human Body 2

1. Where are the ossicles?
2. How many chambers has the heart?
3. Which glands secrete adrenaline?
4. Which organ removes excess water from the blood?
5. What name is given to the small bones which form the spinal column?
6. How many ventricles are there in the human heart?
7. Which organ in the body stores excess sugar as glycogen?
8. A deficiency of which vitamin can cause scurvy?
9. What is the scientific name for the tube connecting the mouth with the stomach?
10. When might a person show rapid eye movement (REM)?

Answers on page 476

SCIENCE

Human Body 3

1. Which teeth are the third molars, and are always the last to erupt?
2. What is the average human body temperature when taken by a thermometer under the tongue?
3. What beats more than 2,000 million times during an average lifetime – or about 72 beats per minute?
4. What is secreted by the pancreas to regulate blood sugar levels?
5. What are the two main veins in the neck, returning blood from the brain to the heart?
6. Which parts of the body are formed by the bones of the metatarsals and phalanges?
7. Where in the body are the cerebellum, the medulla and the hypothalamus?
8. What is the term for a series of uncontrollable intakes of air caused by sudden spasms of the diaphragm?
9. What are the very narrow blood vessels which form a network between arteries and veins?
10. What makes up 60–70% of human body weight?

Answers on page 476

SCIENCE

Human Body 4

1. What is the name of the membrane enclosing the fluid around the fetus?
2. Which part of the eye contains about 137 million light-sensitive cells in one square inch?
3. What is the fluid that lubricates and cushions the movable joints between the bones?
4. Which is the only vein in the body to carry oxygenated blood?
5. What is the ring of bones at the hip called?
6. Which human body organ weighs about 2 kilos?
7. What are the chemicals produced by the endocrine glands to control body functions?
8. What is the more common name for the tympanic membrane?
9. What is the oxygen-carrying protein found in the red blood cells of the body?
10. What is the colourless liquid, consisting of plasma and white cells, which bathes the body tissues?

Answers on page 476

SCIENCE

Human Body 5

1. What tube connects the kidney to the bladder?
2. Where in the human body do you find the alveoli?
3. A bone is joined to a muscle by which structure?
4. What is the threshold of noise-induced pain, measured in decibels?
5. What is the name for a red blood cell?
6. Which organ makes bile?
7. In which organ are faeces formed?
8. Which name is given to the heart chamber which receives blood?
9. What name is given to the genetic make-up of an individual?
10. What is the biggest bone in the body?

Answers on page 476

SCIENCE

Human Body 6

1. Which of the retina's cells can distinguish between different wavelengths of light?
2. Where is the pituitary gland?
3. What is the name of the large buttock and thigh muscle?
4. What kind of joint is the hip?
5. What is the name of the structural tissue found in the ear, the nose, and in between the vertebral discs?
6. Which organ of the body secretes insulin?
7. Which hormone causes male sexual development?
8. Where are the semicircular canals?
9. What is the scientific name for the windpipe?
10. What is the name of the enzyme produced in the mouth?

Answers on page 476

SCIENCE

Human Body 7

1. Which glands secrete oestrogen?
2. What is the function of the islets of Langerhans?
3. Where do the Graafian follicles develop?
4. Which tissue secretes progesterone during the second half of the menstrual cycle?
5. What term is given to the lymphocytes which mature in the thymus?
6. Which part of the brain controls the heart rate?
7. What is the scientific name for the heart's pacemaker?
8. Which artery supplies the kidney with blood?
9. Which part of the gut absorbs water from the food?
10. How many genes are there in the human genome?

Answers on page 477

SCIENCE

Human Body 8

1. When the egg is released from the ovary, what is left behind?
2. Where is the sinoatrial node?
3. Which hormone helps control ovulation?
4. Where would you find the carotid arteries?
5. Which organ destroys old red blood cells?
6. The pituitary controls many hormones. But what controls the pituitary?
7. Where would you find the islets of Langerhans?
8. What hormone was discovered by John Jacob Abel?
9. Which gland secretes the corticosteroids?
10. Which part of the body produces the excretory product urea?

Answers on page 477

SCIENCE

Human Body 9

1. Where would you find the pisiform bone?
2. What are the natural pain-killing substances produced in the brain and pituitary gland?
3. What is an overgrowth of fibrous tissue, usually produced at the site of a scar?
4. Which protein forms hair and nails?
5. What is the coloured muscle that responds involuntarily to light?
6. What is the substance produced by hard exercise and oxygen debt, causing stiffness in the muscles?
7. Which three bones are collectively known as the auditory ossicles?
8. What is the pigment that colours skin?
9. Of what do we have 52 in a lifetime, 20 of which are deciduous?
10. What is the substance that the body over-produces in an allergic reaction to pollen?

Answers on page 477

SCIENCE

Senses 1

1. Which part of the eye contains light-sensitive cells?
2. Which composer wrote much of his finest music when he was deaf?
3. Which nerve carries information from the eye to the brain?
4. How do bats 'see in the dark'?
5. Which part of the eye gives it colour?
6. Which part of the eye gets smaller when the lights go on?
7. What name is given to the colour-sensitive sense cells in the eye?
8. What phenomenon is characterized by constant sound in the ears?
9. How many basic tastes can the human tongue distinguish?
10. What is the medical term for not being able to smell?

Answers on page 477

Science

Senses 2

1. Fish use the lateral line system for sensing which kind of stimulus?
2. Which part of the ear helps you balance?
3. Which eye defect is caused by loss of elasticity of the lens?
4. What is the term for being sensitive to light?
5. How many colour pigments are there in the human retina?
6. Which nerves are responsible for smell?
7. Which part of the eye is responsible for focusing the lens?
8. Which human sense organ may be sensitive to magnetic fields?
9. Which light-sensitive pigment in plants is involved in the regulation of flowering?
10. Which sense does the Venus Flytrap use in order to capture prey?

Answers on page 477

Science

Medicine and Health 1

1. In a surgical operation which kind of doctor is responsible for putting the patient to sleep?
2. During a transfusion which tissue is given to the patient?
3. What kind of drug prevents the spread of a bacterial infection through the body?
4. When was hormone-replacement therapy first used?
5. Too much of which type of beverage can cause high blood cholesterol levels?
6. Which type of fat is recommended for healthy eating?
7. What is the maximum number of units of alcohol the government says is safe for a man to drink each week?
8. Someone with gastroenteritis is having problems with which organ?
9. The blood problem anaemia is sometimes cured by extra doses of which mineral?
10. Which parts of the body concern an ENT specialist?

Answers on page 477

SCIENCE

Medicine and Health 2

1. What type of microbe causes the common cold?
2. Which insect transmits malaria?
3. What is the main organ affected by a stroke?
4. Who developed vaccination against smallpox?
5. Which agency of the United Nations exists to fight and eradicate disease?
6. Diabetes results from a failure to secrete which hormone?
7. What kind of food poisoning can be caused by eating half-cooked poultry?
8. What kind of contraceptive is the best protection against sexually transmitted diseases?
9. Which body fluid is affected by thalassaemia?
10. What is the disease in which normal clotting of the blood is slowed or stopped completely?

Answers on page 478

Science

Medicine and Health 3

1. Who pioneered the use of antiseptics, which resulted in a dramatic reduction in the death rate during surgery?

2. What is the term for a physical change resulting from disease or injury?

3. What is the viral disease, named after a West African village, for which there is no known cure?

4. What is the Latin for 'I will please', a word used to mean a sugar pill that has no active effect?

5. What is the common name for the infectious disease whose medical name is rubeola?

6. What is a more common name for Hansen's disease?

7. Which species of macaque monkey gave its name to the blood-group system of humans?

8. Which disease is the single biggest cause of blindness worldwide?

9. What is the pneumonia-like disease named after the people who caught it while attending an American Convention in Philadelphia in 1976?

10. What has the technical name dyspepsia, a disorder causing abdominal pain?

Answers on page 478

Science

Medicine and Health 4

1. Which surgeon performed the world's first heart transplant in 1967?
2. An embolism is a blockage. But where?
3. Multiple sclerosis is a disease of which system?
4. Beta-blockers affect which organ of the body?
5. Osteoporosis affects which part of the body?
6. Which phobia is the fear of heights?
7. Diabetes is caused by a malfunction of cells in which organ of the body?
8. Barium sulphate is taken into the body by which method?
9. Interferon defends the body from which kind of microbe attack?
10. What do we call the swelling on the neck caused by an iodine deficiency or over-activity of the thyroid gland?

Answers on page 478

Science

Medicine and Health 5

1. What is the medical term for inflammation or stiffness of the joints and muscles?
2. Which hormones are used in hormone–replacement therapy?
3. What does the acronym 'IVF' mean?
4. AZT is used in the treatment of which disease?
5. What is the technical name for chronic fatigue syndrome?
6. Which organ is affected by emphysema?
7. Which bacterium causes toxic shock syndrome?
8. Which antimalarial drug is extracted from the bark of the cinchona tree?
9. What causes Down's syndrome?
10. Beriberi results from a lack of which vitamin?

Answers on page 478

SCIENCE

Medicine and Health 6

1. The tree *Salix alba* was used in the preparation of which drug?
2. What is the name given to a statistician who calculates life expectancy, etc. for an insurance company?
3. *Diabetes insipidus* affects which organ?
4. Which disease, targeted by the World Health Organization, was eradicated by 1980?
5. Malarial parasites live in which part of the mosquito?
6. Dopamine acts on which part of the body?
7. Amniocentesis is used in which field of medicine?
8. Hodgkin's disease is what type of disease?
9. The T cells of the human immune system mature in which gland?
10. English writer D H Lawrence died of which disease?

Answers on page 478

SCIENCE

Planet Earth 1

1. Which Australian mammal lays eggs?
2. Which animal has been hunted almost to extinction because of its horn?
3. What name is given to the hard white material of elephant tusks?
4. Which gas, released by car exhausts, stops the blood haemoglobin from working properly?
5. Which chemical, commonly used to increase crop yield, sometimes contaminates drinking water?
6. What is the term used for something that will break down naturally?
7. Where is the Glacier Bay national park?
8. Acid rain is caused by which polluting gas?
9. What device is added to a car's exhaust system to reduce pollution?
10. When you recycle a drinks can, which metal are you likely to be conserving?

Answers on page 478

SCIENCE

Planet Earth 2

1. Which is the most common gas in the atmosphere?
2. What is the Earth's core made of?
3. Which Indian state is at the eastern end of the Himalayas?
4. Which fuel is formed by the fossilization of plants?
5. What is the world's deepest ocean?
6. What is the name of the liquid rock which pours from a volcano?
7. Oxygen forms approximately what proportion of the atmosphere?
8. What is the term applied to the process of gathering together weather forecasts from various recording stations?
9. What kind of tide occurs at full Moon?
10. What kind of natural phenomenon 'meanders'?

Answers on page 479

SCIENCE

Planet Earth 3

1. What is the term given to the study of the weather?
2. What is a cloud?
3. Which is the largest animal ever to have inhabited the Earth?
4. Which gas forms 80% of the Earth's atmosphere?
5. What is the second most common gas in the atmosphere?
6. In which mountain chain would you find Mount Everest?
7. What is the collective name for rain, hail, snow, and sleet?
8. What is the name of the atmospheric gas which screens out the sun's harmful ultraviolet radiation?
9. What is the name given to the outermost layer of the Earth?
10. What is the hardest natural substance known?

Answers on page 479

SCIENCE

Planet Earth 4

1. What once covered 14% of the Earth's land area, but by 1991 over half had been destroyed?

2. Which country produces the world's largest quantity of municipal waste per person per year at over five-sixths of a ton?

3. What was the name of the ship that spilt 85,000 tonnes of oil off the Shetland Islands in 1993?

4. What is the collective term for substances such as coal, oil and natural gas, the burning of which produces carbon dioxide?

5. Which environmental pressure group was founded in the UK in 1971?

6. Which is the largest national park in Europe?

7. What contributes to the greenhouse effect at lower atmospheric levels, but in the upper atmosphere protects life on Earth?

8. What is the collective noun for crows?

9. What is the name for land in Britain officially designated 'not to be built on but to be preserved as open space'?

10. What is dispensed from the green pump, and must be used if a car has a catalytic converter?

Answers on page 479

Science

Planet Earth 5

1. Which sea is so highly polluted that the Barcelona Convention was set up in 1976 to try and clean it up?
2. What are the three main greenhouse gases?
3. What natural feature covers approximately 6% of the Earth's land surface, and harbours 40% of the Earth's species?
4. What is the name of the process by which substances are washed out of the soil?
5. 25% of which traditional British feature was cut down between 1945 and 1985 because of agricultural mechanization?
6. What was the viral disease controversially introduced into Britain during the 1950s to reduce the rabbit population?
7. Who was director of the environmental pressure group Friends of the Earth 1984–90?
8. Which European country is committed to decommissioning all of its nuclear reactors?
9. Which inland sea between Kazakhstan and Uzbekistan is fast disappearing because the rivers that feed it have been diverted and dammed?
10. What is the name of Britain's nuclear-fuel reprocessing plant?

Answers on page 479

SCIENCE

Planet Earth 6

1. Which Canadian city gave its name to the 1987 world agreement on protection of the ozone layer?
2. The damaged Chernobyl nuclear power station is situated in which country?
3. What name is given to the huge growths of algae sometimes seen in polluted lakes and rivers?
4. What is the collective noun for larks?
5. What was the name of the dioxin-containing defoliant used during the Vietnam war by the USA army?
6. Five-legged creatures have damaged which 1250 mi-long wonder of the world?
7. In which area of the world do tropical rainforests occur?
8. What is the maximum speed of a garden snail: 0.03 mph, 0.3 mph, or 3 mph?
9. CITES is an international agreement on which environmental problem?
10. The dodo was a native bird of which island?

Answers on page 479

Science

Planet Earth 7

1. What type of rock is granite?
2. What is the approximate circumference of the Earth?
3. What is the name given to the study of earthquakes?
4. What is the name given to the geological time period of 363–290 million years ago during which coal measures were formed?
5. What is the scientific scale for measuring the hardness of rocks?
6. Which is further north, the tropic of Cancer or the tropic of Capricorn?
7. Which gas in the atmosphere can be turned into fertilizer by some microbes?
8. What does a barometer measure?
9. Someone who studies tectonics is probably an expert in which field?
10. What name is given to your angular distance on the Earth's surface relative to the equator?

Answers on page 479

Science

Planet Earth 8

1. How do igneous rocks form?
2. Which landlocked Asian country is described as 'the world's highest rubbish dump' because of all the refuse left behind by expeditions?
3. What prevents the Earth's atmosphere from floating out into space?
4. What common mineral is formed by the fossilization of vegetation?
5. What is the difference between *weathering* and *erosion*?
6. What type of a rock is basalt?
7. What is the basic chemical composition of malachite?
8. How many carats is pure gold?
9. What is the world's smallest continent?
10. When and where was the Mount Pinatubo eruption?

Answers on page 480

SCIENCE

Planet Earth 9

1. What element gives amethyst its violet colour?
2. What name is given to the layer of the atmosphere closest to the surface of the Earth?
3. Which gas forms approximately 1% of the atmosphere?
4. Which clouds only occur above 10,000 metres?
5. Which layer of the Earth is believed to be formed of molten iron and nickel?
6. Which theory compares the Earth to a living organism?
7. Marble is formed by the metamorphosis of which rock?
8. What is the main constituent of natural gas?
9. What is the term for a fold of the Earth's crust in which the layers of rock dip inwards?
10. What name is given to the Earth's single continent, which existed 250 million years ago?

Answers on page 480

Science

Planet Earth 10

1. What is the term for nutrient enrichment of lakes?
2. Which common water pollutant is believed to be harmful to newborn babies?
3. What component of CFCs causes destruction of ozone?
4. In which part of the atmosphere is the ozone layer?
5. What is the name of the organization which controls whaling?
6. Which of the emissions from cars are acidic?
7. Which is the world's largest nature reserve?
8. What is the term for the energy obtained from hot, underground rocks?
9. How large is the area seated within the project BioSphere 2?
10. Why is lead in petrol dangerous?

Answers on page 480

SCIENCE

Planet Earth 11

1. Where might you find an aurora?
2. What name is given to the rocks swallowed by dinosaurs to assist their digestion?
3. Which of the Earth's atmospheric layers reflects radio waves?
4. What is the collective noun for rhinoceri?
5. What name is given to the rock formations used as a source of water?
6. Which radioactive substance sometimes occurs naturally in spring water?
7. Where are you likely to come across a laccolith?
8. What kind of a person might study a podzol?
9. What type of rock is formed by the rapid cooling of molten lava?
10. Which quarry in the Italian region of Tuscany is renowned for the quality of its marble?

Answers on page 480

SCIENCE

Space 1

1. How long does it take for the Earth to spin once on its axis?
2. What is the name of the force which keeps the planets in orbit around the sun?
3. Which planet is the closest to the Sun?
4. Which is the largest planet in the solar system?
5. Which is the only planet in the solar system to have life on its surface?
6. Which planet is covered by clouds of sulphuric acid?
7. What is the smallest planet in the solar system?
8. How long does it take for the Earth to go once round the Sun?
9. Which planet is named after the Roman god of war?
10. Which is the brightest comet in the solar system?

Answers on page 480

SCIENCE

Space 2

1. What would you find if you travelled to the centre of the solar system?
2. Which two planets take less time than Earth to orbit the Sun?
3. Which planet is named after the Roman goddess of love?
4. Which planet is named after the sky-god who was father of the Titans?
5. What kind of extraterrestrial object has been named after the 17th-century astronomer Edmond Halley?
6. Which planet has a day which lasts eight months?
7. Visible sunspots vary in number according to a cycle of how many years?
8. What is the term for a natural satellite?
9. Which planet is usually the furthest from the Sun, but sometimes not?
10. How many planets are there in the solar system?

Answers on page 480

SCIENCE

Space 3

1. What was the first artificial satellite?
2. Who was the first living creature in space?
3. Who was the first man in space?
4. What was the name of the American mission to land a man on the Moon?
5. Which country built the *Saturn V* rocket?
6. Who was the first man to walk on the Moon?
7. Which was the first space probe to leave the solar system?
8. What is the name of the space shuttle destroyed in midair 28 Jan 1986?
9. What was the name of the American space station?
10. How many US space shuttles are there?

Answers on page 481

SCIENCE

Space 4

1. From which areas of space can there be no escape?
2. What is the Milky Way?
3. What is the approximate temperature at the surface of the Sun?
4. What units are used for measuring distances in the universe?
5. Where is the chromosphere?
6. What is the name for the study of the structure of the universe?
7. What force bends light rays travelling through the universe?
8. Which objects in space emit energy in pulses?
9. What, ultimately, will the Sun become?
10. What is another name for a shooting or falling star?

Answers on page 481

SCIENCE

Space 5

1. Which planet takes almost 30 Earth years to orbit the Sun?
2. What travels around the Sun at an average speed of 185 miles per second?
3. Which planet has one moon called Charon?
4. What is almost halfway through its 10-billion-year life, will expand to become a red giant and then shrink to become a white dwarf?
5. What was the name of two space probes launched in 1977 which sent back remarkable pictures of Jupiter, Saturn, Uranus and Neptune?
6. Which planet orbits the Sun four times in the time it takes the Earth to go round once?
7. What are the clouds of interstellar dust, said to be the birthplace of stars?
8. What is the Latin name for the North Star?
9. What is the astronomical unit equal to 32.616 light years?
10. Which gas forms 30% of the Sun's mass?

Answers on page 481

SCIENCE

Space 6

1. Which force is nothing more than the bending of space and time?
2. Scientists study the red shift to investigate which aspect of cosmology?
3. Which star is as bright as 23 Suns, and is orbited by the Pup?
4. What is the defining feature of a neutron star?
5. What name was given to the invisible material once thought to occupy all space?
6. What name is given to the explosive death of a star?
7. What is the most distant object visible to the naked eye?
8. Which is the nearest star to the solar system?
9. Which is the second lightest element in the universe?
10. Which scientist first determined how stars make elements?

Answers on page 481

SCIENCE

Space 7

1. Which planet is the densest?
2. How many moons has Neptune?
3. Which is the second largest planet in the solar system?
4. Which planet possesses the Galilean satellites?
5. Which planet is covered with frozen methane?
6. Which planet has an atmosphere composed mainly of oxygen and nitrogen in a ratio of 1 to 4?
7. Which is the largest moon in the solar system?
8. Where would you find the Caloris Basin?
9. What is the name of the largest moon of Uranus?
10. Where would you find the Aphrodite Terra?

Answers on page 481

SCIENCE

Space 8

1. What is brighter than a hundred million suns?
2. What exists within ten dimensions?
3. Which planet has been the focus of investigations for signs of life?
4. What is the name given to the superdense stars that sometimes result from a supernova?
5. What is a red giant?
6. What name is given to the thousands of small bodies which orbit the Sun?
7. What is the largest asteroid, orbiting the Sun every 46 years?
8. Which galaxy is closest to the Milky Way?
9. In which constellation can Betelgeuse be found?
10. Where is the Palomar telescope?

Answers on page 481

SCIENCE

Space 9

1. The red shift is an example of what effect?
2. What is a pulsar?
3. Which constellation is named after the mother of Andromeda?
4. Where, theoretically, might one find objects squeezed to an infinite density?
5. Who developed the 'aperture synthesis' method of radioastronomy?
6. When did the Big Bang take place?
7. What is the Hertsprung–Russell diagram?
8. What is the name given to the study of the origins of the cosmos?
9. What is the name of the theory that the universe appears the same wherever and whenever viewed?
10. In the general theory of relativity what causes space-time to be modified?

Answers on page 482

SCIENCE

Space 10

1. Which planet was located only in 1930?
2. Which planet has the lowest density?
3. Which planet has the Great Red Spot?
4. Which planet, apart from the Earth, was the first to be orbited by a human-made object?
5. How far does the Sun's gravitational influence extend?
6. Which planet has a Great Dark Spot?
7. Which space probes failed to find life on Mars?
8. How strong is the Moon's gravity, compared with the Earth's?
9. Which is the largest moon of Saturn?
10. Which planet has the largest number of moons?

Answers on page 482

SCIENCE

Space 11

1. Who was the first Cambridge professor of radioastronomy?
2. Who is the current Astronomer Royal in Britain?
3. What can contract to give birth to a star?
4. What is a parsec?
5. Whose theories for ever banished the ether from science?
6. Superstrings exist in a universe of how many dimensions?
7. Which type of celestial object emits bursts of energy at regular intervals?
8. Which theory suggested that the universe had no beginning?
9. What shape is the Milky Way?
10. The energy of the Sun is produced by which kind of reaction?

Answers on page 482

Science

Space 12

1. Saturn's ring has how many sections?
2. Which planet is composed of an inner core, a mantle, and an outer crust?
3. When was the first *Pioneer* space probe?
4. Which was the first crewed *Apollo* spacecraft to orbit the Earth?
5. Proteus and Nereid are moons of which planet?
6. Europa is a moon of which planet?
7. Which gas gives Neptune its blue colour?
8. Who discovered Uranus?
9. Jupiter is largely composed of hydrogen and which other gas?
10. Which was the last *Apollo* mission?

Answers on page 482

SCIENCE

Technology and Transport 1

1. Which company bought Alfa Romeo in 1985?
2. Which canal was built to link Manchester and the Potteries?
3. Which saint's emblem is a wheel?
4. Which early civilization developed the potter's wheel?
5. At what speed do TGV trains travel a) 275 kph/170 mph b) 300 kph/185 mph c) 325 kph/200 mph?
6. What nationality was the racing driver Ayrton Senna?
7. Which maker in 1972 introduced safety tyres, which seal themselves after a puncture?
8. How many wheels had a hansom cab?
9. In which country is the purpose-built Monza motor-racing circuit?
10. Which famous car with front-wheel drive, transverse engine, and independent rubber suspension was introduced in 1959?

Answers on page 482

Science

Technology and Transport 2

1. What part of a car's engine conveys electricity to the spark plugs?
2. Which development in information technology uses light waves to transfer information?
3. Which electrical device is used to increase or decrease voltage?
4. What name is given to the heavy spinning plate used in some engines to smooth the power output?
5. What term describes the adaptation of advanced technology for undeveloped countries?
6. What does FM stand for?
7. In a sound system, which device is used to increase the strength of the signal from the CD player?
8. Which device in a motor car controls the transmission of power from the gear box to the wheels?
9. What name is given to the study of airflow over moving objects?
10. In computing, what do the letters RAM stand for?

Answers on page 482

SCIENCE

Technology and Transport 3

1. What technology is used by aeroplanes for locating other objects in the sky?
2. What name is given to the device used to produce an intense and narrow beam of light?
3. What device produces the air/petrol mix used in internal combustion engines?
4. What name is given to the type of engine where a stream of hot gases provides propulsion?
5. What name is given to the displays commonly seen in notebook computers and pocket calculators?
6. What is 'maglev' an abbreviation for?
7. What technology is used by submarines for detecting other objects under water?
8. What did the transistor replace?
9. What was the principle power source during the British Industrial Revolution?
10. What is the name given to the methods used to make an aircraft hard to detect?

Answers on page 483

SCIENCE

Technology and Transport 4

1 When did Marconi transmit the first radio signals across the Atlantic?

2 What was the name of the ship in which Captain Scott and his expedition sailed to the Antarctic in 1900?

3 What form of transport was initially a form of hobby-horse?

4 What was the name of the three-stage rocket used in the Apollo series of moonshots?

5 Which two British engineers got together in 1905 to design and produce cars?

6 What term denotes the communications and weather satellites that appear to stay above one point on the Earth?

7 Which American aviator was the first woman to fly the Atlantic solo in 1932?

8 Which computer language is an acronym of the name of the world's first computer programmer?

9 What is the name of the industrial city on Honshu Island, Japan, and also that of a motorcycle manufactured there?

10 What do Americans call the jet fuel paraffin?

Answers on page 483

SCIENCE

Technology and Transport 5

1. Which Rolls-Royce car was produced between 1906 and 1925?
2. Which vertical take-off jet made its first flight in 1966?
3. In which field was Sir Mortimer Wheeler famous?
4. Which two activities beside cycling are involved in the triathlon?
5. Who produced the world's first petrol-driven motor vehicle?
6. Where did William Morris begin manufacturing cars in 1910?
7. What does TT mean in the Isle of Man's TT motor cycle races?
8. Which was France's first mass-producer of cars?
9. What was the former name of the Tour of Britain cycle race?
10. What material is used to make the microphone of a telephone?

Answers on page 483

SCIENCE

Technology and Transport 6

1. What kind of material is treated by 'tempering'?
2. The introduction of the pendulum greatly improved the accuracy of which kind of device?
3. Which device bends as the temperature changes?
4. The technique of dialysis is used in which type of medical technology?
5. A transgenic animal is liable to result from which type of technology?
6. What kind of effect is used by a solenoid switch?
7. Warp and weft are found in which kind of a machine?
8. What does the abbreviation AM mean?
9. What is a cyclotron?
10. In a front-engined motor car what is the name of the device which connects the drive shaft to the rear axle?

Answers on page 483

SCIENCE

Technology and Transport 7

1. The bobbing device invented by Stephen Salter to harness wave power was named after which bird?
2. What was the occupation of Robert Stirling, inventor of the Stirling Engine?
3. Where in aeroplanes are the ailerons positioned?
4. When was the first transatlantic telephone cable laid?
5. Spinnerets are used in the manufacture of which type of material?
6. What name is given to the technique of moulding metal?
7. In the baking industry fermentation is used to produce which gas?
8. Which technology is commonly used for checking the growth of the fetus?
9. The external-combustion engine is best seen in which type of engine?
10. Which part of the motorcar engine provides the high-tension current necessary for sparking?

Answers on page 483

SCIENCE

Technology and Transport 8

1 In which country did the first organized motor race occur?

2 How many Ford Model T cars were produced between 1908 and 1927 – 7 million, 11 million or 15 million?

3 What is the device that allows a car's driving wheels to turn at different speeds when cornering?

4 How did car manufacturer Charles Stewart Rolls die?

5 Who designed the Volkswagen Beetle?

6 Which company created history with the first front-wheel drive in 1934?

7 Which company took over Bugatti following Ettore Bugatti's death in 1947?

8 Which company won the Le Mans 24-hour race five times from 1951 to 1958?

9 What kind of mechanical aid is now frequently used in assembly lines?

10 Which company withdrew from motor sport for more than 30 years after a crash involving one of its cars killed 80 spectators at Le Mans?

Answers on page 483

Science

Discovery and Invention

1. Who invented the spinning jenny?
2. Who invented the cyclotron?
3. What was the surname of the German engineer who patented the diesel engine?
4. Richard Leakey made his discoveries in which area of science?
5. Which French philosopher is known for his principle in hydraulics, and his triangle in mathematics?
6. Which Frenchman's single-image photographic process was superseded by Talbot's negative/positive system?
7. Who coined the word 'cell' in biology?
8. Who discovered that the blood circulates around the body?
9. Which 18th century English priest/scientist discovered that plants absorb air?
10. Who invented the electric light bulb?

Answers on page 484

Science

Computers

1. Who devised the first general-purpose calculating machine?
2. What is the basic unit of memory?
3. Which type of memory is 'volatile'?
4. Who invented a test designed to reveal the moment when a machine becomes as intelligent as a human?
5. Which computer manufacturing company is descended from the Tabulating Machine Company?
6. Which medical condition sometimes occurs among the keyboarding community?
7. Text displayed graphically is described by which acronym?
8. Who invented the term 'cyberspace'?
9. An interpreter translates a program into which kind of language?
10. When was Windows 3 released?

Answers on page 484

QUIZLINK

Introduction

The *Hutchinson Quizlink* is a different type of quiz where you not only have to answer the questions, you also have to work out what links the answers together.

Each set of questions constitutes one round, and the answers to each round contain a link of some kind. This link, the quizlink, could be a word or words, or the names of people. It may be something very straightforward and immediately obvious, or something a little more devious.

A typical round would be:

1 Which singer had a number 1 hit in 1974 with a song called 'Gonna Make You A Star'?
2 What was the alias used by Superman while working as a reporter for the *Daily Planet* newspaper?
3 Which English actress played the part of Fleur in the television production of John Galsworthy's *The Forsythe Saga*?
4 Which bowler took nine wickets in an innings for the England cricket team in a test match against South Africa in 1994?
5 Which British author wrote the novel *Of Human Bondage*?

The answers are as follows:
1 David ESSEX
2 Clark KENT
3 Susan HAMPSHIRE
4 DEVON Malcolm
5 SOMERSET Maugham

Quizlink = Names of English COUNTIES

As you see, the link between the answers is that they all contain the name of an English county. Easy, isn't it? This example may be, but be warned! They are not all such giveaways.

How to play

Quizlink has been specially devised for team play – but can be used in any way you like. You will need somebody to act as quizmaster. It is possible to do this yourself if there are only two people playing, but it will be very difficult to avoid seeing the answers to future questions when looking for the answer you want.

Each game consists of six complete rounds. Teams should consist of an equal number of players on each side. The team that goes first will select a number corresponding to one of the question numbers in Round 1. The quizmaster will read the question and the team answering (Team A) will be given 30 seconds to answer.

If they answer correctly they are awarded two points and are given an opportunity to identify the quizlink (what it is that links the answers together). Should they successfully identify the link they are awarded a further three points.

A team shall be deemed to have correctly identified the link if their answer contains the keyword given in the quizlink. The keyword is the word or words given in capital letters after the = sign. In the example given earlier (Quizlink = Names of English COUNTIES) the keyword is COUNTIES.

Should Team A be unable to answer the original question however, it should be passed to their opponents (Team B) who will be given a further 15 seconds to provide a correct answer for a one-point bonus. A correct answer will entitle them to try to identify the quizlink. Again, three points are awarded for a successful identification.

If both teams are unable to answer the original question correctly, the quizmaster should NOT divulge the answer, as these questions will be returned to after the link has been identified. If, after the link has been identified, a question has been asked to both teams a second time and they are still unable to answer, the quizmaster can then reveal the answer.

Team B should then select a number corresponding to one of the unanswered questions from Round 1, and the same procedure as for the previous question is followed. In all cases an attempt at identifying the quizlink will only be awarded after a team has given a correct answer to a question.

The same pattern is followed for the remaining questions in Round 1. If and when the link is identified, the remaining questions should still be asked to the teams in turn, and the scoring system of two points or one bonus point maintained. This is to ensure that each team receives the same number of questions. It also makes the questions a little easier to answer, as you already know the link.

If both teams are unable to identify the link after all questions have been asked, the quizmaster should reveal the link to both teams.

The team with most points after Round 6 is of course the winner.

The section contains 20 complete games of six rounds each.

QUIZLINK

Game 1

Round 1
1 Which mountain was believed by the ancient Greeks to be the source of poetic inspiration and home of the Muses?
2 Which character did Nerys Hughes play in the television comedy show *The Liver Birds*?
3 What was the name of the intellectual circle of writers and artists that flourished in London in the 1920s?
4 Which British prime minister assumed the title Earl of Stockton?
5 Which villain did Danny de Vito play in the 1992 film *Batman Returns*?

Round 2
1 Who was Peter Bowles' co-star in the television series *Perfect Scoundrels*?
2 What was the name of the Venetian traveller who visited Kublai Khan in the 13th century?
3 In an industrial context, for what are the initials ICI an abbreviation?
4 What type of weapon was the Zulu assegai?
5 Angie Dickinson starred in the title role in the television drama *Police Woman*. What was the name of the character she portrayed?

Round 3
1 What name is given to a garden shack which is generally used as a store for tools and seedlings?
2 The list of the 92 naturally occurring chemical elements arranged according to their atomic numbers is known as what ?
3 What was dismantled and reassembled in Arizona in the USA during the 1960s?
4 Who was the original lead vocalist with rock band Led Zeppelin ?
5 What was the title of Ronald Reagan's 1991 autobiography?

Answers on page 485

QUIZLINK

Game 1

Round 4
1. Who became the 41st president of the USA?
2. Which well-known fictional detective was created by the novelist Dashiell Hammett?
3. Where, according to tradition, was Sir Francis Drake playing bowls when he was warned of the impending invasion of the Spanish Armada?
4. What name is given to the process by which the world's atmosphere is becoming continually warmer?
5. Who was the Wolverhampton Wanderers footballer who made 49 appearances for England between the years of 1955 and 1966?

Round 5
1. What was the nickname given to King Edward I of England?
2. What is the name of Deirdre's daughter in the TV soap *Coronation Street*?
3. Which English general was killed on the Plains of Abraham in 1759?
4. Which world boxing champion forced Muhammad Ali to retire after the tenth round of their fight in 1980?
5. In the US television show *Dynasty*, who was the first husband of Alexis Colby?

Round 6
1. Who played the part of Chief Inspector Barlow in the television show *Softly, Softly*?
2. There are two varieties of artichoke. One of them is called the Jerusalem artichoke; what is the name of the other?
3. Which English humorist is remembered for his *Book of Nonsense* which popularized the limerick?
4. What was the name of the bank manager's secretary in the television comedy show *The Beverly Hillbillies*?
5. What was the title of the second Top 10 hit for the group Dire Straits; the song reaching number 8 in the charts in 1981?

Answers on page 485

QUIZLINK

Game 2

Round 1
1 Which Elizabethan hero was executed in 1618?
2 Who played the role of Samantha Stevens in the television comedy show *Bewitched*?
3 Who was nicknamed 'the Iron Chancellor'?
4 Which fantastic bird is said to have risen from its own ashes?
5 What was the name of the character played by Walter Matthau in the film *The Odd Couple*?

Round 2
1 Who was the lead singer with the pop group Slade?
2 What was the nickname of jazz musician Charles Christopher Parker?
3 In which county is the port of Southampton?
4 What name is given to the areas in both New York and London that are frequented by musicians?
5 Which character was created by Len Deighton and played in a series of films by Michael Caine?

Round 3
1 Who were the supporters of Charles I during the English Civil War?
2 What do astronomers call an exploding star?
3 What is the name of the satellite used by Sky Television?
4 In which film does Marlon Brando become president of Mexico?
5 Who is credited with the invention of the parking meter; the first ones being used in Oklahoma in 1935?

Answers on page 486

QUIZLINK

Game 2

Round 4
1. What is the correct name of the building which is usually referred to as the Houses of Parliament?
2. Which football club defeated Leeds United in a replay to win the 1970 FA Cup?
3. Who wrote the book *Call of the Wild*?
4. What is the traditional venue for the promenade concerts?
5. Which famous battle was fought in the year 1815?

Round 5
1. Who succeeded Neil Kinnock as leader of the Labour Party?
2. What was the popular name of the Locomotives and Highways Act passed by parliament in 1865?
3. Which famous scientist formulated the theory of relativity?
4. Which historical conflict occurred on 21 Oct 1805?
5. Which football team were beaten in the FA Cup final three times during the 1960s?

Round 6
1. What name is given to a mound of rough stones set up as a monument or landmark?
2. Who was the founder of the Quaker religion?
3. Which stretch of water lies between Liverpool and the Isle of Man?
4. What is the name of the foodstuff made from a batter of milk, eggs, and flour that is traditionally served with roast beef?
5. On which island off the British coast is Portree the major town?

Answers on page 486

QUIZLINK

Game 3

Round 1
1. What was the name of the cartoonist who was well known for his drawings of complex machinery designed to perform everyday tasks?
2. Who was the brother of singer Peter Sarstedt who had a number 1 hit in the British charts with a song called 'Well I Ask You'?
3. According to David Bowie's 'Space Oddity', who were ground control attempting to contact?
4. Which Arsenal and Scotland goalkeeper became a television presenter?
5. In the book *The Adventures of Tom Sawyer* by Mark Twain, what was the name of Tom's sweetheart?

Round 2
1. Which television programme with a sporting connection is presented by David Baddiel and Frank Skinner?
2. Who is the longest-reigning occupant of the British throne?
3. For which book was Kingsley Amis awarded the 1986 Booker Prize?
4. Of what is the majority of the Great Barrier Reef composed?
5. In which book by Charles Dickens does the character Scrooge appear?

Round 3
1. What is the name of the cartoon cat created by Jim Davis?
2. Who wrote *The Shining* and *Misery*?
3. Who plays the part of Curly Watts in *Coronation Street*?
4. Which horse race completes the so-called Spring Double along with the Grand National?
5. Which Irish dramatist wrote the play *Waiting For Godot*?

Answers on page 487

QUIZLINK

Game 3

Round 4
1. Which US general planned Operation Desert Storm in 1991?
2. Who played the title role in the 1971 film *Klute*?
3. What is the capital city of the Dominican Republic?
4. Which Scottish physician discovered that citrus fruits could cure and prevent scurvy?
5. Which female singer with the group Bucks Fizz later became a television presenter?

Round 5
1. What was the name of Han Solo's spaceship in the film *Star Wars*?
2. In which television quiz show hosted by Paul Daniels did three couples compete in an attempt to win more time than the others?
3. What was the title of the first winning song sung by Irishman Johnny Logan in the Eurovision Song Contest?
4. What was the title of Lena Martell's 1979 number 1 hit?
5. Which television show first broadcast in 1963 became known as *TW3*?

Round 6
1. In which well-known film do a group of children mistake an escaped convict for Jesus?
2. Which English bowler took seven West Indies wickets in the second innings of his test match debut in June 1995?
3. Which member of the English peerage is known for his advocacy of prison reform?
4. Which well-known fictional doctor was created by Max Brand and played in a series of films by Lew Ayres before moving to television in the 1960s?
5. Which US actor appeared in all the following films: *Jesse James*, *The Sun Also Rises*, and *The Black Swan*?

Answers on page 487

QUIZLINK

Game 4

Round 1

1. In the original television adaptation of the book *Rich Man, Poor Man*, Nick Nolte played the part of the poor man. Who played the rich man?
2. What was the name of the character in *Are You Being Served?* played by Wendy Richards?
3. In which television comedy series did Liza Goddard play the part of a piano teacher?
4. Who played Daisy Duke in *The Dukes of Hazzard*?
5. Who wrote the world famous book *The Compleat Angler*?

Round 2

1. Which two countries united in 1964 to form the country of Tanzania?
2. Which children's TV cartoon show was about a janitor with a double life as an accident-prone, kung-fu practising, super detective?
3. In which city could you sunbathe on Copacabana beach?
4. Which British colony was founded by Sir Stamford Raffles?
5. What was the title of Sir Thomas More's book about a perfect society?

Round 3

1. Which television quiz game hosted by Michael Barrymore involves the use of a number of televisions?
2. Where, according to the Beatles, did somebody keep his fire engine clean with a clean machine?
3. Which actress played Rebecca in the US comedy show *Cheers*?
4. Which small metallic fastener was invented by the US inventor Walter Hunt?
5. Which accessory carried by a motorist could you also have around your midriff?

Answers on page 488

QUIZLINK

Game 4

Round 4
1 In which well-known film does the character played by Paul Newman eat 50 eggs?
2 Which female group had a 1981 hit with the song 'Slow Hand'?
3 What name is given to an annual statement of accounts produced by a business?
4 What is the name of the Chinese snack consisting of a pancake filled with vegetables, rolled up, and then fried?
5 Which Alfred Hitchcock film starred Ray Milland and Grace Kelly?

Round 5
1 What was the full name of the musician who was nicknamed 'Jellyroll'?
2 By what name did the ancient Romans know Britain?
3 In which film did Alec Guinness play eight roles?
4 Who was the mistress of Horatio Nelson?
5 Which gangster was portrayed on film by Warren Beatty in 1967?

Round 6
1 To which organization have David Nixon, Tommy Cooper, and Paul Daniels all belonged?
2 *As Seen On TV* starred whom?
3 What do the initials DC stand for in Washington DC?
4 One of the most important events in crown green bowling is named after the Blackpool hotel where it is staged. What is it called?
5 Which anniversary did Queen Victoria celebrate in 1897?

Answers on page 488

Quizlink

Game 5

Round 1

1. In which musical work does the character Lieutenant Pinkerton appear?
2. Aboard which vessel did Sir Francis Chichester complete a circumnavigation of the globe in 1967?
3. Which is the world's smallest species of bird?
4. What was the name of the group of gangsters who drove one of the cars in the television cartoon show *Wacky Races*?
5. In which film of 1987 did Harrison Ford play an inventor?

Round 2

1. What name is given to the hydrated form of calcium sulphate that sets hard when it is mixed with water?
2. Which Dutch football team were European champions in three consecutive years of the early 1970s?
3. What is the name of the strong fibrous cord that connects the calf muscle to the heel?
4. Who was the female star of the television show *The Duchess of Malfi*?
5. Who composed the *Symphonie Fantastique*?

Round 3

1. In which novel does the gang leader Colleoni appear?
2. What is the nickname of Coventry City football club?
3. Which singer had a number 1 hit in 1976 with 'Don't Give Up On Us'?
4. In which Charles Dickens novel does Inspector Bucket appear?
5. Which film is generally accepted to be the first 'talkie'?

Answers on page 489

QUIZLINK

Game 5

Round 4
1. What is the name of the world's largest monolith?
2. What was the name of the television show in which Tom Baker read and reviewed books for children?
3. What is the common name for the astronomical phenomenon commonly known as the *aurora borealis*?
4. Which group first entered the charts with a song called 'I Get Around'?
5. What was the full name of Alan B'stard's personal assistant in the television comedy show *The New Statesman*?

Round 5
1. In which 1957 film did Frank Sinatra play the part of a night-club entertainer working in San Francisco?
2. What is undoubtedly the most famous novel written by Muriel Spark?
3. Which phrase, originating from the name of a Cambridge horse dealer, means in essence that you get what you are given?
4. Who played the part of the Joker in the *Batman* television series of the 1960s?
5. Which cartoon director created the character of Droopy?

Round 6
1. Who did British boxer Nigel Benn defeat in one round in the first defence of his world middleweight title?
2. What was the title of the only number 1 hit for the group T'Pau?
3. Which British show jumper rode a horse called Mandingo?
4. What was the pen name of writer Jacques Thibault?
5. Who in 1953 founded the organization known as the Samaritans?

Answers on page 489

QUIZLINK

Game 6

Round 1
1. What was the name of the Scottish heroine remembered for her part in the escape of Bonnie Prince Charlie in 1746?
2. Who was the first person ever to appear on a postage stamp?
3. What was the stage name of the British music hall entertainer Matilda Alice Powles who specialized in male impersonation?
4. What is the name of the damaged sculpture of Aphrodite discovered on the island of Melos in 1820?
5. What was the title of the controversial book about a member of the British royal family published by Andrew Morton in June 1992?

Round 2
1. In which novel by Oliver Goldsmith does the character of Doctor Primrose appear?
2. Which group had a Top 10 hit in 1988 with a song called 'Real Gone Kid'?
3. Whose record of most goals in an English season has stood for over 60 years?
4. Which British rock band was involved in a US court case over subliminal lyrics in the late 1980s?
5. Which British poet and satirist wrote the well-known phrase 'Fools rush in where angels fear to tread'?

Round 3
1. Which song did Frank Ifield take to number 22 in the 1963 charts?
2. In which film was Richard Harris captured by Indians?
3. Which method of mail transportation was operated in the USA in 1860–61?
4. Who is credited with the invention of the revolver?
5. Which television show featured Globelink News?

Answers on page 490

QUIZLINK

Game 6

Round 4
1. By what name is the singer Stanley Burrell better known?
2. Which was the first of the Harry Palmer film trilogy?
3. What is the name of the cocktail consisting of vodka and orange juice?
4. Which one word can be all of the following: a small West African monkey; a type of heavy cotton cloth; and a marine mollusc closely related to the whelk?
5. Who was the partner of Chaka Demus on hit songs of the 1990s?

Round 5
1. In which card game are all the cards under seven not used?
2. What was the name of the man known as the 'Old Pretender'?
3. What was the name of the soothsayer in Frankie Howerd's television comedy show *Up Pompeii*?
4. In which film did Sean Connery play a Russian submarine captain?
5. Who was the British lead singer with the pop group the Monkees?

Round 6
1. What is the slang word for a trifling amount of money?
2. Which former member of the duo Soft Cell recorded a hit record with Gene Pitney?
3. Which is the only South American country whose official national language is Portuguese?
4. What name is given to a male swan?
5. Which female singer recorded 'Eighth Day' and 'Will You'?

Answers on page 490

QUIZLINK

Game 7

Round 1
1. British actor Anthony Hopkins won an Oscar in 1991 for his portrayal of which character?
2. What alternative name is given to the Sepoy rebellion of 1857–58?
3. In which film is the central character called Charlie Allnut?
4. What was the title of the 1982 number 1 hit for Paul McCartney and Stevie Wonder?
5. Which *Emmerdale Farm* character died after he accidentally shot himself with his own shotgun?

Round 2
1. In which television show did David Hasselhof drive a car called KITT?
2. Which building replaced St James's Palace in 1837?
3. Who is well known for saying 'Hello, good evening and welcome'?
4. What was the name of singing cowboy Gene Autrey's horse?
5. Who on television shared a prison cell with Lennie Godber?

Round 3
1. Which queen of England reigned for only nine days?
2. Who played the title role in the television series *Sharpe*?
3. In which country were the first ever Commonwealth Games held?
4. Which actor plays the robot in *Star Trek The Next Generation*?
5. In which Ealing comedy film of 1957 did Alec Guinness play the part of a seasick sailor who takes charge of a Victorian pier?

Answers on page 491

QUIZLINK

Game 7

Round 4
1. Where did Tolkien set his *Lord of the Rings* trilogy?
2. In which 1971 film did Dustin Hoffman play a character living in Cornwall?
3. Almost 500 British soldiers died in one action on 25 Oct 1854. How is this incident known today?
4. Who served as general secretary of the TUC from 1970–74?
5. What was the title of the second number 1 hit for the Hollies?

Round 5
1. What is the SI unit of illumination?
2. Jan and Dean had a 1963 hit in the British charts with a song whose title was concerned with a particular water sport. What was the title of the song?
3. Who was the flighty spirit in the Shakespeare play *The Tempest*?
4. What name is given to the electric decorations used on Christmas trees?
5. In the printing trade, which word is used to describe text which is thicker than usual in order to give it prominence?

Round 6
1. Who was the female star of the film *The Woman in Red*?
2. Which politician during the 1960s and 1970s served at various times as chancellor of the Exchequer, home secretary, foreign secretary, and prime minister?
3. What is the better-known title of the man who is also Duke of Cornwall?
4. Which television show of the 1980s was written by, directed by, and also starred the actor Michael Landon?
5. What name is given to an arrangement of ropes and pulleys used for hoisting or hauling?

Answers on page 491

QUIZLINK

Game 8

Round 1
1. Which French queen was the daughter of a famous Florentine ruler and patron of the arts?
2. What was the name of the character played by Rodney Bewes in the television comedy show *The Likely Lads*?
3. Which novel is set in the magic land of St Brandan's Isle?
4. In which film do John Wayne and Kirk Douglas plan to ambush a mining contractor's gold shipment?
5. Which football team lost their league status in 1972?

Round 2
1. With which historical event was *The Iliad* concerned?
2. What was the well-known invention of Frank Whittle?
3. Which character did Ronald Allen play in the now defunct television soap, *Crossroads*?
4. Which ship was sunk after an explosion in Auckland harbour, New Zealand, in July 1985?
5. What is the better-known name of the plant belladonna?

Round 3
1. Who said that the report of his death was an exaggeration?
2. What did Shylock want to satisfy the debt owed to him in Shakespeare's play, *The Merchant of Venice*?
3. What name is given to the punctuation mark that consists of two dots, one above the other?
4. Who was the Italian film director best known for his work on the so-called spaghetti westerns?
5. Which British woman won an Olympic long jump gold medal in 1964?

Answers on page 492

Quizlink

Game 8

Round 4
1. What name is given to the Chinese method of cooking where small pieces of food are mixed together and cooked rapidly in hot oil?
2. On television, what is the name of Aidensfield's police constable?
3. What is the name of the traditional Scottish breakfast dish of boiled oatmeal?
4. What was the title of the first British hit song for Suzi Quatro?
5. What is a ewer?

Round 5
1. Chuck Connors played the title role in the television western show *The Rifleman*. What was the name of his character?
2. Who composed *A German Requiem* in 1868?
3. What is the name of a house or flat owned by a sovereign and granted free of rent to a person to whom the sovereign wishes to express gratitude?
4. Who created the slobbish cultural attaché Les Patterson?
5. Who is remembered for his transposition of the initial letters of words, resulting in such phrases as 'A scoop of boy trouts'?

Round 6
1. Which actor played one of the seven in *The Magnificent Seven* and also appeared in the film *Von Ryan's Express*?
2. Which device for lifting water was invented by, and named after, an ancient Greek mathematician?
3. Who has played television characters called Oz and Spender?
4. Which single word is used to describe equipment used in horse riding?
5. Which indoor game is governed in the USA by the ABC?

Answers on page 492

Quizlink

Game 9

Round 1
1. What is the name of the 250 metre high hill situated close to Holyrood House and overlooking the city of Edinburgh?
2. Who composed the overture *Fingal's Cave*?
3. What is the last letter of the Greek alphabet?
4. What name is given to the long spikes of flowers found hanging on trees such as the hazel or willow?
5. According to the Old Testament, which royal female visited King Solomon?

Round 2
1. Who was the Roman equivalent of Eros?
2. Who replaced Barbara Bel Geddes in the TV show *Dallas*?
3. What is visible to people on Earth once every 76 years?
4. Which US all-girl group had their first British chart success in 1987 with a song called 'Edge of a Broken Heart'?
5. As what did Anna Pavlova become famous?

Round 3
1. Which group had a hit with the song 'To Know Him Is To Love Him'?
2. What was the title of the first in the series of *Indiana Jones* films?
3. Which group had a hit with the song 'Lyin' Eyes'?
4. Which people invaded England in the year AD 792?
5. What were the names of the rival gangs in the musical film *West Side Story*?

Answers on page 493

Quizlink

Game 9

Round 4
1. Who said 'This is not the end, it is not even the beginning of the end'?
2. Who was the lead singer with the 1980s pop group Altered Images?
3. What is the name of the authority that controls lighthouses and buoys around the coast of England and Wales?
4. What are the names of the two different breeds of corgi dog?
5. Which television comedy character played by Bill Maynard frequently said 'Magic our Maurice'?

Round 5
1. The biblical brothers James and John were known as the 'sons of thunder'. Who was their father?
2. Which well-known author wrote *Under Milk Wood*?
3. Who carried a pet owl around in her pocket during the Crimean War?
4. In which irreverent comedy film was the title role played by Graham Chapman?
5. Which former television news reader went on to present a Channel 4 programme for senior citizens?

Round 6
1. Which famous Englishman said shortly before his death, 'I thank God that I have done my duty'?
2. Who played the part of Huggy Bear in the television show *Starsky And Hutch*?
3. Which explorer was killed by natives in the Philippines in 1521?
4. In which television show is there a character called Eddie Hitler?
5. Who was the 1960 Olympic light heavyweight boxing champion?

Answers on page 493

QUIZLINK

Game 10

Round 1
1. Which actress plays the character Dorian Green on television?
2. Which station do you pass first at the start of a game of Monopoly?
3. Which US woman was killed in a notorious car crash at Chappaquiddick in 1969?
4. What does the road sign showing a cow inside a red circle signify?
5. Who starred opposite Bruce Willis in the television show *Moonlighting*?

Round 2
1. What is the adopted name of the singer Roberta Joan Anderson?
2. Who played the detective Frank Cannon on television?
3. Who had companions called Wilson, Bowers, Evans, and Oates?
4. Who wrote the novel *Rich Man, Poor Man*?
5. What was the middle name of the famous general who died with his troops at the Battle of Little Bighorn in 1876?

Round 3
1. Who played the part of the wife in the television show *Macmillan And Wife*?
2. Where could you see the burial place known as Poets' Corner?
3. In which historical film of 1968 did Katharine Hepburn and Peter O'Toole play a married couple?
4. Who rode 100/1 outsider Foinavon to victory in the 1967 Grand National?
5. What is the traditional gift for a 15th wedding anniversary?

Answers on page 494

QUIZLINK

Game 10

Round 4
1. Which horse won the King George VI Chase three times in the 1980s?
2. What is the name of the snooty character played by Patricia Routledge in the television comedy show *Keeping Up Appearances*?
3. What name is given to the system of connecting computer devices in a series, so that the first device is connected to the second, the second to the third, and so on?
4. Which Canadian group had a hit with a song called 'Which Way You Going Billy' in 1970?
5. Which female character in literature often threatened to 'scream and scream and scream'?

Round 5
1. Which British heavyweight boxer was knocked out in world title fights by both Floyd Paterson and Muhammad Ali?
2. Which former member of the Eagles released a solo album entitled *Building the Perfect Beast*?
3. What was the name of the television character played by Ralph Waite in a series set in the US depression?
4. What is the capital city of Jamaica?
5. What was the real name of actor John Carradine who died in 1988?

Round 6
1. Which fictional character made his first appearance in the 1929 story *The Roman Hat Mystery*?
2. Which film of 1973 starring Robert Redford and Paul Newman won the Oscar for best picture?
3. In which 1989 film did Rick Moranis play an inventor who had trouble with his children?
4. What was the title of the early television comedy show in which Charlie Drake played an unemployable layabout?
5. Which word describes a pilotless, radio controlled aircraft?

Answers on page 494

QUIZLINK

Game 11

Round 1
1. Which author created the character Tarzan?
2. Who was the well-known co-writer of Richard Rogers who collaborated with him on musicals such as *South Pacific* and *The Sound of Music*?
3. Who starred with Roger Moore in the television show *The Persuaders*?
4. Who is the jazz singer wife of Johnny Dankworth?
5. Who is the champagne-guzzling friend of Edina, played by Joanna Lumley, in the television comedy series *Absolutely Fabulous*?

Round 2
1. Which Compton Mackenzie novel centres on a 1943 shipwreck?
2. What is the capital city of Trinidad and Tobago?
3. In which variation of a well-known card game does each player receive ten cards?
4. In the book *Treasure Island* which line follows 'Fifteen men on the dead man's chest'?
5. Which girl's name gave the Four Seasons a hit in 1962?

Round 3
1. Which singer's only British number 1 hit was 'Runaway'?
2. Who plays the part of Lacey in the television show *Cagney and Lacey*?
3. Which device protecting the city of London was operated for the first time in 1984?
4. Who played Uncle Mort in the television comedy show *I Didn't Know You Cared*?
5. Who played the part of Princess Leia in the first of the *Star Wars* series of films?

Answers on page 495

QUIZLINK

Game 11

Round 4
1. Which famous woman committed suicide after the Battle of Actium in 31 BC?
2. What is the old name for the chemical element now called sulphur?
3. Which Greek god was the son of Zeus and brother of Artemis?
4. For which man was Hampton Court built?
5. Which character in the television comedy series *Are You Being Served?* was played by Frank Thornton?

Round 5
1. What 'burst' in 1720, causing the financial ruin of thousands of investors?
2. In which stretch of water is the island of Lundy situated?
3. In which Spanish city can you see the Alhambra, a Moorish citadel and palace?
4. Who was the Australian cricket captain on the 1993 tour of England?
5. Which word describes any one of the imaginary lines connecting the North and South Poles and running at right angles to the equator?

Round 6
1. Which US tennis player did Bjorn Borg beat to win his fourth consecutive Wimbledon singles title?
2. Which creature gives its name to a protein found in human blood?
3. Who has always been the presenter of the teenage quiz show *Blockbusters*?
4. Which Latin term means 'an equal exchange or substitution'?
5. Which equine creature is particularly associated with the Shetland Islands?

Answers on page 495

Quizlink

Game 12

Round 1
1. Who kidnapped Helen of Troy and precipitated the Trojan War?
2. By what title was Arthur Wellesley better known?
3. Which song was the highest placed chart entry for Ultravox?
4. In the USA in 1949, Mrs I Toguri d'Aquino was sentenced to ten years in prison for treason. By what name was she known during World War II?
5. Which character did Peter Lorre play in the film *The Maltese Falcon*?

Round 2
1. On which date does St George's day fall?
2. Who wrote *Adolf Hitler, My Part In His Downfall*?
3. What was the name of the nurse lusted after by Arkwright in the television comedy show *Open All Hours*?
4. What was the title of the first British hit for Buddy Holly?
5. Which British soldier of the 18th century spent most of his life in India?

Round 3
1. Which television quiz show presented by Bob Monkhouse was based on the game of bingo?
2. In which film did Clint Eastwood play an Arizona sheriff charged with taking an escaped killer back to New York?
3. What was the title of the sequel to the television show *Porridge*?
4. What was the name of the pet dog owned by Elizabeth Barrett Browning?
5. How were Lenny Henry, Tracy Ullman, and David Copperfield known collectively in a television comedy show?

Answers on page 496

QUIZLINK

Game 12

Round 4
1. Which Australian painter is well known for his portraits of the outlaw Ned Kelly?
2. On which day of the year is the Eton wall game traditionally played?
3. In which television show did Max Baer and Donna Douglas play brother and sister?
4. What name was given to the flight of Chinese communists led by Mao Zedong in 1934?
5. When Armstrong and Aldrin walked on the Moon for the first time in 1969, who remained in the command module?

Round 5
1. What in mythology was suspended by a single horse hair?
2. Which 1924 play by Sean O'Casey tells of life in a Dublin slum?
3. Which is the largest city in the state of Nebraska?
4. What was the title of Freda Payne's number 1 hit?
5. In which state of the USA is Salt Lake City?

Round 6
1. Born in 1820, she became famous for her pioneering medical work during the Crimean War. Who was she?
2. Born in 1812, at the age of 12 he was put to work in Warren's boot blacking factory. He became one of England's most celebrated novelists. Who was he?
3. Born in 1642, he devised the three laws of motion and is credited with the discovery of gravity. Who was he?
4. Born in 1781, he built the famous *Rocket* steam locomotive. Who was he?
5. Born in 1632, he designed 51 churches, the most famous being St Paul's Cathedral in London. Who was he?

Answers on page 496

QUIZLINK

Game 13

Round 1
1. Which *Coronation Street* character was widowed when her husband was killed by armed raiders at his place of work?
2. Who wrote the series of *Lassie* books?
3. Which pair of private detectives were played on television by Derek Martin and Nigel Planer?
4. Which group made the 1976 album *A Day at the Races*?
5. Who won the first of 20 Wimbledon titles in 1966?

Round 2
1. Which Brazilian motor racing driver was formula one world champion in 1981, 1983, and 1987?
2. Which film of 1977 is concerned with the disastrous allied landings at Arnhem during World War II?
3. Which US rap duo reached number 1 in the British charts in 1990 with a song called 'The Power'?
4. What is the common name of the flower *kniphofia*?
5. Where are the headquarters of British horse racing?

Round 3
1. Which song was a number 1 hit for Enya in 1988?
2. Who was the successful British commander at the Battle of Waterloo?
3. After Jersey and Guernsey, which is the next largest of the Channel Islands?
4. Of which country is Sofia the capital city?
5. Which US national park covers part of the states of Wyoming, Idaho, and Montana and contains the famous geyser known as Old Faithful?

Answers on page 497

QUIZLINK

Game 13

Round 4
1. What was the surname of Richard and Karen, the singing duo who had several hits in the British charts during the 1970s?
2. Who lost his British heavyweight boxing title to Joe Bugner in 1971?
3. Who plays the character Betty Turpin in the TV show *Coronation Street*?
4. Who did Kenneth Clarke succeed as home secretary in 1992?
5. Who was the leader of the mutiny against Captain William Bligh aboard *HMS Bounty* in 1789?

Round 5
1. Which football team plays its home matches at the Manor Ground?
2. Which company manufactured the famous Electra Glide motorcycle?
3. Who once married a lady called Teresa Draco?
4. In which film of 1936 did Fred Astaire sing 'Let's face the music and dance'?
5. A famous US actress, she died in 1942. Her last three films were *They Knew What She Wanted*, *Mr and Mrs Smith*, and *To Be Or Not To Be*. Who was she?

Round 6
1. Who is the leader of the Monster Raving Loony Party?
2. Minnie Riperton had a number 2 hit in 1975. With which song?
3. Which well-known artist painted *The Haywain*?
4. Which book by Boris Pasternak was made into a film starring Julie Christie?
5. If you are unfortunate enough, you may be given a dose of nitrous oxide at the dentist's. What is the more common name of nitrous oxide?

Answers on page 497

QUIZLINK

Game 14

Round 1
1. Which 1983 film of a Graham Greene novel starred Michael Caine and Richard Gere?
2. What name is shared by mountain ranges in Spain and the USA?
3. Which Spanish word describes a religious festival or celebration especially on a Saint's Day?
4. Which constellation is depicted as the Hunter?
5. In which murder film of 1960 did Noel Trevarthan play an out-of-work actor?

Round 2
1. What is advertised as 'the mint with the hole'?
2. Which West End musical was written by an ex-member of ABBA?
3. Which group had a hit with 'It's Raining'?
4. Its scientific name is *Gryllus campestris*; what is it?
5. Which school did Tom Brown attend in the novel by Thomas Hughes?

Round 3
1. Which character did Linda Thorson play in the television series *The Avengers*?
2. Which Scottish football club is nicknamed 'the Accies'?
3. Who won the Oscar as best supporting actor for his role in the film *Cool Hand Luke*?
4. What was the name of the bus driver played by Reg Varney in the TV comedy show *On The Buses*?
5. Which red-haired Irish actress starred with John Wayne in the film *The Quiet Man*?

Answers on page 498

QUIZLINK

Game 14

Round 4
1. Which property on a Monopoly board is immediately to the left of Kings Cross Station?
2. Who created the comic characters Stavros and Loadsamoney?
3. What name is commonly given to the line of longitude lying at 0 degrees?
4. What is the official residence of the archbishop of Canterbury?
5. What is Cockney rhyming slang for the word 'hair'?

Round 5
1. Which US male/female duo had a British Top 10 hit in 1986 with a song called 'I Can't Wait'?
2. Who played Mariette Larkin on television?
3. Which film starring Charlton Heston is concerned with the aftermath of germ warfare?
4. Which North Sea oil rig exploded in 1988, resulting in the tragic deaths of 167 men?
5. Which word describes the flat area of alluvial deposits at the mouth of some rivers?

Round 6
1. What was the name of the maid played by Connie Booth in the television comedy series *Fawlty Towers*?
2. Who famously became lost during the Paris–Dakar rally of 1982?
3. Which line follows 'Oh, East is East and West is West'?
4. What is the slang term describing a drink containing a drug to render the drinker unconscious?
5. Who created the characters Samuel Whiskers and Mrs Tiggywinkle?

Answers on page 498

QUIZLINK

Game 15

Round 1
1. What name was given to the political uprising that took place in China in 1900?
2. Which television show featured a character called Richard de Vere?
3. What name is given to the drink consisting of a mixture of advocaat and lemonade?
4. Which well-known historical figure first described England as a nation of shopkeepers?
5. Who had a Top 10 hit with a song called 'What is Love?' in 1983?

Round 2
1. What name was given to the sacred gold-covered wooden chest identified by the Hebrews with God?
2. Who became prime minister of Great Britain on the resignation of Lord Salisbury in 1902?
3. Who died when his speedboat *Bluebird* crashed on Coniston Water in 1967?
4. Which song by Paul McCartney spent nine weeks at number 1 in the British charts during the winter of 1977–78?
5. Which US actor appeared in the television series *Maverick* as Bat Masterson, and also appeared in the films *Benji* and *A Man For Hanging*?

Round 3
1. In which film did James Cagney proclaim, 'Made it Ma, top of the world'?
2. Which British regiment is particularly associated with the county of Yorkshire?
3. Which oily blister-inducing liquid has been used as a poison during warfare?
4. Who was referred to in a children's comic as 'our Indian chum'?
5. The first English actress to win the Oscar for best actress did so in 1939. What was the name of the character she portrayed?

Answers on page 499

QUIZLINK

Game 15

Round 4
1. Which dog, according to legend, watched over his master's grave for 14 years?
2. What type of fruit is a morello?
3. Which British boxer from the city of York was unsuccessful in challenges to both Nigel Benn and Chris Eubank for their world titles?
4. What was the original name of the character played in *Coronation Street* by Eileen Derbyshire?
5. Which famous British sportsman was champion jockey on 26 occasions between 1925 and 1953?

Round 5
1. Which swimmer won seven gold medals at the 1972 Olympic Games in Munich?
2. Who won a Pulitzer Prize for his novel *The Bridge of San Luis Rey*?
3. Which character did Cameron Mitchell play in the TV western series *The High Chaparral*?
4. What was the title of Ralph McTell's 'capital' hit of 1974?
5. In which region of the Yukon was gold discovered in 1896?

Round 6
1. Which group had a number 1 hit with 'Billy Don't be a Hero'?
2. Who is the chairman of Tottenham Hotspur Football Club and founder of the Amstrad company?
3. By what nickname was actress Jean Harlow known?
4. Which country on the coast of West Africa has a capital city called Yamoussoukro?
5. What was the name of the Lone Ranger's horse?

Answers on page 499

QUIZLINK

Game 16

Round 1
1. In which musical film of 1948 do three of the characters sing the song 'Busy Doin' Nothin''?
2. Which song, written by James Connell in 1889, is considered to be the anthem of the Labour movement?
3. Which government department is responsible for the registration of trademarks and industrial designs?
4. What name is given to the type of competition in which all competitors play each other to decide the winner?
5. Which company advertised itself with the slogan '57 varieties'?

Round 2
1. Which female group had a hit in 1981 with 'Slowhand'?
2. Aboard which ship did Charles Darwin travel from 1831–36?
3. What code name was given to the allied invasion of Sicily in 1943?
4. What was the name of the idiot private in the *Bilko* TV show?
5. What was the occupation of Robert de Niro in the film *Raging Bull*?

Round 3
1. Which horse ridden by Hywel Davies won the 1984 Grand National?
2. In which 1982 film did Julie Andrews pose as a female impersonator?
3. Which football club won the FA Cup in 1961–62 and again in 1981–82?
4. In which 1937 film is Cary Grant visited by two friendly ghosts?
5. Which girl's name gave Barry Manilow a hit song in 1975?

Answers on page 500

QUIZLINK

Game 16

Round 4
1. Of what is pumpernickel a variety?
2. Which character was played by Richard Gibson in the television comedy show 'Allo 'Allo?
3. What name is given to a female swan?
4. Which actor sang the song 'Get Me to the Church on Time' in the film *My Fair Lady*?
5. Which singer had a number 1 hit with 'Space Oddity'?

Round 5
1. Which music hall entertainer was known as 'the Cheeky Chappie'?
2. Who wrote the poem 'The Charge of the Light Brigade'?
3. Which two rivers converge at New York City?
4. Who had a Top 10 hit with 'In Your Eyes' in 1983?
5. What was the real life name of super hero Spiderman?

Round 6
1. Who wrote *The Mill on the Floss*?
2. Which famous film of 1941 was concerned with a statue of a bird?
3. What name did the American Indians give to early steam locomotives in the wild west?
4. What was the name of John Cannon's wife and Manolito's sister in the television western show *The High Chaparral*?
5. What general term is used to describe the 20 republics of Central and South America where the Romance languages are spoken?

Answers on page 500

QUIZLINK

Game 17

Round 1
1. Which terrorist group was responsible for the deaths of 11 competitors at the 1972 Olympic Games in Munich?
2. Which song was a number 1 hit for Pilot?
3. Who was the lead guitarist with the group Queen?
4. Who won an Oscar for his portrayal of Dr Jekyll and Mr Hyde?
5. Who played the wife of Terry Scott on television?

Round 2
1. Who played the short guy in the film *The Tall Guy*?
2. Which day follows Shrove Tuesday?
3. Which of the *Blue Peter* pets was replaced by Kari and Oki?
4. Which was the Beatles' own record label?
5. In which suburb was the Crossroads motel situated in the now defunct television soap *Crossroads*?

Round 3
1. What is the state capital of New Mexico?
2. On which river does the Italian city of Turin stand?
3. Which song was a hit for both the Beatles and Ferry Aid?
4. What was the nickname of tennis great Maureen Connolly?
5. Which song was Dooley Wilson asked to play in the film *Casablanca*?

Answers on page 501

QUIZLINK

Game 17

Round 4
1. Which African country has a capital city called Nouackchott?
2. What symbol is on the back of a UK two pence coin?
3. Which character has been played on television by both Richard Greene and Jason Connery?
4. What was the occupation of Clint Eastwood in the film *For a Few Dollars More*?
5. In which 1981 film starring Sylvester Stallone and Michael Caine do allied prisoners of war play their German captors at football?

Round 5
1. Which general was killed at Khartoum in 1885?
2. Who painted the ceiling of the Sistine Chapel?
3. Who said that he had come to bury Caesar, not to praise him?
4. Which grandma became a well-known US painter?
5. Which Spanish hero had the real name Rodrigo Diaz de Vivar?

Round 6
1. Which planet in our solar system takes over 247 years to orbit the Sun?
2. Which blonde actress appeared in the 1985 television series *CATS Eyes*?
3. What was the name of Benny Hill's milkman?
4. Besides heat, what is always created when you mix an alkali and an acid?
5. What was the nickname of the character with the surname O'Reilly in the television show M*A*S*H*?

Answers on page 501

QUIZLINK

Game 18

Round 1
1 Which film starred Frank Sinatra as a drug addict?
2 Which TV quiz show is hosted by Nicky Campbell and Carol Smillie?
3 What was the invention of the British scientist Joseph Swan?
4 For which film did Gary Cooper win his second Oscar?
5 Which song was a number 3 hit for Status Quo in 1977?

Round 2
1 Which is the world's fastest moving land animal?
2 Which group sang 'I'm the Urban Spaceman' in 1968?
3 Which French monarch was married to Marie Antoinette?
4 On which river does the city of Glasgow stand?
5 Which British boxer was world junior lightweight champion in 1981?

Round 3
1 What was the title of the first Top 10 hit for the group Simply Red?
2 Which word, more often used in Scotland, describes a small plot of land adjoining a house which is worked by the house owner?
3 Who on television played the private investigator Jim Rockford?
4 Which duo had a 1978 Top 10 hit with the song 'Dancing in the City'?
5 Which character was played on television by Lorna Patterson and on film by Goldie Hawn?

Answers on page 502

QUIZLINK

Game 18

Round 4
1. Who was famous for his lavish musicals featuring ornate dance routines with large numbers of dancers?
2. Which man-made construction connects the Pacific and Atlantic Oceans?
3. What is the name of Britain's most poisonous type of mushroom?
4. During which 1854 battle did the famous Charge of the Light Brigade occur?
5. What name is given to a low-roofed concrete emplacement for a machine gun or antitank gun?

Round 5
1. What is the name of the journal produced especially for the medical profession?
2. Which group had the original hit with the song 'Love Don't Live Here Anymore'?
3. Which 1971 film starring Gene Hackman won the Best Picture Oscar?
4. Which stretch of water washes the coasts of Northern Spain and Western France?
5. Who was known as 'the IT girl'?

Round 6
1. Who was the Wimbledon men's singles champion in 1987?
2. Which was the last play published by Joe Orton before his death in 1967?
3. Which was the only number 1 hit for the group Lieutenant Pigeon?
4. Which Carla Lane TV show features the character Freddy Boswell?
5. Which TV show featured the character Bradley Hardacre?

Answers on page 502

QUIZLINK

Game 19

Round 1
1. Which literary character was referred to as 'the fat owl of the remove'?
2. Who in history reputedly singed the king of Spain's beard?
3. Which character in literature was bullied by Flashman?
4. What is the more common name of the star called Sirius?
5. What is the name of the rounded loaf of bread with a cross in the top?

Round 2
1. Which well-known US actor played the title role in the 1960 film *Spartacus*?
2. Who wrote *The Cherry Orchard*?
3. Which sea, part of the Western Pacific, lies between Borneo and the central Philippines?
4. Which US pianist and composer is credited with creating the style of music known as ragtime?
5. Who published *The Commonsense Book of Baby and Child Care* in 1946?

Round 3
1. Who won Britain's only athletics medal during the Montreal Olympics of 1976?
2. Which US president succeeded John F Kennedy?
3. What was the title of Bob Hoskins' animated box office hit of 1988?
4. Which Scottish physicist is credited with the invention of radar?
5. What was the name of the female character who was taught to speak properly in the film *My Fair Lady*?

Answers on page 503

QUIZLINK

Game 19

Round 4
1 Who was British prime minister from 1955–57?
2 Who was the female star of the film *Gregory's Girl*?
3 Who was Bonnie Parker's infamous partner?
4 Who was the little girl who lived in *The Old Curiosity Shop*?
5 Who played Crockett in the television show *Miami Vice*?

Round 5
1 Which Alfred Hitchcock film starred James Stewart and Kim Novak?
2 Which is the nearest planet to the Sun?
3 Which stage in the life cycle of a butterfly follows the pupa?
4 Which company advertised itself as 'simply years ahead'?
5 At which game were Short and Kasparov in opposition in 1993?

Round 6
1 Which US actress received an Academy Award nomination for her role in the 1983 film *Terms of Endearment*?
2 Which US cop was played on television by William Shatner?
3 Where, according to the title of the first of the series, did Marty McFly go?
4 Which novel by Jules Verne features the character Professor Challenger?
5 What is the name given to the function on an electronic recording device, such as a videocassette or tape player, that permits rapid advancement of the tape?

Answers on page 503

QUIZLINK

Game 20

Round 1
1. Which 'game' involves a number of people placing a single bullet in the barrel of a revolver, spinning the chamber and taking it in turns to point the gun at their head and pull the trigger?
2. In which Irish county is the town of Ennis?
3. In which television series did James Bolam star as Jack Ford?
4. Which Rider Haggard novel tells the story of an African queen who holds the secret of eternal life?
5. Which character got married in a 1786 Mozart opera?

Round 2
1. What is the name of the comedy actress who plays Blunderwoman to Russ Abbot's Cooperman?
2. Who played Douglas Bader in the film *Reach for the Sky*?
3. What was the title of Barbra Streisand's 1980 number 1 hit?
4. Who was the Manchester United player who was voted European footballer of the year in 1968?
5. Which television comedy show starred Richard O'Sullivan and Tim Brooke-Taylor?

Round 3
1. Which 1968 film won Katharine Hepburn her third Oscar?
2. Who wrote the novel *Kane and Abel*?
3. Which actress played Sybil Fawlty on TV?
4. What was the title of Madonna's second British Top 10 hit?
5. What name is given to the modern crime of driving motor vehicles through shop windows in order to steal from them?

Answers on page 504

Quizlink

Game 20

Round 4
1. Which singer had a Top 10 hit with the song 'I Remember Elvis Presley'?
2. In which film did Frank Sinatra play a US officer in charge of a group of escaped prisoners of war?
3. Whom, according to Abraham Lincoln, can you not fool all of the time?
4. What was the name given to the medieval protective clothing consisting of riveted metal links or rings?
5. In which film have Janet Gaynor, Judy Garland, and Barbra Streisand all played the lead role?

Round 5
1. Who wrote the novel *The Prisoner of Zenda*?
2. Which trophy is contested annually between the English league champions and the cup holders as a curtain raiser to the new football season?
3. Which group had the 1961 hit 'Pasadena'?
4. Who played the character Sir Lancelot Spratt in the *Doctor* series of films with Dirk Bogarde?
5. What was the title of rock star John Bon Jovi's 1993 album?

Round 6
1. Who rode Aldaniti to victory in the Grand National?
2. What was the nationality of United Nations secretary general U Thant?
3. Which organization has its HQ at Baden Powell House?
4. What did Judas Iscariot receive as payment for his betrayal of Jesus?
5. In which European city can you see the Little Mermaid?

Answers on page 504

ANSWERS

General Knowledge

General Knowledge 1

1. Balaclava helmet
2. 1666 (MDCLXVI)
3. The tomb of the Unknown Soldier
4. Rubik
5. Alphabet
6. Five years
7. Alexander
8. Desmond Tutu
9. Frisbee
10. Credit cards

General Knowledge 2

1. Neil Armstrong
2. Assisi
3. Billionaire
4. Guy Fawkes
5. Gordonstoun School
6. *The Adventures of Pinocchio*
7. Gypsies
8. Interpol
9. Coroner
10. Alibi

General Knowledge 3

1. Dick Turpin
2. Hacking
3. Military intelligence
4. Iron Curtain
5. April Fool's Day/1 April
6. Bedouins
7. Tower of London
8. Cruft
9. Charter
10. Denier

General Knowledge 4

1. Eiffel Tower
2. Bar code
3. National curriculum
4. Pompeii
5. Greece
6. Edinburgh
7. Capital punishment/hanging
8. Ejector seat
9. ECU
10. Hans Christian Andersen

General Knowledge 5

1. New York
2. *Spycatcher*
3. Hill figures
4. *Schindler's List*
5. Footpad
6. Michael Heseltine
7. Independence Day
8. Michaelangelo
9. Rupert Murdoch
10. Milky Way

General Knowledge 6

1. Flute
2. Short tennis
3. Shark
4. Brain
5. Potato
6. Aldous Huxley
7. Actors
8. The chancellor of the Exchequer
9. St Christopher
10. Black Sea

General Knowledge

General Knowledge 7

1. Gymnastics
2. Seven
3. The Pope
4. J S Bach
5. William Caxton
6. Delilah
7. Chihuahua
8. Isosceles
9. Spanish
10. Dogfish

General Knowledge 8

1. Thomas Edison
2. Bridge
3. English Civil War
4. Spaniel
5. Goat
6. Lockheed
7. Blue
8. Old Bailey
9. Excessively long nose
10. Billy Butlin

General Knowledge 9

1. Old Glory
2. Ned Kelly
3. Red
4. Zeus
5. Goat
6. The Red Baron
7. Beatrix Potter
8. Ferdinand Magellan
9. Jupiter
10. Limbo

General Knowledge 10

1. Swastika
2. Domesday Book
3. A whale
4. Midas
5. One
6. Nazareth
7. Lech Walesa
8. Warren Beatty
9. Acre
10. Bug

General Knowledge 11

1. Ninja
2. Renault
3. The Loch Ness monster
4. Rudolph Valentino
5. Marx Brothers
6. Istanbul
7. Salt
8. Windsor
9. Caspian Sea
10. Sumo wrestling

General Knowledge 12

1. Grantham
2. Thor Heyerdahl
3. Earth
4. Isaac Newton
5. Tuberculosis
6. Jodhpur
7. Because they were the seventh, eighth, ninth and tenth months of the Roman calendar
8. Esperanto
9. Bradford
10. Marquess

General Knowledge

General Knowledge 13

1. Crescent moon
2. Elsinore
3. Graffiti
4. Macao
5. Jeremy
6. Denim
7. British Standards Institute
8. Jordan
9. A jewelled egg
10. Canada

General Knowledge 14

1. Caernarvon
2. Horatio
3. Haiti
4. Napoleon Bonaparte
5. 1931
6. Rasputin
7. Chicago
8. Blenheim Palace
9. Tog
10. The press

General Knowledge 15

1. Bridges
2. Mounties
3. Cancer
4. Cartel
5. Kazakhstan
6. Colombia
7. Longleat
8. Anticoagulants
9. Pecan
10. Pope Gregory

General Knowledge 16

1. Rose Theatre
2. Mafia
3. Descartes
4. Breton
5. Hebridean
6. The Thames
7. Geneva
8. GCE 'O' levels; CSE
9. Sir Christopher Wren
10. Summit conference

General Knowledge 17

1. Romania
2. Squint
3. James II
4. Pakistan
5. Orly
6. Mars
7. Spoonerism
8. King
9. Portugal
10. Green

General Knowledge 18

1. Austrian
2. Turkey
3. Venice
4. Joseph Goebbels
5. Triathlon
6. Potomac
7. Oliver Cromwell
8. Brown
9. Ash Wednesday
10. Jack Hobbs

General Knowledge

General Knowledge 19

1. Fiction
2. Brazil
3. Thursday
4. Herring
5. Smallpox
6. Croesus
7. Apollo
8. Islam
9. Denmark and Sweden
10. Topiary

General Knowledge 20

1. Maserati
2. Force 12 or more
3. Musical instrument
4. 64
5. Sternum
6. Magnitude of earthquakes
7. Earl of Essex
8. Aeneas
9. Los Angeles
10. Crow

General Knowledge 21

1. Marie Curie – for discovering radioactivity and radium
2. William Randolph Hearst
3. Charleston
4. 'Stormin' Norman'
5. Chicago
6. Polish
7. A large flightless bird
8. Polaroid
9. Poseidon
10. Rabies

General Knowledge 22

1. Edgar Allan Poe
2. Heath Robinson
3. Four
4. Charles de Gaulle
5. Limestone
6. Italy
7. Pumice
8. St Louis
9. Gunpowder
10. St Kitts

General Knowledge 23

1. Charles II
2. Tea
3. Zurich
4. Lawyer
5. Lizard
6. Rabbi
7. Peru
8. Tofu
9. Pole Star; North Star
10. Luxor, Egypt

General Knowledge 24

1. Information technology
2. Inkatha movement
3. 25 March
4. Grimaldi
5. Westminster Abbey
6. Women
7. Tom
8. Ergonomics
9. Koh-i-noor
10. Khalistan

General Knowledge

General Knowledge 25

1. Ilium
2. Infanta
3. Klondike
4. Yakuza
5. Libra
6. A book
7. A pound coin
8. Romance languages
9. Top the appropriate letter with a short horizontal bar – e.g. $\bar{V}$ is $5 \times 1{,}000 = 5{,}000$)
10. P L Travers

General Knowledge 26

1. Australia
2. Sauna
3. Ruskin
4. Yggdrasil
5. Vivienne Westwood and Malcolm McLaren
6. Bouvier
7. Quango
8. Mir
9. Robben Island
10. Isle of Man

General Knowledge 27

1. Adelaide
2. Benelux
3. Chivalry
4. Froebel
5. Norway
6. Bolshevik and Menshevik
7. UK; USA; Russia; China; France
8. St Cecilia
9. Monaco
10. Friday

General Knowledge 28

1. Lady Godiva
2. Exxon Corporation
3. As coach dogs, protecting occupants of carriages
4. The Getty Museum, Malibu, California
5. Australia
6. A whale
7. So that he could eat without leaving the gaming table
8. Fred Quimby
9. *Calypso*
10. Their shorthand could not be deciphered

General Knowledge 29

1. Abu Dhabi
2. Manhattan Project
3. Garrison Keillor
4. He wraps them
5. Epiphany
6. Abraham Lincoln
7. Quasi-stellar object
8. Tungsten
9. Jean Martinet
10. John Masefield

General Knowledge 30

1. Asgard
2. Dublin
3. Silicon
4. Illinois
5. Ralph Vaughan Williams
6. Pluto
7. Nike
8. Charles Babbage
9. Belshazzar
10. United Kingdom

General Knowledge

General Knowledge 31
1. Spreadsheet
2. John Glenn
3. Islam
4. Kidney
5. Lambada
6. Small desert fox
7. Manet
8. Quisling
9. D
10. The Gambia

General Knowledge 32
1. HIV
2. Money
3. Walter Raleigh
4. Roland
5. A musical instrument
6. William Hurt
7. Rowing
8. Corfu
9. Christopher Fry
10. Ernst Heinkel

General Knowledge 33
1. Ballet
2. Existentialism
3. Nepal
4. Luke
5. Oberon
6. Aikido
7. Pierre Cardin
8. Hardness of minerals
9. Iceland
10. Molière

General Knowledge 34
1. Thomas Gainsborough
2. Athena
3. Milan
4. Frank and Betty Spencer
5. Corinthian
6. Cathedral
7. Vita Sackville-West
8. A bird
9. Amsterdam
10. Richard Trevithick

Mixed Bag

True or False? 1

1. False
2. True
3. True
4. False
5. True
6. True
7. False
8. True
9. True
10. False – he sealed it because he couldn't write

True or False? 2

1. False
2. True
3. False
4. True
5. False
6. True
7. False
8. False
9. True
10. True

True or False? 3

1. True
2. False
3. True
4. True
5. True
6. True
7. False
8. False
9. True
10. False

True or False? 4

1. True
2. True
3. True
4. True
5. False
6. True
7. False
8. False
9. True
10. False

True or False? 5

1. False
2. True
3. True
4. True
5. True
6. True
7. False
8. True
9. True
10. False

True or False? 6

1. True
2. False
3. True
4. True
5. True
6. True
7. False
8. False
9. True
10. True

Mixed Bag

True or False 7

1. True
2. True
3. False
4. False
5. False
6. True
7. True
8. True
9. False
10. False

True or False? 8

1. True
2. False
3. True
4. True
5. False
6. False
7. False
8. True
9. True
10. False

True or False? 9

1. False
2. True
3. True
4. False
5. True
6. True
7. True
8. True
9. True
10. True

True or False? 10

1. False
2. True
3. False
4. False
5. True
6. False
7. True
8. False
9. True
10. True

Choices 1

1. a) Black
2. b) Albania
3. a) Six
4. c) Alaska
5. c) 50 kilos
6. b) Gnomon
7. c) 4876 metres
8. b) Literature
9. c) Dong
10. a) Right arm/right eye

Choices 2

1. c) Embellished waterspouts
2. b) Hals
3. b) Half-man/half-horse
4. b) $74\frac{1}{2}$ miles
5. c) 1,763 days
6. b) Eva Peron
7. a) Henry James
8. c) Greg Norman
9. b) 40 million
10. b) 9 metres

Mixed Bag

Choices 3

1. c) Kirk Douglas
2. a) Italy
3. a) Indonesia
4. a) Derbyshire
5. c) 15,000,000°C
6. a) 397 metres
7. c) Fast railway network
8. b) 130
9. c) 200 mph
10. a) Catalan

Choices 4

1. b) 1908
2. b) Karate
3. b) 90,000,000
4. c) King Zog
5. c) 206 bones
6. b) 6,500,000
7. b) 969
8. c) Football
9. a) Turkey
10. c) Her maid

Choices 5

1. a) Bats
2. c) Michael Caine
3. a) 1860
4. b) US judge
5. b) Empty orchestra
6. a) Pheasant
7. b) 5 cm
8. c) 50,000
9. a) Italy
10. a) 800 million

Choices 6

1. c) 400 square miles
2. c) El Greco
3. b) 113,000
4. c) Australian sheep
5. c) Winchester College
6. a) £70
7. b) Harness racing
8. a) Jenkins
9. c) York
10. b) 70 times

1, 2, 3... 1

1. Dromedary
2. William Shakespeare
3. Jerome K Jerome
4. Rudolph Valentino
5. Pentagon
6. An author
7. The hanging gardens
8. Octave
9. Beethoven
10. Agatha Christie

1, 2, 3... 2

1. Binary system
2. Gary Powers
3. Anton Chekhov
4. Seven
5. Mecca
6. Henry VIII
7. Gluttony
8. Field Marshal Montgomery
9. The Muses
10. Two

Mixed Bag

1, 2, 3...   3

1. Hydrogen
2. India
3. Kurt Weill
4. T S Eliot
5. The Pentateuch
6. Gary Sobers
7. Akira Kurosawa
8. The end of the watch
9. Harrison
10. *Decameron*

Colours   1

1. Red Guards
2. Green belt
3. Black Forest
4. Yellow River
5. Bluebeard
6. Whitehall
7. Lady Jane Grey
8. Gretna Green
9. A white rose
10. Blue Period

Colours   2

1. Legs
2. Mercury
3. Rice
4. White
5. The White Rabbit
6. Pink Floyd
7. Johann Strauss
8. Beatles
9. Suez Canal
10. Denmark

Colours   3

1. Orange
2. Lucinda Green
3. Pink Floyd
4. Red-hot poker
5. Black Prince
6. Capability Brown
7. Black Death
8. Blue
9. White Sea
10. Gold Coast

Colours   4

1. *The Color of Money*
2. Orange
3. Five
4. Large, bright stars
5. Nell Gwyn
6. George Gershwin
7. Kerry Packer
8. *Golden Hind*
9. The Wall Street stock market crashed
10. Disneyland

Colours   5

1. Green Bank
2. Order of the Purple Heart
3. Yellowhammer
4. White
5. Earl Grey
6. Magenta
7. *The Woman in White*
8. Red
9. Green
10. Red and green

Mixed Bag

Colours   6

1. Nathaniel Hawthorne
2. Selborne
3. Rugby
4. Silver
5. Insect
6. Red
7. William II
8. Arthur Bliss
9. Scale insect
10. Duke of Gloucester

Colours in Science

1. Green
2. Red
3. Red
4. Blue
5. Red
6. A plant
7. Blue
8. Astronomy
9. Red
10. Verdigris

Time

1. 3,600
2. Sundial
3. Quartz
4. Atomic clocks
5. Six
6. Greenwich
7. H G Wells
8. Metronome
9. Second
10. Milan in 1353

Money

1. The sucre
2. The Tower of London
3. 21 shillings
4. Lira
5. Mark
6. 1931
7. A plant
8. Sergio Leone
9. Bermuda dollar
10. Its exports become cheaper to buy abroad

Who, What, Where?   1

1. The Pope
2. John F Kennedy
3. Anne Frank
4. Francis Drake
5. Tower of London
6. Saigon
7. Mark Antony
8. Dogs
9. On the road to Damascus
10. McDonald's

Who, What, or Where ?   2

1. Carl Lewis
2. The study of coins
3. Alexander Graham Bell
4. Guinevere
5. A fish
6. Wonderland
7. Julius Caesar
8. Tennis
9. Paris, France
10. Robert Baden-Powell

Mixed Bag

Who, What, or Where?   3

1. Elizabeth Garrett Anderson
2. Wounded Knee
3. An island
4. Paul McCartney
5. Romansch
6. Ujiji
7. Erasmus
8. Cagliari
9. Paris
10. Holman Hunt

Crime

1. Whitechapel
2. Tax evasion
3. Sheriff Pat Garrett
4. Charles Lindbergh
5. Frank and Jesse James
6. John Wilkes Booth
7. Georges Simenon
8. Barabbas
9. Mafia
10. Triad

Catastrophes and Disasters

1. 1986
2. Krakatoa
3. China
4. Tsunami
5. 1912
6. Pudding Lane
7. *Hindenburg*
8. Bhopal
9. William McGonagall
10. Black Monday

Fashion

1. *My Fair Lady*
2. Christian Dior
3. Pierre Cardin
4. From the Pacific atoll where atom bombs were tested
5. Vivienne Westwood
6. Savile Row
7. Halston
8. Emporio
9. Bazaar
10. Amelia Bloomer

Language

1. Farsi
2. Aramaic
3. Computer language
4. Académie Française
5. Received pronunciation
6. Miles Coverdale
7. German
8. China
9. George Bernard Shaw
10. Yes

Water, Water, Everywhere   1

1. H_2O
2. Rabies
3. Pacific
4. Handel
5. To help prevent tooth decay
6. Aquarius
7. Old Faithful
8. *Babies*
9. Tributaries
10. Suffolk

Mixed Bag

Water, Water, Everywhere 2

1 *Mary Rose*
2 Russia
3 Brussels
4 60–70%
5 Richard Adams
6 Colombia
7 Fourteen
8 Narwhal
9 Crystal glass
10 Huron

Archaeology

1 Minoan
2 1922
3 Piltdown man
4 The study of tree rings
5 Round barrows
6 Mortimer Wheeler
7 France
8 Pompeii
9 Winchester
10 Etruscan

Economics

1 The Bretton Woods Conference
2 Thomas Malthus
3 Vilfredo Pareto
4 Household management
5 John Maynard Keynes
6 1957
7 Adam Smith
8 John Stuart Mill
9 Norwegian
10 Leonid Kantorovich

Cats and Dogs 1

1 Peter Sellers
2 St Bernard
3 Sherlock Holmes
4 South America
5 Jones
6 Erwin Rommel
7 July and August
8 No tail
9 Dalmatians
10 Tiger

Cats and Dogs 2

1 Four
2 Puma
3 Jane Fonda
4 Ounce
5 Tiger
6 Pit bull terrier
7 Andrew Lloyd Webber
8 Earth
9 Lion
10 Three

Cats and Dogs 3

1 Luchino Visconti
2 Frederick Forsyth
3 Felix the Cat
4 Suffragettes
5 W H Auden
6 Volkswagen
7 Haile Selassie
8 Miniature
9 Dachshund
10 Miles Davis

Mixed Bag

Name the Year 1

1. 1929
2. 1989
3. 1978
4. 1966
5. 1944
6. 1963
7. 1991
8. 1936
9. 1982
10. 1969

What's in a Name? 2

1. Edward
2. Black
3. Edith
4. Victoria Cross
5. Partisans
6. Shelley
7. Rita Hayworth
8. Fitzgerald
9. Bomber Harris
10. Emma Thompson

Name the Year 2

1. 1957
2. 1912
3. 1985
4. 1949
5. 1974
6. 1959
7. 1975
8. 1933
9. 1965
10. 1980

What's in a Name? 3

1. A mineral
2. Mistinguett
3. Klapka
4. *Thrust 2*
5. Uranus
6. Umberto Eco
7. *Vostok I*
8. Grampus
9. Switch-hitter
10. John Wayne

What's in a Name? 1

1. Catherine
2. Steam engine
3. Ampère
4. *Herald of Free Enterprise*
5. Heartsease
6. Cassius Clay
7. Istanbul
8. Cape Canaveral
9. Blondin
10. Geronimo

Entertainment

General 1

1. Batman
2. James Herriot
3. Beatles
4. Michael Caine
5. Gospel
6. Jeeves and Wooster
7. *Silence of the Lambs*
8. Roald Dahl
9. The Muppets
10. Cats

Music 1

1. Vivaldi
2. Nine
3. Piano
4. Balalaika
5. Schubert
6. Three
7. *Carmen*
8. Waltz
9. Mezzo-soprano
10. Violin

General 2

1. Isadora Duncan
2. Phineas T Barnum
3. Verdi
4. Montreux
5. Peter Cook
6. Bruce Lee
7. Stephen Sondheim
8. The Old Vic
9. Dennis Potter
10. Joy Adamson

Music 2

1. George Harrison
2. Leonard Bernstein
3. Mozart
4. The Beach Boys
5. Oratorios
6. Charlie Parker
7. Woodwind
8. Fender
9. J S Bach
10. Bono Vox

General 3

1. Fringe theatre
2. Gummo
3. Kabuki
4. Kenneth Branagh
5. John Gay
6. L Frank Baum
7. Maurice Chevalier
8. Harry Lauder
9. Benny Goodman
10. Estragon and Vladimir

Music 3

1. Pianoforte
2. Operas
3. The Proms/promenade concerts
4. Gilbert and Sullivan
5. Hungarian
6. Harmonica
7. It wasn't discovered until 1930
8. Concert harp
9. Mozart
10. Harmonium

Entertainment

Music 4

1. Piano
2. George Gershwin
3. Bob Dylan
4. 'Like a Virgin'
5. Czech
6. Oscar Hammerstein
7. The Rolling Stones
8. Miles Davis
9. Janáček
10. Haydn

Music 5

1. Simon Rattle
2. Piano
3. Finnish
4. Prokofiev
5. Thomas Beecham
6. Mendelssohn
7. Ralph Vaughan Williams
8. *The Barber of Seville*
9. Beethoven
10. Debussy

Music 6

1. *Prince Igor*
2. Glyndebourne
3. Scales
4. George I
5. A violin bow
6. (Classical) guitar
7. Operas by Benjamin Britten
8. James Galway
9. *Fidelio*
10. The 'New World' symphony

Music 7

1. Mozart
2. Mahalia Jackson
3. *Parsifal*
4. Dublin
5. John Philip Sousa
6. Folk songs and dances
7. Harrison Birtwistle
8. Metronome
9. Camille Saint-Saëns
10. Hymns

Music 8

1. Organ
2. Louis XIV
3. 1956
4. Arnold Schoenberg
5. Rock and roll
6. Philip Glass
7. Jimi Hendrix
8. Belgian
9. Austrian
10. Michael Jackson

Music 9

1. Paderewski
2. Cremona
3. Messiaen
4. Feedback
5. Faust
6. Viol
7. Malcolm Williamson
8. Stephen Foster
9. Haydn
10. Handel

Entertainment

Jazz 1

1. Ella Fitzgerald
2. Bebop
3. Vibraphone
4. Miles Davis
5. Duke Ellington
6. F Scott Fitzgerald
7. Count Basie
8. Scott Joplin
9. Louis Armstrong
10. Bessie Smith

Popular Music 1

1. Gene Kelly
2. Cliff Richard
3. Beach Boys
4. Paul Simon
5. The Who
6. Glenn Miller
7. Otis Redding
8. Prince
9. Barbra Streisand
10. Sex Pistols

Popular Music 2

1. Frank Sinatra
2. 'Lady in Red'
3. Rodgers and Hammerstein
4. Eric Clapton
5. Motown
6. Phil Spector
7. *Thriller*
8. Buddy Holly
9. Woodstock
10. Paul McCartney

Popular Music 3

1. Elvis Presley
2. Elton John
3. 'Satchmo'
4. The Rolling Stones
5. Bananarama
6. Phil Collins
7. Bob Geldof
8. Tina Turner
9. New York
10. Bill Haley

Popular Music 4

1. Jimi Hendrix
2. Frank Sinatra
3. Guitar
4. Johnny Cash
5. David Bowie
6. Billie Holiday
7. 'The Birdie Song'
8. Grateful Dead
9. Richard Rodgers
10. Vera Lynn

Popular Music 5

1. Joni Mitchell
2. Wilson Pickett
3. Bruce Springsteen
4. The Jackson Five
5. Mark Knopfler
6. Tim Rice
7. Tin Machine
8. Country and western/country music
9. Irving Berlin
10. 'Rock Around the Clock'

Entertainment

Popular Music 6
1. Paul McCartney
2. *The Threepenny Opera/Die Dreigroschenoper*
3. Berry Gordy Jr
4. Ringo Starr
5. 'Cinderella Rockerfella'
6. David Bowie
7. Janis Joplin
8. Trumpet
9. Indie/independent
10. Ragtime

Popular Music 7
1. Harry
2. Bob Marley
3. Sun
4. Rolling Stones
5. Ennio Morricone
6. Bananarama
7. Yesterday
8. Texas
9. Miles Davis
10. M C Hammer

Musical Instruments
1. Marimba
2. Soprano saxophone
3. Jingles
4. Vibraphone
5. Trombone
6. Sousaphone
7. Hammond organ
8. Two
9. Trombone
10. The Who

Cinema and TV 1
1. Alfred Hitchcock
2. Austrian
3. Clark Gable
4. Dustin Hoffman
5. Roger Rabbit
6. *Bullseye*
7. Hepburn
8. It was the first talking picture
9. Sylvester Stallone
10. *Snow White and the Seven Dwarfs*

Cinema and TV 2
1. *The Saint*
2. Sergio Leone
3. *A Hard Day's Night*
4. Sony
5. Madonna
6. Steve McQueen
7. Holly Hunter
8. Anthony Hopkins
9. Jamie Lee Curtis
10. Wendy Richards

Cinema and TV 3
1. A car
2. Lucille Ball
3. Steven Spielberg
4. Kenneth More
5. Sean Connery
6. Laurence Olivier
7. John Logie Baird
8. *A Fistful of Dollars*
9. 'Eh, what's up, Doc?'
10. Red, blue and green

Entertainment

Cinema and TV 4

1. Boris Karloff
2. *The Man in the White Suit*
3. Edward Teller
4. River Phoenix
5. Georges Méliès
6. Walt Disney
7. Cellulose nitrate
8. *The Birds*
9. *The Krypton Factor*
10. *Jaws*

Cinema and TV 5

1. *Santa Claus the Movie*
2. Buster Keaton
3. Woody Allen
4. Telstar
5. Shirley Temple Black
6. Cathode-ray tube
7. Charlie Chaplin
8. Vivien Leigh
9. In a road accident
10. *Carry on Sergeant*

Cinema and TV 6

1. Felix the Cat
2. Tony Curtis
3. *Yentl*
4. Cary Grant
5. *The Last Emperor*
6. 1982
7. Paramount
8. For leaving her husband to have another man's child
9. Alan Bennett
10. David Bowie

Cinema and TV 7

1. Mickey Mouse
2. Ginger Rogers and Fred Astaire
3. Jodie Foster
4. Stan Laurel
5. Marlon Brando
6. Martin Scorsese
7. Akira Kurosawa
8. Richard Burton
9. Alan Partridge
10. Arthur C Clarke

Cinema and TV 8

1. Mary Pickford
2. Francis Ford Coppola
3. *Monsieur Verdoux*
4. *Sapphire and Steel*
5. Wolves (*Dances with Wolves*)
6. Jeffrey Holland
7. Sergei Eisenstein
8. Cary Grant
9. *Heaven's Gate*
10. Faye Dunaway

Cinema and TV 9

1. John Barrymore
2. Bengal
3. Peter Weir
4. Roald Dahl
5. Hilversum
6. Greta Garbo
7. Lillian Gish
8. *Klute*
9. Arthur Miller
10. Goldfish

Entertainment

Cinema and TV — 10

1. *The Empire Strikes Back*
2. 24
3. Lauren Bacall
4. Dopey and Doc
5. High-definition television
6. Auguste and Louis Lumière
7. *True Grit*
8. François Truffaut
9. Three
10. Robert Redford

On the Stage — 1

1. They are played by members of the opposite sex
2. Ray Allen
3. Yes
4. Farce
5. *The Mousetrap*
6. Ruby Keeler
7. Mime
8. Pooh-Bah
9. The Comédie Française
10. Japan

On the Stage — 2

1. Stratford-upon-Avon
2. *St Joan*
3. Bayreuth
4. Barry Humphries
5. Noël Coward
6. Laurence Olivier
7. *The Boy Who Wouldn't Grow Up*
8. Mummers' play
9. Pantomime
10. Sir Toby Belch

On the Stage — 3

1. George Bernard Shaw
2. Ellen Terry
3. Ibsen
4. *A Midsummer Night's Dream*
5. *Hair*
6. *Who's Afraid of Virginia Woolf?*
7. *Dramatis personae*
8. Laurence Olivier
9. Margot Fonteyn
10. Alan Ayckbourn

On the Stage — 4

1. Rita Hayworth
2. Ivor Novello
3. *Patience*
4. Rochdale
5. The Globe
6. David Garrick
7. *Showboat*
8. J B Priestley
9. The 'Great White Way'
10. Sam Shepard

On the Stage — 5

1. *A Long Day's Journey into Night*
2. Richard Burbage
3. Dustin Hoffman
4. Lawrence of Arabia
5. Dionysus
6. Louis XIV
7. Ralph Richardson
8. Architecture
9. Alec Douglas-Home
10. Antonio

Entertainment

On the Stage — 6

1. Vaudeville
2. Julie Andrews
3. T S Eliot
4. *The Playboy of the Western World*
5. *Lysistrata*
6. Verdi
7. Czechoslovakia
8. Neil Simon
9. John Cage
10. *Serious Money*

Comedians and Clowns — 1

1. *Monty Python's Flying Circus*
2. *Hancock's Half Hour*
3. Windor Davies
4. *Fantasia*
5. Bob Hope and Bing Crosby
6. Gauls
7. Three
8. Dudley Moore
9. Chris Tarrant
10. Judy

Comedians and Clowns — 2

1. Superman
2. Alan Bennett
3. The Goons
4. Joseph Grimaldi
5. Stan and Oliver
6. Joe Orton
7. Ealing
8. George Formby
9. Harold Lloyd
10. St Trinian's

Comedians and Clowns — 3

1. Fatty Arbuckle
2. Max Wall
3. *New Yorker*
4. Ben Travers
5. James Thurber
6. Mack Sennett
7. *Punch*
8. Doonesbury
9. Harpo
10. Roadrunner

Sport and Leisure

Sport 1

1. W G Grace
2. The marathon
3. 90 minutes
4. Ben Johnson
5. Breaststroke
6. Bobby and Jack Charlton
7. Slalom
8. Thirteen
9. Roger Bannister
10. A shuttlecock

Sport 2

1. Paul Gascoigne
2. Sumo
3. Deuce
4. Ryder Cup
5. Six
6. Fairway
7. Le Mans
8. Leeds United
9. Surfing
10. Blackburn Rovers

Sport 3

1. Volley
2. At a rodeo
3. Ice hockey
4. Muhammad Ali/Cassius Clay
5. Brown
6. Caber
7. Three-day eventing/eventing
8. Sky-diving
9. Barcelona
10. Freestyle/crawl

Sport 4

1. Sumo wrestling
2. Polo
3. Wimbledon, US Open, Australian Championships, French Championships
4. Harlem Globetrotters
5. Heptathlon
6. The first six
7. Ascot
8. Sydney
9. Curling
10. Gridiron

Sport 5

1. Diego Maradona
2. Boris Becker
3. Tom Watson
4. Stirling Moss
5. Joe Louis
6. Bjorn Borg
7. McLaren
8. Dressage
9. USA
10. Spinners

Sport 6

1. Lawn tennis
2. Joe DiMaggio
3. Bridge
4. Gary Sobers
5. Mark Spitz
6. New Zealand
7. Le Mans
8. Comanche Run
9. Yellow
10. Because the male contestants were naked

Sport and Leisure

Sport 7

1. 26 miles 385 yards
2. Johannesburg
3. Snatch and jerk
4. Yachts
5. India
6. Roller skating
7. Graham Gooch
8. He refused to join the US army
9. Volleyball
10. St Leger

Sport 8

1. Allan Wells
2. Fishing
3. Third man
4. Jonah Barrington
5. Sonja Henie
6. Nine
7. Hockey
8. Sugar Ray Leonard
9. Wrestling
10. Lawn tennis

Sport 9

1. Croquet; polo
2. Scunthorpe United
3. Braemar Gathering
4. American/National Football Conference
5. Kayak; Canadian-style canoe
6. Cricket; Australian rules football
7. Nine
8. Rugby Union
9. Four
10. Luge

Food and Drink 1

1. Champagne
2. Prunes
3. Rum
4. Spinach
5. Peanut
6. Caviar
7. Bacchus
8. A vegan
9. Rice
10. Tuna

Food and Drink 2

1. Black Russian
2. Olive Oyl
3. Chewing gum/bubble gum
4. Granny (Maria Ann) Smith
5. Roughage
6. Haggis
7. Aubergine
8. Avocado
9. Beaujolais *nouveau*
10. Pancakes

Food and Drink 3

1. Garlic
2. Appellation controlée
3. Oysters
4. Nellie Melba
5. Mead
6. Somerset Maugham
7. Sir Walter Raleigh
8. Nuts
9. Soya
10. 17th century

Sport and Leisure

Food and Drink 4

1. Angelica
2. Brine
3. Irradiation
4. Lager
5. Ultra heat treated
6. Roquefort
7. Rice
8. Olives
9. Pasteurization
10. Juniper

Food and Drink 5

1. Sago
2. Plantain
3. Rye
4. Stilton
5. Nonalcoholic
6. Mace
7. Sugar
8. Durum flour
9. Orchids
10. Saffron

Food and Drink 6

1. Phylloxera
2. Sicily
3. Aniseed
4. Halibut
5. Turmeric
6. Vienna
7. Lamprey
8. Truffles
9. Halal food
10. Clarence Birdseye

Games and Pastimes

1. Angling
2. 30
3. The zero gives all stakes to the banker – unless a player bets on it
4. France
5. Macramé
6. India
7. 8
8. To get round a law prohibiting ninepin bowling in New York
9. Cribbage
10. Snooker

Art and Literature

Literature 1

1. Mr Rochester
2. Agatha Christie
3. Kenneth Grahame
4. Dr Watson
5. Mark Twain
6. Sancho Panza
7. The Hobbits
8. The Brontë family
9. Charles Dickens
10. Dracula

Literature 2

1. *The Lord of the Rings*
2. Robert Louis Stevenson
3. Canterbury
4. E M Forster
5. Pacific
6. Westerns
7. *Glory*
8. William Shakespeare
9. Edward Lear
10. H G Wells

Literature 3

1. Richmal Crompton
2. Ernest Hemingway
3. *The Pilgrim's Progress*
4. *Black Beauty*
5. Rabbits
6. Captain Ahab
7. *Verona*
8. Chocolate
9. Twenty thousand leagues
10. Narnia

Literature 4

1. *The Merry Wives of Windsor*
2. Booker Prize
3. Haiku
4. 'The Metamorphosis'
5. Victor Hugo
6. *Gulliver's Travels*
7. Hughes
8. Hiawatha
9. *Nineteen Eighty-Four*
10. Percy Bysshe Shelley

Literature 5

1. Wordsworth
2. Colombian
3. The Count of Monte Cristo
4. P G Wodehouse
5. *The Picture of Dorian Gray*
6. Umberto Eco
7. Norwegian
8. *Roget's Thesaurus of English Words and Phrases*
9. Geoffrey Chaucer
10. Tobias Smollett

Literature 6

1. Australian
2. Wilkie Collins
3. *Edwin Drood*
4. Somerset Maugham
5. John Updike
6. Shelley
7. Disraeli
8. Dante
9. Wystan
10. Lady Windermere's

Art and Literature

Literature 7

1. Plato
2. Horace
3. The *Iliad*
4. Aristophanes
5. Jason
6. Pliny the Younger
7. Sirens
8. Plutarch
9. Ovid
10. Aeschylus

Literature 8

1. *The Last Tycoon*
2. *The Matter*
3. Ovid
4. *Gloucester*
5. Father and son
6. Samuel Taylor Coleridge
7. Patrick White
8. Edgar Allan Poe
9. Pushkin
10. *Prima Donna*

Literature 9

1. G K Chesterton
2. André Gide
3. Lord Tennyson
4. Jonathan Swift
5. Thomas Keneally
6. Robert Frost
7. Eugene O'Neill
8. Tolstoy
9. Goethe
10. Charlotte

Literature 10

1. *Under Milk Wood*
2. Larousse
3. Cordelia
4. Robert Southey
5. Blank verse
6. John Milton
7. Christopher Marlowe
8. Walt Whitman
9. Angry Young Men
10. Tennesee Williams

Literature 11

1. Edward de Bono
2. Mars
3. *Literature and Science*
4. *Dr Jeckyll and Mr Hyde*
5. Jules Verne
6. He turned into an insect
7. The mad hatter
8. Ben Jonson
9. C P Snow
10. Stephen Hawking

Art and Artists 1

1. Vinci
2. Christopher Wren
3. Henry Moore
4. Gauguin
5. Lions
6. The Louvre
7. Pieter Brueghel the Elder
8. Norman/Romanesque
9. The Sydney Opera House
10. L S Lowry

Art and Literature

Art and Artists 2

1. Leonardo da Vinci
2. Florence
3. Henry VIII
4. Egypt
5. Andy Warhol
6. Edvard Munch
7. Michelangelo
8. Spanish
9. George Stubbs
10. Vincent van Gogh

Art and Artists 3

1. Leonardo de Vinci
2. Andy Warhol
3. *The Laughing Cavalier*
4. Impressionism
5. Gainsborough
6. Tenniel
7. Brighton
8. Seventeenth
9. Graham Sutherland
10. Graumann's Chinese Theater

Art and Artists 4

1. Paul Klee
2. Frank Lloyd Wright
3. Abstract
4. Gothic
5. Impressionists
6. Toulouse-Lautrec
7. Salvador Dali
8. Baroque
9. Guernica
10. Jackson Pollock

Art and Artists 5

1. J M W Turner
2. One
3. Paolo Uccello
4. Spanish
5. Fresco
6. John Betjeman
7. John Bratby
8. He took the first photograph
9. Dada
10. Barcelona

Art and Artists 6

1. Auguste Rodin
2. Florence
3. Rembrandt
4. Vermeer
5. Hieronymus Bosch
6. David Hockney
7. Nicolas Poussin
8. Gentile
9. The Pre-Raphaelites
10. Josiah Spode

Art and Artists 7

1. Degas
2. Inigo Jones
3. Yosemite
4. Rubens
5. Tintoretto
6. Graham Sutherland
7. CAD
8. Brussels
9. *Winnie-the-Pooh* stories
10. Ghiberti

Art and Literature

Art and Artists　　　　　　　　8

1. Salvador Dali
2. Pointillism
3. Dresden
4. Edward Hopper
5. Napoleon
6. Jacob Epstein
7. Tempera
8. Barbara Hepworth
9. The Wallace Collection
10. Man Ray

Art and Artists　　　　　　　　9

1. M C Escher
2. Walter Gropius
3. The Graces
4. Edwin Lutyens
5. Rembrandt
6. The Medici family
7. Jacques Louis David
8. Crystal Palace
9. Utrillo
10. Francis Bacon

Art and Artists　　　　　　　　10

1. Albrecht Dürer
2. Einstein
3. Michael Nyman
4. *Discovery*
5. Astronomy
6. Giotto
7. Pietra dura
8. Anatomy
9. Rembrandt
10. Futurism

Around the World

General 1

1. Nile
2. Atlantic and Pacific
3. Danube
4. Sahara
5. Lake Superior
6. Antarctica
7. Australia
8. Belgium
9. Massachusetts
10. Etna

General 2

1. Africa
2. Budapest
3. Anticyclone
4. Amazon
5. Ecuador
6. Niagara river
7. Canada
8. Hungary
9. Anchorage, Alaska
10. Equator

General 3

1. Austria
2. Victoria
3. Crete
4. Liberia
5. Islamabad
6. Mississippi
7. Israel
8. Golden Gate
9. Kildare
10. Milan

General 4

1. Table Mountain
2. China
3. The Camargue
4. Amman
5. Somerset
6. Nagasaki
7. Hawaii
8. The Netherlands
9. Boroughs
10. Danube

General 5

1. Greenland
2. New Hebrides
3. Agra
4. Vladivostok
5. Cuba
6. Tibet
7. New York harbour
8. Rhine and Rhône
9. Borneo
10. Ayers Rock

General 6

1. Mariana Trench
2. Mali
3. The Falkland Islands
4. Genoa
5. The Levant
6. Minnesota
7. Murmansk
8. Venezuela
9. Moraine
10. Australia

Around the World

UK 1

1. Sandwich
2. Avon
3. Sherwood Forest
4. Cumbria
5. Nottingham
6. M6
7. Ireland
8. Wales
9. The Pennines
10. Kinder Scout

UK 2

1. The Potteries
2. Holyhead
3. Lough Neagh
4. Sheffield
5. Isle of Wight
6. Cheviots
7. Birmingham
8. Watling Street
9. By peat-digging
10. Cairngorms

UK 3

1. Belfast
2. Caledonian Canal
3. Menai Strait
4. Middlesex
5. Basalt
6. Liverpool Bay
7. Bracknell
8. Nottinghamshire
9. Royal Leamington Spa; Royal Tunbridge Wells
10. The Peak District

USA and Canada 1

1. The Rockies
2. Ottawa
3. Hollywood
4. Democrat
5. 50
6. George Custer
7. Texas
8. Las Vegas
9. 'Last Frontier'
10. Franklin D Roosevelt

USA and Canada 2

1. Skunk
2. Salt Lake City
3. Florida
4. New England
5. Meg Ryan
6. Maple leaf
7. Oklahoma
8. Gettysburg
9. Albany
10. Pearl Harbor

USA and Canada 3

1. Arkansas
2. Nickel
3. The American Constitution
4. Columbus
5. Judy Garland
6. J Edgar Hoover
7. Ronald Reagan
8. Wyoming
9. Glenn Miller
10. Memphis

Around the World

USA and Canada 4

1. St Lawrence
2. Philadelphia
3. Arizona
4. James Wolfe
5. Pierre Trudeau
6. Orville and Wilbur Wright
7. Sandwich Islands
8. Watching a play
9. California
10. Québec

USA and Canada 5

1. Johnson
2. Crazy Horse and Sitting Bull
3. Kansas
4. Impeachment
5. J Paul Getty
6. Prohibition
7. President
8. Irangate
9. Gerald Ford
10. Secretary of State

USA and Canada 6

1. Montréal
2. New Amsterdam
3. Paul Revere
4. Colorado
5. San Andreas fault
6. Utah
7. Lake Ontario
8. Atlanta
9. Rio Grande
10. Minneapolis

USA and Canada 7

1. Meriwether Lewis and William Clark
2. Theodore Roosevelt
3. Quebec
4. Basketball
5. Mount McKinley
6. Colorado and Wyoming
7. Yukon
8. Grover Cleveland
9. *The Birth of a Nation*
10. Saskatchewan

USA and Canada 8

1. Labrador
2. Liberty Island
3. Elizabeth II
4. San Antonio
5. Montezuma II
6. Delaware
7. Continental Congress
8. Rhode Island
9. Irving Berlin
10. Detroit

USA and Canada 9

1. New Mexico
2. Warren Commission
3. Lake Michigan
4. Ronald Reagan
5. The first ten amendments of the Constitution
6. Berkeley
7. Michael Collins
8. London Bridge
9. The Manhattan Project
10. President Andrew Johnson

Around the World

Africa 1
1. Suez Canal
2. Egypt
3. Kenneth Kaunda
4. Dutch
5. Zaire, formerly Congo
6. Dohomey
7. African National Congress
8. Uganda
9. Morocco
10. South Africa

Africa 2
1. Southern Rhodesia, now Zimbabwe
2. Green
3. Burkina Faso
4. Tutankhamen
5. Sadat
6. Kenya
7. Kilimanjaro
8. Strait of Gibraltar
9. Blue Nile; White Nile
10. Congo

Africa 3
1. Morocco
2. Gordon
3. Zambia and Zimbabwe
4. Dinar
5. Humphrey Bogart
6. Portugal
7. Alan Paton
8. Nairobi
9. Great Rift Valley
10. Bartolomeu Diaz

Africa 4
1. Khartoum
2. Atlas Mountains
3. Sudan
4. Burkina Faso
5. Somalia
6. Tanzania
7. Kenya
8. Winnie Mandela
9. Zimbabwe
10. Freetown

Africa 5
1. Richard Burton
2. Niger
3. Karen Blixen
4. Limpopo
5. Marcus Garvey
6. Algeria
7. Ghana
8. A cereal
9. Togo
10. Tunisia

Africa 6
1. Nigeria
2. James Monroe
3. Sharpeville
4. Uganda
5. Egypt
6. Kalahari
7. A letter R
8. Abuja
9. Cairo
10. Albert Luthuli

Around the World

Asia 1

1. Khyber Pass
2. Siam
3. Lawrence of Arabia
4. Ganges
5. Nepal
6. 1,450
7. Abu Dhabi
8. Yak
9. Rupee
10. Seoul

Asia 2

1. Persia
2. India
3. Lebanon
4. Miniature trees
5. Genghis Khan
6. China
7. Soya
8. Jordan
9. New Guinea
10. Red

Asia 3

1. Vasco da Gama
2. Jute
3. Malaysia
4. Hirohito
5. Victoria
6. Scheherazade
7. Egypt
8. Yellow Sea
9. Amritsar
10. Yemen

Asia 4

1. Riyadh
2. Ho Chi Minh
3. Uttah Pradesh
4. Damascus
5. Maldives
6. Calcutta
7. Tiananmen Square
8. Iran and Iraq
9. Honda
10. Nepalese

Asia 5

1. Shah Jahan
2. Tamerlane
3. Honshu
4. 1839–42
5. Caspian Sea
6. Rabindranath Tagore
7. Myanmar
8. Kemal Atatürk
9. Dien Bien Phu
10. Iran

Asia 6

1. Assisted by wind
2. Indonesia
3. Bahrain
4. Mekong
5. Iran
6. Jumna
7. Porcelain
8. Vietnam
9. Sanskrit
10. Laos

Around the World

Australasia 1
1. Eucalyptus tree
2. Indonesia
3. Mel Gibson
4. Kiwi fruit
5. *Kon-Tiki*
6. Brisbane
7. Back
8. Great Barrier Reef
9. Sydney
10. New South Wales

Australasia 2
1. A politician
2. Tasmania
3. 1956
4. 'Waltzing Matilda'
5. Butterfly
6. Coral Sea
7. Western Australia
8. The Tropic of Capricorn
9. To watch an eclipse
10. Crime

Australasia 3
1. Errol Flynn
2. Robert Menzies
3. A marsupial
4. Four times
5. Van Diemen's Land
6. 'Long daylight'
7. Ernest Rutherford
8. Oval
9. Joan Sutherland
10. Nullarbor Plain

Australasia 4
1. Joey
2. *Rainbow Warrior*
3. Errol Flynn
4. Abel Tasman
5. Kiri Te Kanawa
6. Bob Hawke
7. Tonga
8. Cook Strait
9. Melbourne
10. Solomon Islands

Australasia 5
1. Judy Davis
2. Robert O'Hara Burke and William Wills
3. Germaine Greer
4. Murray
5. Capt William Bligh
6. Lake Dumbleyung
7. Perth
8. Hobart
9. Amelia Earhart
10. South Australia and Victoria

Australasia 6
1. A marsupial
2. India
3. Donald Bradman
4. Society Islands
5. *Aurora australis*
6. Ernest Rutherford
7. Anzac day
8. Patrick White
9. Fremantle
10. New Britain

Around the World

Europe 1

1. Bay of Biscay
2. Mont Blanc
3. Eire
4. Poland
5. Bulgarian
6. The Hague
7. Corsica
8. Andorra
9. Austria
10. Sicily

Europe 2

1. Bonn
2. Ireland
3. Danube
4. Switzerland and Austria
5. Denmark
6. Portugal
7. Loire
8. Switzerland
9. Andorra
10. Munich

Europe 3

1. Malta
2. Strasbourg
3. Red and white
4. Gdansk
5. Milan
6. Andalusia
7. Germany
8. Czechoslovakia
9. Denmark
10. Rome

Europe 4

1. Po
2. 1990
3. Paphos
4. Aachen
5. Louis XVI
6. Spain
7. Helsinki
8. Copenhagen
9. Blue and white
10. Portugal

Europe 5

1. Byron
2. Finland
3. Third crusade
4. Fjords
5. Vltava
6. Eagle
7. Luxembourg
8. Portuguese
9. Adige
10. Náxos

Europe 6

1. The Hague
2. La Manche
3. St Basil's
4. Norway
5. Piedmont
6. Finland
7. Charlemagne
8. The Left
9. Yalta
10. Switzerland

Around the World

South America and the Caribbean 1

1. Portuguese
2. The Strait of Magellan
3. Rio de Janeiro
4. Caracas
5. Pampas
6. 2,000
7. Brasilia
8. Gabriela Sabatini
9. Port-au-Prince
10. Orinoco

South America and the Caribbean 2

1. Argentina
2. Falkland Islands
3. Bogotá
4. Tobago
5. Tierra del Fuego
6. Bolivia and Paraguay
7. Panama
8. Sugar Loaf mountain
9. Haiti
10. Caribbean

South America and the Caribbean 3

1. Simon Bolívar
2. Shining Path
3. The Netherlands
4. Dominican Republic
5. Bolivia and Peru
6. Colombia
7. Actress
8. Bay of Pigs
9. Argentina
10. Guatemala City

South America and the Caribbean 4

1. Venezuela
2. Carmen Miranda
3. Quito
4. Peru
5. Devil's Island
6. 1988
7. The Galapagos Islands
8. Brazil and Colombia
9. Chile
10. Chinchilla

South America and the Caribbean 5

1. Cape Horn
2. Managua
3. La Paz, Bolivia
4. Atahualpa
5. Valparaiso
6. Architecture
7. Pelé
8. Argentina
9. Uruguay
10. Paraguay

South America and the Caribbean 6

1. Santo Domingo
2. Uruguay
3. Bajan
4. Salvador Allende
5. Honduras
6. Brazilian
7. El Salvador and Honduras
8. Spanish and Quechua
9. White
10. Destroyer of boats

Around the World

Built World 1

1. Alcatraz
2. Wailing Wall or Western Wall
3. Richard Rogers
4. Mecca
5. Pudding Lane
6. Wall Street
7. Buckinghamshire
8. Iron
9. Beijing
10. Hadrian's Wall

Built World 2

1. Eiffel
2. James Stirling
3. Uganda
4. Lighthouses
5. Blackpool
6. To cover scars after a fire
7. Pompidou Centre
8. Istanbul
9. Arch
10. Gothic

Built World 3

1. World Trade Center
2. Petra
3. Crystal Palace
4. Le Corbusier
5. Istanbul
6. Bailey
7. London and New York
8. Temple of Artemis
9. Hampton Court Palace
10. Bell tower

Built World 4

1. Toronto
2. Boulder Dam
3. Bosporus
4. Edwin Lutyens
5. Rance
6. The Statue of Liberty
7. Alhambra
8. Sir Walter Scott
9. Port Sunlight
10. Ziggurat

Built World 5

1. Abu Simbel
2. Nicholas Hawksmoor
3. Les Invalides
4. Cambridge
5. Seville
6. Pakistan and China
7. Arizona
8. Holyrood House
9. The prison
10. Zambezi

History and Politics

History 1

1. Elephants
2. Calcutta
3. England and France
4. Nelson Mandela
5. Viscount Montgomery of Alamein
6. George Washington
7. Molotov
8. Mayor of London
9. Elba
10. Czechoslovakia

History 2

1. Lenin
2. Crimean War
3. Lady Jane Grey
4. Joan of Arc
5. Gaius Julius Caesar
6. Empress Josephine
7. Fidel Castro
8. Dunkirk
9. Boudicca/Boadicea
10. Solidarity

History 3

1. Victoria and Albert
2. Hadrian's Wall
3. Domesday Book
4. Excommunicate
5. The Great Plague
6. Christopher Columbus
7. England and Scotland
8. American Civil War
9. Hardy
10. Crimean War

History 4

1. Alexander the Great
2. Julius Caesar
3. Carthage
4. Mary, Queen of Scots
5. Farouk
6. Persia
7. Parthenon
8. Constantine the Great
9. Pompey
10. Buddhism

History 5

1. Cadiz
2. Alfred Dreyfus
3. American Civil War
4. No
5. Earl of Warwick
6. Malta
7. Roger Casement
8. Geneva Convention
9. William Pitt the Elder
10. Napoleon Bonaparte

History 6

1. 1816
2. Medici
3. James 1
4. Holy Roman Emperor
5. Jamestown
6. Mao Zedong
7. France
8. Spinning cotton
9. Jomo Kenyatta
10. France

History and Politics

History 7

1. Abraham Lincoln
2. The Commonwealth
3. Russia
4. Battle of Bosworth
5. Gauls
6. Catherine Parr
7. Adolf Hitler
8. Czechoslovakia
9. Battle of Hastings
10. Italy

History 8

1. James I
2. 1948
3. Hendrik Verwoerd
4. Battle of Actium
5. House of Lancaster
6. The Great Leap Forward
7. Booker T Washington
8. Charles II and James II
9. Amritsar
10. Gustavus Adolphus

History 9

1. Hadrian
2. War of Spanish Succession
3. Visigoths
4. Robespierre
5. Valley Forge
6. Switzerland
7. Martin Luther
8. Culloden
9. Hermann Goering
10. Salvador Allende

History 10

1. Scutari
2. King Idris
3. Pierre de Villeneuve
4. Gibraltar
5. Henrietta (Maria)
6. Rosetta Stone
7. Richard Nixon
8. Saladin
9. Joseph Stalin
10. Stephen

History 11

1. The French under Napoleon
2. Bunker Hill
3. Jacobite rebellion
4. American Civil War
5. 1941
6. 1984
7. Versailles
8. War of Spanish Succession
9. 1950
10. New Mexico, California and Texas

Kings and Queens 1

1. Six
2. Tudor
3. Juan Carlos
4. William II
5. First century BC
6. The 'Sun King'
7. Anne Boleyn
8. Greece
9. Henry V
10. Lear

History and Politics

Kings and Queens 2

1. Canute
2. Punctuality
3. Belgium
4. Charles II
5. Richard III
6. Spain
7. George III
8. The Netherlands
9. William IV
10. Wilhelm II

Kings and Queens 3

1. Canute
2. Isle of Wight
3. Bohemia
4. Scrofula
5. Charles
6. Caroline of Brunswick
7. Habsburg or Hapsburg
8. Ptolemy
9. Romania
10. Mercia

Politics 1

1. Jimmy Carter
2. Cambodia
3. Mussolini
4. Elysée Palace
5. East India Company
6. Ben-Gurion
7. Amnesty International
8. Adolf Hitler
9. Drug trafficking
10. Every four years

Politics 2

1. Edward Heath
2. Democratic and Republican
3. Nazi party
4. Harold Wilson
5. 18
6. Apartheid
7. 1920
8. Goebbels
9. Home secretary
10. Speaker

Politics 3

1. Neil Kinnock
2. House of Commons
3. Douglas Hurd
4. Shadow cabinet
5. European Parliament
6. Neville Chamberlain and Winston Churchill
7. Hansard
8. Paddy Ashdown
9. Three
10. Poll tax/community charge

Politics 4

1. London
2. Franklin Roosevelt
3. Aneurin Bevan
4. Plaid Cymru
5. Proportional representation
6. 1776
7. Winter of discontent
8. Ombudsman
9. Ecology Party
10. James Ramsey MacDonald

History and Politics

Politics 5

1. Robert Peel
2. Charles de Gaulle
3. National Party
4. 1990
5. Dan Quayle
6. Dáil éireann/the Dáil
7. Chancellor of the Exchequer
8. Francis Bacon
9. Portugal
10. Ken Livingstone

Politics 6

1. Sebastian Coe
2. 50
3. Edward Heath
4. Federalism
5. Citizen's Charter
6. Hugh Gaitskell
7. Speaker
8. Glenda Jackson
9. Deselection
10. Peter Jay

Politics 7

1. Kate Millett
2. Michael Troughton
3. Pakistan People's Party
4. Opposing Quebec separatism
5. *The North Briton*
6. Gough Whitlam
7. Lady Falkender
8. Harry S Truman
9. 1991
10. Suez Crisis

Politics 8

1. She threw herself under the king's horse in the Derby
2. Veto
3. Thomas Paine
4. Electoral college
5. Chancellor of the Exchequor
6. Hunger marches
7. Milton Friedman
8. Chauvinism
9. First past the post
10. Bill of Rights

Politics 9

1. Lord Chancellor
2. Treaties of Rome
3. Gladstone
4. John Major
5. Chairman of the party
6. David Steel
7. Poll tax
8. 1928
9. Cornwall
10. Secretary of state for the environment

People

General 1

1. Lewis Carroll
2. Classifying books
3. Dr Watson
4. John Paul I
5. Maoris
6. Elvis Presley
7. Census
8. Freddie Mercury
9. Grace Kelly
10. Walter Raleigh

General 2

1. Thomas More
2. Venice
3. William
4. Ballet
5. Mormons
6. Philistines
7. Four
8. Charles de Gaulle
9. Samuel Johnson
10. In a cave

General 3

1. Mikhail Gorbachev
2. Clarence House
3. Little Bighorn
4. Edward VIII
5. The 'Little Sparrow'
6. Thomas Minton
7. Danny Kaye
8. Spartacus
9. Yuri Gagarin
10. Stonewall

General 4

1. George IV
2. Nelson
3. Martin Luther King
4. Joe McCarthy
5. Veronica Lake
6. James Watt
7. Ireland
8. Dutch
9. Cars
10. A J P Taylor

General 5

1. Lichfield
2. Harry Gordon Selfridge
3. Dr Benjamin Spock
4. Coco Chanel
5. Dynamite
6. Francis Chichester
7. St Peter
8. Monks
9. Nepalese
10. Benjamin Franklin

General 6

1. Samuel Johnson
2. His ear
3. Charles Blondin
4. Peter Fabergé
5. Hawley Crippen
6. Crown Jewels
7. P T Barnum
8. Beau Brummell
9. Andrew Carnegie
10. Samuel Goldwyn

People

General 7

1. Berber
2. Héloïse
3. Earl Marshal
4. Adlai Stevenson
5. Photography
6. Photography
7. New York
8. Gabrielle
9. La Pasionaria
10. Thomas Malthus

Murders and Assassinations 1

1. John F Kennedy
2. Christopher Marlowe
3. Sweden
4. Jack the Ripper
5. Al Capone
6. Agatha Christie
7. John Lennon
8. Hamlet
9. Guillotine
10. Sarajevo

Murders and Assassinations 2

1. Taking a bath
2. Ice pick
3. Rajiv Gandhi
4. Philippines
5. Russia
6. Cain
7. Edmund Campion
8. Adolf Hitler
9. James I
10. Actor

Murders and Assassinations 3

1. Rasputin
2. Michael Collins
3. Indira Ghandi
4. Spencer Perceval
5. James Garfield
6. Malcolm X
7. Edward the Martyr
8. In the Senate house
9. Anastasia
10. St Bartholomew's Day

Conquerors and Explorers 1

1. 55 BC
2. Roald Amundsen
3. Roald Amundsen
4. St Helena
5. Attila
6. Napoleon I
7. Third Reich
8. Conquistador
9. *Golden Hind*
10. Marco Polo

Conquerors and Explorers 2

1. Goths
2. Amerigo Vespucci
3. Angel Falls
4. Christmas Day
5. *Niña*, *Pinta* and *Santa Maria*
6. Matterhorn
7. Ivan the Terrible
8. Francisco Pizzaro
9. Leif Ericsson
10. Hawaii

People

Partners

1. Eleanor
2. Oliver Hardy
3. Marie Antoinette
4. Ballooning
5. Desdemona
6. Castor and Pollux/Polydeuces
7. Mr Hyde
8. Romulus and Remus
9. Nelson Mandela and F W de Klerk
10. Cain and Abel

Who Said It? 1

1. Benjamin Franklin
2. John Lennon
3. Diego Maradona
4. George Bush
5. Geoffrey Chaucer
6. Madonna
7. Mickey Mouse
8. *The Three Musketeers*
9. Richard Nixon
10. *Gone With the Wind*

Who Said It? 2

1. Charlie Chaplin
2. Colonel Tom Parker
3. Robert Baden-Powell
4. Muhummad Ali
5. Chuck Berry
6. Alfred Hitchcock
7. Benito Mussolini
8. Charles Darwin
9. Robert Burns
10. Jules Verne

Who Said It? 3

1. W C Fields
2. *Pinocchio*
3. History
4. Queen Victoria
5. Greta Garbo
6. Martin Luther King
7. A little learning
8. Alamein
9. Alexander Graham Bell
10. Roald Dahl

Who Said It? 4

1. Laurence Oates
2. A house
3. The Panama Canal
4. Life
5. Oscar Wilde
6. Advertising
7. Desperation
8. Abraham Lincoln
9. Magna Carta
10. Existentialism

Who Said It? 5

1. Mark Twain
2. Cole Porter
3. Marco Polo
4. An imitation of herself
5. Bob Hope
6. Mae West
7. At the entry to Hell
8. Edgar Rice Burroughs
9. The Rubicon
10. Gertrude Stein

Ideas and Beliefs

General 1

1. Judas Iscariot
2. Mahatma Gandhi
3. Hippies
4. Hinduism
5. Maundy Thursday
6. Confucius
7. Jupiter
8. *On the Origin of Species*
9. Revelation
10. Four

General 2

1. Hindu
2. Dalai Lama
3. Austrian
4. Martin Luther
5. Plato
6. The Mormon church
7. Desmond Tutu
8. Albert Einstein
9. Minaret
10. Jewish

General 3

1. Sikhism
2. Easter
3. Islam
4. Judaism
5. Charlemagne
6. Adventists
7. Hinduism
8. Presbyterianism
9. Quakers/Society of Friends
10. Nirvana

General 4

1. Mary Baker Eddy
2. Osiris
3. Quakers
4. Yang
5. Sistine Chapel
6. John Stuart Mill
7. Nicene
8. Freemasons
9. Korea
10. Mecca

General 5

1. Socrates
2. Epiphany
3. Ayatollah
4. Copernicus
5. Six
6. Plymouth Brethren
7. Beatification
8. Nineteenth
9. Hirohito
10. Karma

General 6

1. Mormon
2. Islam
3. Lourdes
4. Mardi Gras
5. Echo
6. Ecumenical movement
7. Mistletoe
8. Holy Grail
9. Jesuits
10. Shinto

Ideas and Beliefs

General 7

1. Friedrich Nietzsche
2. Franklin D Roosevelt
3. Carl Gustav Jung
4. Jehovah's Witnesses
5. Aleister Crowley
6. Milton Friedman
7. The Divine Light Mission
8. The Oxford Movement
9. Jacob
10. Jainism

General 8

1. Taoism
2. Liberation theology
3. Diggers
4. Jainism
5. Trotsky
6. The head of the Jesuits
7. Palamedes
8. Salvation Army
9. Pantheism
10. Johann Kepler

General 9

1. The recapture and rededication of the Temple of Jerusalem
2. Nemesis
3. *Mahabharata*; *Ramayana*
4. Epigram
5. Canonization
6. Archbishop of York
7. The Anointed One
8. Io
9. Ramadan
10. Edict of Nantes

Bible 1

1. Lot
2. Jacob
3. David
4. His hair
5. King James Bible
6. Mary Magdalene
7. Pontius Pilate
8. Medicine
9. Dancing
10. Lion's den

Bible 2

1. John
2. Lazarus
3. Aaron
4. Garden of Gethsemane
5. Proverbs
6. Genesis
7. Jericho
8. Judas Iscariot
9. Psalms
10. Adam

Bible 3

1. The Ten Commandments
2. Frankincense and myrrh
3. Shem; Ham; Japheth
4. John's Gospel
5. David
6. Mammon
7. Absalom
8. Genesis; Exodus; Leviticus; Numbers; Deuteronomy
9. The Evangelists
10. In the belly of a whale

Ideas and Beliefs

Bible 4

1. Luke
2. Aramaic
3. Elisabeth
4. New Testament
5. Philistine
6. Saul; David
7. Ruth
8. Deborah
9. Bishop of Ephesus
10. Ruth; Esther

Mythology 1

1. Camelot
2. Pegasus
3. Flute
4. Tom Thumb
5. Bram Stoker
6. Icarus
7. Thor
8. Macbeth
9. October 31
10. Copenhagen

Mythology 2

1. His nose grows longer
2. Mars
3. Merlin
4. Rip Van Winkle
5. Robin Hood
6. Vampire
7. Valhalla
8. Black magic
9. His heel
10. *The Wonderful Wizard of Oz*

Mythology 3

1. Winchester and Canterbury
2. Labyrinth
3. Osiris
4. Gorgons
5. 'Hansel and Gretel'
6. Narcissus
7. Olympus
8. Valhalla, in Norse myth
9. Centaur
10. Odysseus

Mythology 4

1. Carefully targeted drugs
2. Eurydice
3. Capricorn
4. Jackal
5. Cyclops
6. Libra
7. Elizabeth I
8. Rhine
9. Cassandra
10. *The Rime of the Ancient Mariner*

Mythology 5

1. The brothers Grimm
2. Aries
3. The cup used by Jesus at the Last Supper
4. Voodoo
5. Griffin
6. Orestes
7. El Dorado
8. The Valkyrie
9. Faust
10. Adonis

Ideas and Beliefs

Mythology 6

1. Nymphs
2. Hope
3. River Styx
4. Seals/dugongs
5. Aeneas
6. Tintagel
7. Demeter
8. Ambrosia
9. Pax
10. Balder

Mythology 7

1. Apollo
2. Aleister Crowley
3. Charles Perrault
4. Thomas Malory
5. Graces
6. Salem
7. May 1
8. Dennis Wheatley
9. Leda
10. Babylonian

Mythology 8

1. Beowulf
2. January
3. Baron Münchhausen
4. Oberon
5. The Argonauts
6. Egyptian
7. Harry Houdini
8. Orion
9. 78
10. Abraxas

Mythology 9

1. Kali
2. Amaterasu
3. Aegis
4. India
5. Pygmalion
6. The Fates
7. Asgard
8. Nereids
9. Kwannon/Kwanyin
10. Elysium

Science

General 1

1. Lignite
2. Sand
3. Iris
4. Lanolin
5. Collagen
6. Cellulose
7. Teflon
8. Enamel
9. Six
10. Cast iron

General 2

1. Decibel
2. Arachnids
3. Electron
4. Joule
5. Acoustics
6. Halogens
7. Nucleus
8. Evaporation
9. Reptile
10. Aspirin

General 3

1. Six
2. Branch of medicine concerning cancer
3. Count von Zeppelin
4. International Standards Organization
5. Fungus
6. 100° Celsius
7. Magma
8. Penicillin
9. Vitamin C
10. The eye

General 4

1. Alloys
2. Arithmetic
3. Hypotenuse
4. Legionnaire's disease
5. Computer science
6. Heredity/inheritance
7. Angles
8. Hydrogen
9. Native elements
10. Hardware

General 5

1. Linus Pauling
2. Rosalind Franklin
3. Leo Szilard
4. James Chadwick
5. Marie Curie
6. Princeton
7. Quantum mechanics
8. Punctuated equilibrium
9. Superconductivity
10. Fred Hoyle

General 6

1. Richard Owen
2. Archimedes
3. A theory of evolution
4. Medicine
5. Ballistics
6. Atomic bomb
7. Leibniz
8. Linnaeus
9. Röntgen
10. Mendelevium

Science

General 7

1. The crab
2. Robert Fitzroy
3. Special theory of relativity in 1905
4. Alchemy
5. Galileo Galilei
6. Ovid
7. Cryonics
8. Dalton
9. William Bragg
10. Richard Owen

General 8

1. Gravity; electromagnetic force; strong nuclear force; weak nuclear force
2. Kinetics
3. Family
4. Helix
5. Magnitude
6. Sulphuric acid
7. Hermaphrodite
8. Square
9. Relative humidity
10. Bearing

General 9

1. James Hutton
2. William of Occam
3. Thomas Kuhn
4. Fritz Haber
5. Empiricism
6. Logical positivism
7. C P Snow
8. Paul Feyerabend
9. Robert Oppenheimer
10. The problem of induction

General 10

1. Bakelite
2. A mycoprotein
3. Iron oxide
4. Swedish
5. Ketone
6. Ammonia
7. Cytoplasm
8. Gold
9. Bismuth
10. Glass

General 11

1. Cryogenics
2. Hans Oersted
3. Chitin
4. Aluminium
5. Inside a cell
6. A type of reproduction among flowering plants
7. Two
8. Ontogeny
9. Alkali metals
10. The potato

General 12

1. Genetic fingerprinting
2. Bionics
3. Mendeleyev
4. Alfred Wallace
5. Lichen
6. Scalene
7. Mega
8. Computer
9. Pitchblende
10. Lavoisier

Science

General   13

1. Four
2. Cubit
3. SI
4. An obsolete unit of depth used by seafarers and miners
5. 1,000
6. The unit for expressing frequency
7. 1,000 kg
8. Eight
9. 1,760
10. Hand

Physics   1

1. Archimedes Principle
2. Meltdown
3. 625
4. Anders Celsius
5. Amplifier
6. Lens
7. Conductor
8. Seven
9. Calorie
10. Inertia

Physics   2

1. Equilibrium
2. Speed of light
3. Frequency
4. Inductance
5. Standard temperature and pressure
6. Diode
7. Momentum
8. Friction
9. Solenoid
10. Ultrasonics

Physics   3

1. Vector quantity
2. Amadeo Avogadro
3. Allotropic
4. Viscosity
5. Very low temperatures
6. Einstein
7. Tesla
8. Holography/holograms
9. Microwave amplification by stimulated emission of radiation
10. Plasma

Chemistry   1

1. Graphite
2. Methane
3. Stalactites
4. Solid, liquid and gas
5. Gypsum
6. Bronze
7. Chlorine
8. Gunpowder
9. Diamond
10. China

Chemistry   2

1. Arsenic
2. Tin
3. Mohs' scale
4. Iodine
5. Radioactive
6. Dry ice
7. Sublimation
8. Iron
9. Halogens
10. Nitrogen

Science

Chemistry 3

1. Water
2. Corundum
3. Tungsten
4. Polyesters
5. Radon
6. Iridium
7. Cinnabar
8. Polyvinylchloride
9. Titration
10. Benzene

Elements 1

1. Hydrogen
2. Hydrogen
3. Silicon
4. Calcium
5. Zinc
6. Aluminium
7. Rare earth
8. Gold
9. Magnesium
10. Carbon

Elements 2

1. Phosphorus
2. Aluminium
3. Iron
4. Gold
5. Fluorine
6. Aluminium
7. Fluorine
8. Sulphur
9. Zinc
10. Silver

Elements 3

1. Noble gases
2. Uranium
3. Deuterium
4. Carbon
5. 12
6. Lead
7. Plutonium
8. Iron
9. Silver
10. Calcium

Energy 1

1. From light
2. Oxygen
3. Ultraviolet radiation
4. Glucose
5. Potential energy
6. Zero
7. Nuclear fusion
8. Michael Faraday
9. Ultraviolet radiation
10. Kinetic energy

Energy 2

1. Mass
2. The law of conservation of energy
3. Respiration
4. Sun
5. Photon
6. Bioluminescence
7. Gamma rays
8. Mechanical energy
9. Carbon dioxide
10. Photoelectric effect

Science

Energy 3

1. Mitochondria
2. Adenosine triphosphate
3. A battery or cell
4. 5,530° Celsius
5. Albedo
6. The Romans
7. Fovea
8. Reykjavik
9. Sodium
10. Heat energy

Instruments and Techniques of Science 1

1. Transpiration stream in a plant
2. Gas
3. Small lengths
4. Scanning electron microscope
5. Telescope
6. Pea plants
7. With electro magnetic coils
8. Spectroscopy
9. The age of a rock, fossil or other sample
10. Geiger counter

Instruments and Techniques of Science 2

1. Telemetry
2. A bathyscaph
3. Medicine
4. Device used before the sextant for navigation
5. Hydrogen maser clock
6. Archaeology
7. Separating molecules of different sizes
8. Astrometry
9. Detection of electric charge
10. Chromatography

Animals and Plants 1

1. Bark
2. 3 metres
3. To absorb oxygen
4. Water
5. Cheetah
6. Bamboo shoots
7. Adam
8. An ostrich
9. Octopus
10. Mulberry

Animals and Plants 2

1. Omnivores
2. Chlorophyll
3. Citric acid
4. An American monkey
5. Algae
6. Pups
7. Ornithology
8. Cactus
9. Yew
10. Hemlock

Animals and Plants 3

1. Penguins
2. Tadpole
3. Flamingo
4. Alligator
5. Owl
6. Crab
7. Lodge
8. Plankton
9. Roadrunner
10. Migration

Science

Animals and Plants 4
1. Ant
2. Appendix
3. Kangaroos
4. Froghopper/spittlebug
5. Hummingbirds
6. Squirrel
7. Cellulose
8. Condor
9. Fungi
10. Kelp

Animals and Plants 5
1. Phloem
2. Ganesh
3. Ethology
4. Chloroplast
5. The outside
6. Skull
7. Gymnosperms
8. Arachnid
9. Sharks
10. Crop

Animals and Plants 6
1. Krill
2. Bryophyta
3. Mesophyll
4. Stationary
5. Leaf
6. Ginkgo
7. It doesn't have one
8. Root
9. Stomata
10. Lenticels

Animals and Plants 7
1. Leaf
2. Prehensile
3. Nacre
4. Oxalic acid
5. Reproduce
6. Latex
7. Kookaburra
8. Hydrophytes
9. Aestivation
10. Beaver

Animals and Plants 8
1. A Himalayan pheasant
2. Light reaction
3. Perfume
4. Muscle tissue
5. Mandrake
6. Bach
7. A horse
8. Fungus
9. Yew
10. Narcissus

Animals and Plants 9
1. Sporophyte
2. An ornithologist
3. Protozoa
4. *Rafflesia arnoldiana* or stinking corpse lily
5. Punctuated equilibrium
6. Archaeopteryx
7. Phloem
8. Classes
9. One
10. A crustacean

Science

Human Body 1
1. Shoulder blade
2. Patella
3. Hypothalamus
4. Stomach
5. Brain
6. Pancreas
7. Diaphragm
8. Kidney
9. The neck
10. Coccyx

Human Body 2
1. In the ear
2. Four
3. Adrenal glands
4. Kidney
5. Vertebrae
6. Two
7. Liver
8. Vitamin C
9. Oesophagus
10. During sleep

Human Body 3
1. Wisdom teeth
2. 37°C / 98.4°F
3. Heart
4. Insulin
5. Jugular veins
6. Feet
7. Brain
8. Hiccups
9. Capillaries
10. Water

Human Body 4
1. Amnion; amniotic membrane
2. Retina
3. Synovial fluid
4. Pulmonary vein
5. Pelvic girdle
6. Liver
7. Hormones
8. Ear drum
9. Haemoglobin
10. Lymph

Human Body 5
1. Ureter
2. Lung
3. Tendon
4. 140 dB
5. Erythrocyte
6. Liver
7. Colon
8. Atrium
9. Genotype
10. Femur

Human Body 6
1. Cone cells
2. In the brain
3. Gluteus maximus
4. Ball-and-socket
5. Cartilage
6. Pancreas
7. Testosterone
8. The inner ear
9. Trachea
10. Salivary amylase

Science

Human Body 7
1. Ovaries
2. They secrete insulin
3. Ovaries
4. Corpus luteum
5. T cells
6. Medulla oblongata
7. Sinoatrial node
8. Renal artery
9. Colon
10. 80,000

Human Body 8
1. Corpus luteum
2. Heart
3. Luteinizing hormone
4. Neck
5. Spleen
6. Hypothalamus
7. Pancreas
8. Adrenaline
9. Adrenal
10. Liver

Human Body 9
1. Wrist
2. Endorphins
3. Keloid
4. Keratin
5. Iris
6. Lactic acid
7. Hammer; anvil; stirrup
8. Melanin
9. Teeth
10. Histamine

Senses 1
1. Retina
2. Beethoven
3. Optic nerve
4. Echolocation
5. Iris
6. Pupil
7. Cones
8. Tinnitus
9. Four
10. Anosmia

Senses 2
1. Vibrations
2. Semicircular canals
3. Presbyopia
4. Photophobia
5. Three
6. Olfactories
7. Ciliary body
8. Nose
9. Phytochrome
10. Touch

Medicine and Health 1
1. Anaesthetist
2. Blood
3. Antibiotic
4. In the 1970s
5. Alcohol
6. Polyunsaturated fat
7. 28
8. Stomach; intestine
9. Iron
10. Ear, nose, and throat

Science

Medicine and Health 2

1. Virus
2. Mosquito
3. Brain
4. Jenner
5. World Health Organization
6. Insulin
7. Salmonella poisoning
8. Condom
9. Blood
10. Haemophilia

Medicine and Health 3

1. Joseph Lister
2. Lesion
3. Lassa fever
4. Placebo
5. Measles
6. Leprosy
7. Rhesus monkey
8. Trachoma
9. Legionnaire's disease
10. Indigestion

Medicine and Health 4

1. Christian Barnard
2. Blood vessel
3. Nervous system
4. Heart
5. Skeleton
6. Acrophobia
7. Pancreas
8. Swallowing
9. Virus
10. Goitre

Medicine and Health 5

1. Rheumatism
2. Oestrogen and progesterone
3. In vitro fertilization
4. AIDS
5. ME
6. Lung
7. *Staphylococcus aureus*
8. Quinine
9. An extra chromosome
10. Vitamin B_1

Medicine and Health 6

1. Aspirin
2. Actuary
3. Kidney
4. Smallpox
5. Salivary glands
6. Brain
7. Obstetrics
8. Cancer
9. Thymus
10. Tuberculosis

Planet Earth 1

1. Duck-billed platypus
2. Rhinoceros
3. Ivory
4. Carbon monoxide
5. Nitrate
6. Biodegradable
7. S E Alaska
8. Sulphur dioxide
9. Catalytic converter
10. Aluminium

Science

Planet Earth 2

1. Nitrogen
2. Molten iron and nickel
3. Assam
4. Coal
5. Pacific
6. Lava
7. 20%
8. Synoptic forecasting
9. Spring tide
10. A river

Planet Earth 3

1. Meteorology
2. Water vapour condensed into droplets
3. Blue Whale
4. Nitrogen
5. Oxygen
6. Himalayas
7. Precipitation
8. Ozone
9. Crust
10. Diamond

Planet Earth 4

1. Rainforest
2. USA
3. *Braer*
4. Fossil fuel
5. Friends of the Earth
6. Hohe Tauern in Austria
7. Ozone
8. Murder
9. Green belt
10. Unleaded petrol

Planet Earth 5

1. Mediterranean Sea
2. Carbon dioxide; methane; chlorofluorocarbons
3. (Tropical) rainforest
4. Leaching
5. Hedges/hedgerows
6. Myxomatosis
7. Jonathon Porritt
8. Sweden
9. Aral Sea
10. Sellafield

Planet Earth 6

1. Montréal
2. Ukraine
3. A bloom
4. Exhalation
5. Agent Orange
6. Great Barrier Reef
7. On or near the equator
8. 0.03 mph
9. The trade in endangered species
10. Mauritius

Planet Earth 7

1. Igneous
2. 24,900 miles
3. Seismology
4. Carboniferous
5. Mohs' scale
6. Tropic of Cancer
7. Nitrogen
8. Atmospheric pressure
9. Movement of continental plates
10. Latitude

Science

Planet Earth 8

1. From cooling volcanic lava
2. Nepal
3. Gravity
4. Coal
5. In erosion, particles of rock are transported away by wind or rain
6. Igneous
7. Copper carbonate
8. 24
9. Australia
10. In the Philippines, north of Manila, in 1991

Planet Earth 9

1. Manganese
2. Troposphere
3. Argon
4. Cirrus
5. Outer core
6. Gaia hypothesis
7. Limestone
8. Methane
9. Syncline
10. Pangaea

Planet Earth 10

1. Eutrophication
2. Nitrate
3. Chlorine
4. Stratosphere
5. The International Whaling Commission or IWC
6. Nitrogen oxides
7. Etosha Reserve in Namibia
8. Geothermal energy
9. 3.5 acres
10. It can affect the development of the nervous system, especially in children

Planet Earth 11

1. The polar skies
2. Gastroliths
3. Ionosphere
4. Crash
5. Aquifers
6. Radon
7. In igneous rock
8. A soil scientist
9. Obsidian
10. Carrara

Space 1

1. One day
2. Gravity
3. Mercury
4. Jupiter
5. Earth
6. Venus
7. Pluto
8. A year
9. Mars
10. Halley's comet

Space 2

1. The Sun
2. Mercury and Venus
3. Venus
4. Uranus
5. A comet
6. Venus
7. Eleven
8. Moon
9. Pluto
10. Nine

Science

Space 3

1. *Sputnik 1*
2. Laika, a dog on board the *Sputnik 2*
3. Yuri Gagarin
4. Apollo project
5. USA
6. Neil Armstrong
7. *Pioneer 10*
8. *Challenger*
9. *Skylab*
10. Four: *Columbia, Endeavour, Discovery, Atlantis*

Space 4

1. Black holes
2. The local galaxy
3. 5,800 K (5,530°C)
4. Light years
5. Sun
6. Cosmology
7. Gravity
8. Pulsars
9. A white dwarf
10. Meteor

Space 5

1. Saturn
2. Earth
3. Pluto
4. The Sun
5. *Voyager I* and *II*
6. Mercury
7. Nebulae
8. Polaris
9. Parsec
10. Helium

Space 6

1. Gravitational force
2. The expansion of the universe
3. Sirius
4. Great density
5. Ether
6. Supernova
7. Andromeda galaxy
8. Alpha Centauri
9. Helium
10. Fred Hoyle

Space 7

1. Earth
2. Eight
3. Saturn
4. Jupiter
5. Pluto
6. Earth
7. Ganymede
8. Mercury
9. Titania
10. Venus

Space 8

1. A supernova
2. Superstring
3. Mars
4. Neutron stars
5. A large, old, bright star
6. Asteroids
7. Ceres
8. Large Magellanic Cloud
9. Orion constellation
10. Mount Palomar, California

Science

Space 9

1. Doppler effect
2. A rapidly rotating neutron star
3. Cassiopaea
4. In a black hole
5. Martin Ryle
6. Approximately 15 billion years ago
7. A graph plotting the luminosities of stars against their temperatures
8. Cosmogony
9. Steady-state theory
10. Mass

Space 10

1. Pluto
2. Saturn
3. Jupiter
4. Mars
5. About 1.5 light years
6. Neptune
7. *Viking* probes
8. One-sixth as strong
9. Titan
10. Saturn

Space 11

1. Martin Ryle
2. Arnold Wolfendale
3. A nebula
4. A unit of distance
5. Albert Einstein
6. Ten
7. Pulsar
8. Steady-state theory
9. Spiral
10. Fusion

Space 12

1. Three
2. Earth
3. 1958
4. *Apollo 7*
5. Neptune
6. Jupiter
7. Methane
8. William Herschel
9. Helium
10. *Apollo 17*

Technology and Transport 1

1. Fiat
2. Grand Union Canal
3. Catherine
4. Egyptian
5. b) 300 kph/185 mph
6. Brazilian
7. Dunlop
8. Two
9. Italy
10. Mini

Technology and Transport 2

1. Distributor
2. Fibre optics
3. Transformer
4. Flywheel
5. Intermediate technology
6. Frequency modulation
7. Amplifier
8. Clutch
9. Aerodynamics
10. Random-access memory

Science

Technology and Transport 3
1. Radar
2. Laser
3. Carburettor
4. Jet engine
5. Liquid crystal display
6. Magnetic levitation
7. Sonar
8. Thermionic valve
9. Steam engine
10. Stealth technology

Technology and Transport 4
1. 1901
2. *Discovery*
3. Bicycle
4. *Saturn V*
5. Rolls and Royce
6. Geostationary
7. Amelia Earhart
8. ADA
9. Kawasaki
10. Kerosene

Technology and Transport 5
1. Silver Ghost
2. Harrier
3. Archaeology
4. Running and swimming
5. Karl Benz
6. Cowley
7. Tourist Trophy
8. Citroën
9. Milk Race
10. Carbon granules

Technology and Transport 6
1. Steel
2. Clock
3. Bimetallic strip
4. Kidney machine
5. Genetic engineering
6. Electromagnetic effect
7. Loom
8. Amplitude modulation
9. A particle accelerator
10. Differential

Technology and Transport 7
1. Duck
2. Priest
3. Wing
4. 1956
5. Nylon
6. Casting
7. Carbon dioxide
8. Ultrasound
9. Steam engine
10. Coil

Technology and Transport 8
1. France
2. 15 million
3. Differential
4. In a flying accident
5. Ferdinand Porsche
6. Citroën
7. Hispano Suiza
8. Jaguar
9. Robot; robotic arm
10. Mercedes Benz

Science

Discovery and Invention 1

1. Hargreaves
2. Ernest Lawrence
3. Diesel
4. Human palaeontology
5. Pascal
6. Daguerre
7. Robert Hooke
8. William Harvey
9. Stephen Hales
10. Thomas Edison

Computers 1

1. Charles Babbage
2. Byte
3. RAM
4. Alan Turing
5. IBM
6. RSI
7. WYSIWYG
8. William Gibson
9. Machine code
10. 1990

QUIZLINK

Game 1

Round 1
1. HELICON
2. Sandra HUTCHINSON
3. BLOOMSBURY group
4. Harold MACMILLAN
5. The PENGUIN

   Quizlink = Names of PUBLISHERS

Round 2
1. Bryan MURRAY
2. Marco POLO
3. IMPERIAL Chemical Industries
4. It was a kind of SPEAR
5. PEPPER Anderson

   Quizlink = Types of MINTS

Round 3
1. POTTING Shed
2. The Periodic TABLE
3. London BRIDGE
4. Robert PLANT
5. *Where's The REST Of Me?*

   Quizlink = Terms used in SNOOKER (accept billiards or pool)

Round 4
1. George BUSH
2. Sam SPADE
3. Plymouth HOE
4. GREENHOUSE Effect
5. Ron FLOWERS

   Quizlink = Things you might find in a GARDEN

Round 5
1. The HAMMER of the Scots
2. TRACY
3. James WOLFE
4. Larry HOLMES
5. BLAKE Carrington

   Quizlink = Surnames of fictional DETECTIVES (Mike Hammer; Dick Tracy; Nero Wolfe; Sherlock Holmes; Sexton Blake)

Round 6
1. STRATFORD Johns
2. The GLOBE artichoke
3. Edward LEAR
4. Miss Jane HATHAWAY
5. 'ROMEO AND JULIET'

   Quizlink = WILLIAM SHAKESPEARE (Stratford-upon-Avon; the Globe Theatre; King Lear; Anne Hathaway)

QUIZLINK

Game 2

Round 1
1. Sir Walter RALEIGH
2. Elizabeth MONTGOMERY
3. Otto BISMARCK
4. The PHOENIX
5. Oscar MADISON

Quizlink = US STATE CAPITALS (Raleigh, North Carolina; Montgomery, Alabama; Bismarck, North Dakota; Phoenix, Arizona; Madison, Wisconsin)

Round 2
1. Noddy HOLDER
2. 'BIRD'
3. HAMPSHIRE
4. Tin Pan ALLEY
5. Harry PALMER

Quizlink = Surnames of first-class cricket UMPIRES (John Holder; Dickie Bird; John Hampshire; Bill Alley; Ken Palmer)

Round 3
1. CAVALIERS
2. A superNOVA
3. ASTRA
4. *VIVA Zapata*
5. CARLTON Magee

Quizlink = Models of VAUXHALL CARS

Round 4
1. The Palace of WESTMINSTER
2. CHELSEA
3. Jack LONDON
4. The Royal ALBERT Hall
5. The Battle of WATERLOO

Quizlink = BRIDGES over the River Thames

Round 5
1. John SMITH
2. RED Flag Act
3. ALBERT Einstein
4. The Battle of TRAFALGAR
5. LEICESTER City

Quizlink = Names of well-known SQUARES

Round 6
1. A CAIRN
2. George FOX
3. IRISH Sea
4. YORKSHIRE pudding
5. SKYE

Quizlink = Breeds of TERRIER

QUIZLINK

Game 3

Round 1
1. HEATH Robinson
2. EDEN Kane
3. MAJOR Tom
4. Bob WILSON
5. Becky THATCHER

Quizlink = Surnames of British PRIME MINISTERS

Round 2
1. FANTASY Football League
2. Queen VICTORIA
3. *The Old DEVILS*
4. CORAL
5. *A CHRISTMAS Carol*

Quizlink = Names of ISLANDS

Round 3
1. GARFIELD
2. Stephen KING
3. Kevin KENNEDY
4. LINCOLN Handicap
5. Samuel BECKETT

Quizlink = Surnames of people who were ASSASSINATED (James Garfield; Martin Luther King; John F and Robert Kennedy; Abraham Lincoln; Thomas à Becket)

Round 4
1. Norman SCHWARZKOPF
2. Donald SUTHERLAND
3. Santo DOMINGO
4. James LIND
5. Cheryl BAKER

Quizlink = Surnames of famous OPERA SINGERS (Elizabeth Schwarzkopf; Joan Sutherland; Placido Domingo; Jenny Lind; Janet Baker)

Round 5
1. *The MILLENNIUM Falcon*
2. *Every SECOND Counts*
3. *'What's Another YEAR?'*
4. *'One DAY at a time'*
5. *That Was The WEEK That Was*

Quizlink = Periods of TIME

Round 6
1. *Whistle DOWN the Wind*
2. Dominic CORK
3. Lord LONGFORD
4. Doctor KILDARE
5. TYRONE Power

Quizlink = Names of IRISH COUNTIES

Quizlink

Game 4

Round 1
1. Peter STRAUSS
2. Miss BRAHMS
3. *Roll Over BEETHOVEN*
4. Catherine BACH
5. Isaak WALTON

Quizlink = Surnames of COMPOSERS

Round 2
1. Tanganyika and ZANZIBAR
2. *HONG KONG Phooey*
3. RIO de Janeiro
4. SINGAPORE
5. *UTOPIA*

Quizlink = Destinations in the series of ROAD FILMS starring Bob Hope and Bing Crosby

Round 3
1. *STRIKE it Lucky*
2. Penny LANE
3. Kirsty ALLEY
4. Safety PIN
5. SPARE tyre

Quizlink = Terms used in TEN PIN BOWLING

Round 4
1. *Cool HAND Luke*
2. The POINTER Sisters
3. BALANCE sheet
4. SPRING roll
5. *DIAL M For Murder*

Quizlink = Parts of a WATCH or CLOCK

Round 5
1. Ferdinand 'Jellyroll' MORTON
2. ALBION
3. *Kind HEARTS and Coronets*
4. Emma HAMILTON
5. CLYDE Barrow

Quizlink = Names of Scottish FOOTBALL TEAMS

Round 6
1. The Magic CIRCLE
2. VICTORIA Wood
3. DISTRICT of Columbia
4. WATERLOO Cup
5. Diamond JUBILEE

Quizlink = Names of lines on the London UNDERGROUND

QUIZLINK

Game 5

Round 1
1. *Madame BUTTERFLY*
2. *Gipsy MOTH IV*
3. BEE humming bird
4. The ANT Hill Mob
5. *MOSQUITO Coast*

   Quizlink = INSECTS

Round 2
1. Plaster of PARIS
2. AJAX of Amsterdam
3. ACHILLES tendon
4. HELEN Mirren
5. HECTOR Berlioz

   Quizlink = Participants in the TROJAN WAR or SIEGE OF TROY

Round 3
1. *Brighton ROCK* by Graham Greene
2. 'The Sky BLUES'
3. David SOUL
4. *Bleak HOUSE*
5. *The JAZZ Singer*

   Quizlink = Types of MUSIC

Round 4
1. Ayers ROCK (in Australia)
2. *The Book TOWER*
3. The Northern LIGHTS
4. The BEACH Boys
5. PIERS Fletcher-Dervish

   Quizlink = Things associated with the seaside resort of BLACKPOOL

Round 5
1. *PAL Joey*
2. *The PRIME of Miss Jean Brodie*
3. Hobson's CHOICE
4. CESAR Romero
5. TEX Avery

   Quizlink = brands of DOG FOOD

Round 6
1. IRAN Barkley
2. 'CHINA in Your Hand'
3. Jean GERMANY
4. Anatole FRANCE
5. CHAD Varah

   Quizlink = Names of COUNTRIES

QUIZLINK

Game 6

Round 1
1. FLORA Macdonald
2. Queen VICTORIA
3. VESTA Tilley
4. VENUS de Milo
5. DIANA: Her True Story

   Quizlink = Names of Roman GODDESSES

Round 2
1. *The VICAR of Wakefield*
2. DEACON Blue
3. Dixie DEAN
4. Judas PRIEST
5. Alexander POPE

   Quizlink = Various offices of CLERGY or RELIGION

Round 3
1. 'MULE Train'
2. *A Man Called HORSE*
3. The PONY Express
4. Samuel COLT
5. *Drop The Dead DONKEY*

   Quizlink = Names of EQUINE creatures

Round 4
1. HAMMER (formerly M C Hammer)
2. *The Ipcress FILE*
3. SCREWDRIVER
4. DRILL
5. PLIERS

   Quizlink = Kinds of TOOLS

Round 5
1. PIQUET
2. James STEWART
3. SENNA
4. *The HUNT For Red October*
5. Davy JONES

   Quizlink = Surnames of WORLD MOTOR RACING CHAMPIONS (Nelson Piquet; Jackie Stewart; Ayrton Senna; James Hunt; Alan Jones)

Round 6
1. PEANUTS
2. Marc ALMOND
3. BRAZIL
4. COB
5. HAZEL O'Connor

   Quizlink = Types of NUT

QUIZLINK

Game 7

Round 1
1. HANNIBAL Lecter
2. The INDIAN Mutiny
3. *The AFRICAN Queen*
4. 'Ebony and IVORY'
5. Jackie MERRICK

Quizlink = All words connected with the ELEPHANT (Hannibal reputedly led a herd of elephants across the Alps 218 BC; John Merrick became known as the Elephant Man)

Round 2
1. *KNIGHT Rider*
2. BUCKINGHAM Palace
3. David FROST
4. CHAMPION
5. Norman Stanley FLETCHER (in *Porridge*)

Quizlink = Names of GRAND NATIONAL-winning JOCKEYS (Steve Knight; John Buckingham; Jimmy Frost; Bob Champion; and Brian Fletcher)

Round 3
1. Lady Jane GREY
2. Sean BEAN
3. CANADA
4. BRENT Spiner
5. *BARNACLE Bill*

Quizlink = Types of GEESE

Round 4
1. MIDDLE Earth
2. *STRAW Dogs*
3. The Charge of the LIGHT Brigade
4. Vic FEATHER
5. 'He Ain't HEAVY He's My Brother'

Quizlink = BOXING WEIGHTS

Round 5
1. LUX
2. 'SURF City'
3. ARIEL
4. FAIRY lights
5. BOLD

Quizlink = Brand names of WASHING POWDERS

Round 6
1. KELLY Le Brock
2. James CALLAGHAN
3. The Prince of WALES
4. *HIGHWAY To Heaven*
5. BLOCK and tackle

Quizlink = Characters played in films by CLINT EASTWOOD (Kelly in *Kelly's Heroes*; Callaghan in the 'Dirty Harry' series; Wales in *The Outlaw Josey Wales*; Highway in *Heartbreak Ridge*; and Block in *Tightrope*)

QUIZLINK

Game 8

Round 1
1. CATHERINE de' Medici
2. Bob FERRIS
3. *The WATER Babies* by Charles Kingsley
4. *The War WAGON*
5. BARROW

   Quizlink = Types of WHEEL

Round 2
1. The TROJAN War
2. The JET engine
3. David HUNTER
4. The Greenpeace ship *Rainbow WARRIOR*
5. Deadly NIGHTSHADE

   Quizlink = Names of television's GLADIATORS

Round 3
1. MARK Twain
2. A POUND of flesh
3. COLON
4. Sergio LEONE
5. Mary RAND

   Quizlink = World CURRENCIES (Mark – Germany; Pound – UK; Colon – El Salvador; Leone – Sierra Leone; Rand – South Africa)

Round 4
1. STIR frying
2. NICK Rowan (played by Nick Berry in *Heartbeat*)
3. PORRIDGE
4. 'CAN the Can'
5. A large water JUG

   Quizlink = Slang terms for PRISON or JAIL

Round 5
1. LUCAS McCain
2. Johannes BRAHMS
3. GRACE-and-favour
4. Barry HUMPHRIES
5. William SPOONER

   Quizlink = Surnames of characters from the television comedy show *ARE YOU BEING SERVED?*

Round 6
1. BRAD Dexter
2. Archimedes SCREW
3. Jimmy NAIL
4. TACK
5. Ten PIN bowling

   Quizlink = Types of FASTENER

QUIZLINK

Game 9

Round 1
1. ARTHUR'S seat
2. FELIX Mendelssohn
3. OMEGA
4. CATKINS
5. The queen of SHEBA

Quizlink = Brands of CAT FOOD

Round 2
1. CUPID
2. DONNA Reed
3. Halley's COMET
4. VIXEN
5. Ballet DANCER

Quizlink = Names of REINDEER employed by Santa Claus

Round 3
1. The Teddy BEARS
2. *RAIDERS Of The Lost Ark*
3. The EAGLES
4. The VIKINGS
5. The JETS and the Sharks

Quizlink = Nicknames of AMERICAN FOOTBALL TEAMS (Chicago Bears; Los Angeles Raiders; Philadelphia Eagles; Minnesota Vikings; New York Jets)

Round 4
1. Sir Winston CHURCHILL
2. CLARE Grogan
3. TRINITY House
4. Cardigan and PEMBROKE
5. SELWYN Froggitt

Quizlink = Names of COLLEGES at CAMBRIDGE UNIVERSITY

Round 5
1. ZEBEDEE
2. DYLAN Thomas
3. FLORENCE Nightingale
4. *The Life Of BRIAN*
5. Robert DOUGAL

Quizlink = Characters from the children's television puppet show THE MAGIC ROUNDABOUT

Round 6
1. HORATIO Nelson
2. ANTONIO Fargas
3. FERDINAND Magellan
4. *BOTTOM*
5. CASSIUS Clay

Quizlink = SHAKESPEAREAN CHARACTERS (Horatio – Hamlet; Antonio – The Merchant Of Venice; Ferdinand – The Tempest; Bottom – A Midsummer Night's Dream; Cassius – Julius Caesar)

QUIZLINK

Game 10

Round 1
1. Leslie JOSEPH
2. KINGS Cross Station
3. MARY Jo Kopechne
4. CATTLE crossing
5. Cybil SHEPHERD

Quizlink = All present in the stable where JESUS was born

Round 2
1. Joni MITCHELL
2. William CONRAD
3. Robert Falcon SCOTT
4. IRWIN Shaw
5. ARMSTRONG (George Armstrong Custer)

Quizlink = ASTRONAUTS who have walked on the MOON

Round 3
1. Susan ST JAMES
2. WESTMINSTER Abbey
3. *The Lion In WINTER*
4. John BUCKINGHAM
5. CRYSTAL

Quizlink = Names of well-known PALACES

Round 4
1. Desert ORCHID
2. HYACINTH Bucket
3. DAISY chaining
4. The POPPY Family
5. VIOLET Elizabeth Bott

Quizlink = FLOWERS

Round 5
1. Brian LONDON
2. Don HENLEY
3. John WALTON
4. KINGSTON
5. RICHMOND Reed

Quizlink = Places situated on the RIVER THAMES

Round 6
1. Ellery QUEEN
2. *The STING*
3. *HONEY, I Shrunk The Kids*
4. *The WORKER*
5. DRONE

Quizlink = Words connected with BEES

Quizlink

Game 11

Round 1

1. EDGAR Rice-Burroughs
2. OSCAR Hammerstein II
3. TONY Curtis
4. CLEO Lane
5. PATSY

Quizlink = AWARDS made in the USA (the Edgar is for mystery writing; the Oscar for films; the Tony is awarded in theatre; the Cleo for television commercials; and the Patsy for performances by animals)

Round 2

1. WHISKY Galore
2. PORT of Spain
3. GIN rummy
4. 'Yo ho ho and a bottle of RUM!'
5. SHERRY

Quizlink = ALCOHOLIC DRINKS

Round 3

1. Del SHANNON
2. TYNE Daly
3. The THAMES flood barrier
4. Robin BAILEY
5. Carrie FISHER

Quizlink = Names of SHIPPING FORECAST AREAS

Round 4

1. CLEOPATRA
2. BRIMSTONE
3. APOLLO
4. CARDINAL Wolsey
5. Captain PEACOCK

Quizlink = Species of BUTTERFLY

Round 5

1. The SOUTH sea bubble
2. The Bristol CHANNEL
3. GRANADA
4. Allan BORDER
5. MERIDIAN

Quizlink = Names of independent TELEVISION COMPANIES

Round 6

1. Roscoe TANNER
2. The Rhesus MONKEY
3. BOB Holness
4. QUID pro quo
5. Shetland PONY

Quizlink = Slang terms for particular amounts of MONEY (Tanner = 6 old pence; Monkey = £500; Bob = 1 old shilling or 12 old pence; Quid = £1; and Pony = £25)

QUIZLINK

Game 12

Round 1
1. PARIS
2. Duke of WELLINGTON
3. 'VIENNA'
4. TOKYO Rose
5. Joel CAIRO

   Quizlink = CAPITAL CITIES

Round 2
1. 23 APRIL
2. SPIKE Milligan
3. GLADYS Emmanuel
4. 'PEGGY Sue'
5. Robert CLIVE

   Quizlink = Names of characters from the television show HI-DE-HI

Round 3
1. Bob's FULL HOUSE
2. Coogan's BLUFF
3. Going STRAIGHT
4. FLUSH
5. THREE OF A KIND

   Quizlink = Terms used in the game of POKER

Round 4
1. Sydney NOLAN
2. St ANDREW'S Day
3. The BEVERLY Hillbillies
4. The long MARCH
5. Michael COLLINS

   Quizlink = Surnames of well-known SISTERS (the Nolan, Andrews, and Beverly sisters are all singing groups; the March sisters featured in the book *Little Women;* and the Collins sisters are Jackie, the writer, and Joan, the actress)

Round 5
1. The SWORD of Damocles
2. *JUNO and the Paycock*
3. OMAHA
4. 'Band of GOLD'
5. UTAH

   Quizlink = CODE NAMES given to the BEACHES used in the D Day landings of World War II

Round 6
1. FLORENCE NIGHTINGALE
2. CHARLES DICKENS
3. ISAAC NEWTON
4. GEORGE STEPHENSON
5. CHRISTOPHER WREN

   Quizlink = All people whose portraits appear or have appeared in the past on British BANK NOTES

Quizlink

Game 13

Round 1
1. Emily BISHOP
2. Eric KNIGHT
3. KING and CASTLE
4. QUEEN
5. Billie Jean KING

Quizlink = CHESS pieces

Round 2
1. Nelson PIQUET
2. *A BRIDGE Too Far*
3. SNAP
4. Red hot POKER
5. NEWMARKET

Quizlink = CARD GAMES

Round 3
1. 'ORINOCO Flow'
2. The Duke of WELLINGTON
3. ALDERNEY
4. BULGARIA
5. YELLOWSTONE National Park

Quizlink = Names of WOMBLES from the children's television show *The Wombles*

Round 4
1. CARPENTER
2. Henry COOPER
3. Betty DRIVER
4. Kenneth BAKER
5. FLETCHER Christian

Quizlink = OCCUPATIONS

Round 5
1. OXFORD United
2. HARLEY Davidson
3. James BOND
4. *Follow the FLEET*
5. Carole LOMBARD

Quizlink = Famous LONDON STREETS

Round 6
1. SCREAMING Lord Sutch
2. 'LOVING You'
3. John CONSTABLE
4. *DOCTOR Zhivago*
5. LAUGHING gas

Quizlink = Titles of films in the *CARRY ON* series

QUIZLINK

Game 14

Round 1
1. *The Honorary CONSUL*
2. SIERRA Nevada
3. FIESTA
4. ORION
5. *ESCORT For Hire*

Quizlink = Makes of FORD CARS past or present

Round 2
1. POLO
2. CHESS
3. DARTS
4. CRICKET (the insect)
5. RUGBY

Quizlink = GAMES or SPORTS

Round 3
1. TARA King
2. HAMILTON Academicals
3. George KENNEDY
4. Stan BUTLER
5. Maureen O'HARA

Quizlink = *GONE WITH THE WIND* by Margaret Mitchell (Scarlett O'Hara lived at Tara; Charles Hamilton, Frank Kennedy, and Rhett Butler were her three husbands)

Round 4
1. The Angel ISLINGTON
2. Harry ENFIELD
3. The GREENWICH Meridian
4. LAMBETH Palace
5. BARNET fair

Quizlink = Names of LONDON BOROUGHS

Round 5
1. NU Shooz
2. Catherine ZETA Jones (in *The Darling Buds of May*)
3. *The OMEGA Man*
4. *Piper ALPHA*
5. DELTA

Quizlink = LETTERS of the GREEK ALPHABET

Round 6
1. POLLY
2. Mark THATCHER
3. 'And never the TWAIN shall meet' in The Ballad of East and West by Rudyard Kipling
4. Mickey FINN
5. Beatrix POTTER

Quizlink = *The Adventures of TOM SAWYER* by Mark Twain (Polly was Tom's aunt; Huckleberry Finn his friend. Together they witnessed a murder of which Muff Potter, was accused. Becky Thatcher was Tom's sweetheart in the book by Mark Twain)

QUIZLINK

Game 15

Round 1
1. The BOXER rebellion
2. *To The MANOR Born*
3. SNOWBALL
4. NAPOLEON Bonaparte
5. Howard JONES

Quizlink = *ANIMAL FARM* by George Orwell (Boxer was a horse; Napoleon and Snowball were pigs; Mr Jones owned Manor Farm)

Round 2
1. The Ark of the COVENANT
2. Arthur James BALFOUR
3. Donald CAMPBELL
4. 'MULL of Kintyre'
5. Peter BRECK

Quizlink = *KIDNAPPED* by Robert Louis Stevenson (*Covenant* was the ship onto which David Balfour was taken after being kidnapped; Alan Breck was his companion. They witnessed the murder of Colin Campbell on the island of Mull)

Round 3
1. *WHITE Heat*
2. The GREEN Howards
3. MUSTARD gas
4. Little PLUM
5. SCARLETT O'Hara (in *Gone With the Wind*)

Quizlink = Characters from the game of CLUEDO

Round 4
1. GREYFRIARS Bobby
2. A CHERRY
3. Henry WHARTON
4. Emily NUGENT
5. Sir Gordon RICHARDS

Quizlink = 'BILLY BUNTER' stories (Greyfriars was Bunter's school where his schoolmates were Harry Wharton, Bob Cherry, and Frank Nugent; in the stories by Frank Richards)

Round 5
1. Mark SPITZ
2. THORNTON Wilder
3. BUCK Cannon
4. 'Streets of LONDON'
5. The KLONDIKE

Quizlink = *CALL OF THE WILD* by Jack London (Spitz and Buck were dogs; Buck was rescued by John Thornton; went to live wild in the Klondike; in the book by Jack London)

Round 6
1. Paper LACE
2. Alan SUGAR
3. 'The PLATINUM Blonde'
4. IVORY Coast
5. SILVER

Quizlink = Traditional gifts for WEDDING ANNIVERSARIES

QUIZLINK

Game 16

Round 1
1. A Connecticut YANKEE in King Arthur's Court
2. 'The Red FLAG'
3. The PATENT Office
4. ROUND ROBIN
5. HEINZ

Quizlink = Types of multiple BETS in HORSE RACING

Round 2
1. The POINTER Sisters
2. HMS *BEAGLE*
3. Operation HUSKY
4. Duane DOBERMAN
5. He was a BOXER

Quizlink = Breeds of DOG

Round 3
1. Hallo DANDY
2. *VICTOR, Victoria*
3. Tottenham HOTSPUR
4. *TOPPER*
5. MANDY

Quizlink = Names of children's COMICS

Round 4
1. BREAD
2. Herr FLICK
3. PEN
4. STANLEY Holloway
5. David BOWIE

Quizlink = Types of KNIVES

Round 5
1. MAX Miller
2. ALFRED Lord Tennyson
3. The HUDSON and the East
4. George BENSON
5. Peter PARKER

Quizlink = Names of television BUTLERS or CHAUFFEURS (Max was the chauffeur in *Hart to Hart*; Alfred was the butler in *Batman*; Hudson was the butler in *Upstairs, Downstairs*; Benson was the butler in Soap; and Parker was Lady Penelope's chauffeur in *Thunderbirds*)

Round 6
1. GEORGE Eliot
2. *The MALTESE Falcon*
3. IRON Horse
4. VICTORIA Cannon
5. LATIN America

Quizlink = Types of CROSS

Quizlink

Game 17

Round 1
1. Black SEPTEMBER
2. 'JANUARY'
3. Brian MAY
4. Fredric MARCH
5. JUNE Whitfield

Quizlink = MONTHS of the year

Round 2
1. ROWAN Atkinson
2. ASH Wednesday
3. WILLOW
4. APPLE
5. Kings OAK

Quizlink = TREES

Round 3
1. Santa FE
2. River PO
3. 'Let it BE'
4. Little MO
5. 'AS Time Goes By'

Quizlink = CHEMICAL SYMBOLS (Fe is the symbol for iron; Po for polonium; Be for beryllium; Mo for Molybdenum; and As for arsenic)

Round 4
1. MAURETANIA
2. PRINCE OF WALES feathers
3. Robin HOOD
4. BOUNTY hunter
5. *Escape to VICTORY*

Quizlink = Names of famous SHIPS

Round 5
1. GENERAL GORDON
2. MICHAELANGELO
3. MARC ANTONY
4. MOSES
5. EL CID

Quizlink = All have been played in films by CHARLTON HESTON

Round 6
1. PLUTO
2. Leslie ASH
3. ERNIE
4. SALT
5. RADAR

Quizlink = Words that are ACRONYMS (words composed of the initial letters of other words; PLUTO stands for Pipe Line Under The Ocean; ASH is for Action on Smoking and Health; ERNIE is the machine that draws the winning premium bond numbers and stands for Electronic Random Number Indicating Equipment; SALT means Strategic Arms Limitation Talks; and RADAR stands for Radio Detection and Ranging)

QUIZLINK

Game 18

Round 1
1. *The Man With the Golden ARM*
2. *WHEEL of Fortune*
3. The ELECTRIC lamp
4. *HIGH Noon*
5. 'ROCKING all over the World'

Quizlink = Types of CHAIR

Round 2
1. The CHEETAH
2. BONZO Dog Doo Dah Band
3. LOUIS XVI
4. River CLYDE
5. CORNELIUS Boza-Edwards

Quizlink = Names of film APES (Cheetah was the chimpanzee in the Tarzan films; Bonzo appeared in films such as *Bedtime for Bonzo* with Ronald Reagan; Louis was king of the apes in *The Jungle Book*; Clyde appeared in the *Any Which Way* films with Clint Eastwood; and Cornelius was one of the apes in the *Planet of the Apes* films)

Round 3
1. 'HOLDING Back the Years'
2. CROFT
3. James GARNER
4. MARSHALL Hain
5. Private BENJAMIN

Quizlink = Surnames of West Indian CRICKETERS or FAST BOWLERS

Round 4
1. BUSBY Berkeley
2. The PANAMA Canal
3. Death CAP mushroom
4. Battle of BALACLAVA
5. A PILLBOX

Quizlink = Types of HATS

Round 5
1. The LANCET
2. ROSE Royce
3. *The FRENCH Connection*
4. The BAY of Biscay
5. Clara BOW

Quizlink = Types of WINDOWS

Round 6
1. Pat CASH
2. *LOOT*
3. 'Mouldy Old DOUGH'
4. *BREAD*
5. *BRASS*

Quizlink = Slang words for MONEY

Quizlink

Game 19

Round 1
1. BILLY Bunter
2. Sir Francis DRAKE
3. TOM Brown
4. The DOG star
5. COB

   Quizlink = Names for MALE ANIMALS

Round 2
1. KIRK Douglas
2. Anton CHEKHOV
3. SULU Sea
4. SCOTT Joplin
5. Benjamin SPOCK

   Quizlink = Characters from the TV show STAR TREK

Round 3
1. Brendan FOSTER
2. Lyndon B JOHNSON
3. *WHO Framed Roger Rabbit*
4. Robert WATSON-Watt
5. Eliza DOLITTLE

   Quizlink = Names of famous DOCTORS (of fact and fiction)

Round 4
1. Anthony EDEN (accept the Earl of AVON)
2. DEE Hepburn
3. CLYDE Barrow
4. Nell TRENT
5. DON Johnson

   Quizlink = Names of British RIVERS

Round 5
1. *VERTIGO*
2. MERCURY
3. CHRYSALIS
4. PHILIPS
5. CHESS

   Quizlink = Names of RECORD LABELS

Round 6
1. Debra WINGER
2. T J HOOKER
3. *BACK To the Future*
4. *Journey to the CENTRE of the Earth*
5. Fast FORWARD

   Quizlink = Positions in the game of RUGBY

QUIZLINK

Game 20

Round 1
1. Russian ROULETTE
2. CLARE
3. WHEN the Boat Comes In
4. SHE
5. FIGARO

Quizlink = Titles of NUMBER 1 HIT SONGS

Round 2
1. BELLA Emberg
2. Kenneth MORE
3. 'A WOMAN in Love'
4. George BEST
5. ME and My Girl

Quizlink = Titles of WOMEN'S MAGAZINES

Round 3
1. The LION in Winter
2. Jeffrey ARCHER
3. Prunella SCALES
4. 'Like a VIRGIN'
5. RAM raiding

Quizlink = Words describing SIGNS OF THE ZODIAC

Round 4
1. Danny MIRROR
2. Von Ryan's EXPRESS
3. All of the PEOPLE
4. Chain MAIL (or just MAIL)
5. A STAR is Born

Quizlink = NEWSPAPERS

Round 5
1. Anthony HOPE
2. The CHARITY Shield
3. The TEMPERANCE Seven
4. James Robertson JUSTICE
5. Keep the FAITH

Quizlink = Five of the seven traditional VIRTUES

Round 6
1. Bob CHAMPION
2. BURMESE
3. The SCOUT Association
4. 30 pieces of SILVER
5. COPENHAGEN

Quizlink = Names of famous HORSES (from fact or fiction) (Champion was the name of singing cowboy Gene Autrey's horse; Burmese was ridden by Queen Elizabeth II at several state functions; Scout and Silver belonged to Tonto and the Lone Ranger respectively; and Copenhagen was ridden by the Duke of Wellington at the Battle of Waterloo in 1815)